THE ESSENTIAL
MARGARET FULLER

THE ESSENTIAL MARGARET FULLER

DOVER THRIFT EDITIONS

Margaret Fuller

DOVER PUBLICATIONS, INC.
MINEOLA, NEW YORK

DOVER THRIFT EDITIONS

GENERAL EDITOR: SUSAN L. RATTINER
EDITOR OF THIS VOLUME: MICHAEL CROLAND

Bibliographical Note

This Dover edition, first published in 2019, is a new selection of works reprinted from standard texts. A new introductory Note has been specially prepared for this volume. Minor inconsistencies and other style vagaries derive from the original sources and have been retained for the sake of authenticity.

Library of Congress Cataloging-in-Publication Data

Names: Fuller, Margaret, 1810–1850, author.
Title: The essential Margaret Fuller / Margaret Fuller.
Description: Mineola, New York : Dover Publications, Inc., 2019. | Series:
    Dover thrift editions | "This Dover edition, first published in 2019, is a
    new selection of works reprinted from standard texts. A new introductory
    Note has been specially prepared for this volume."
Identifiers: LCCN 2018054581 | ISBN 9780486834092 | ISBN 0486834093
Subjects: LCSH: American literature—Women authors—19th century.
Classification: LCC PS2502 2019 | DDC 818/.309—dc23
LC record available at https://lccn.loc.gov/2018054581

Manufactured in the United States by LSC Communications
83409301   2019
www.doverpublications.com

Note

MARGARET FULLER was born on May 23, 1810, in Cambridgeport (now Cambridge), Massachusetts. Timothy Fuller—her father, a lawyer, and, later, a congressman—was disappointed that his firstborn child was a girl. She was a precocious child, and he gave her a rigorous home education. He taught her to read at age 3 and Latin by age 6, and she learned Greek, Italian, and French as well. "To excel in all things should be your constant aim; mediocrity is obscurity," he advised when she was 10. She blamed his grueling education for the depression and headaches that plagued her throughout her life. Formal education was limited for girls at that time, and she did not attend school until she was 14.

After her father died in 1835, Fuller, her mother, one sister, and five brothers were transferred to the custody of her uncle. At 25, she resisted the idea of going from one man's care to another's. Instead, she supported her immediate family through teaching and writing. She often worked to the point of exhaustion.

Fuller developed her ideology through her literary endeavors and events. In 1839, she published a translation of *Eckermann's Conversations with Goethe.* From 1839 to 1844, in Boston, she led "conversations" that empowered women. Attendees discussed women's roles in society, in addition to literature, education, mythology, and philosophy. From 1840 to 1842, she was the editor of *The Dial,* a Transcendentalist quarterly magazine, for which she wrote poetry, reviews, and critiques.

In 1845, Fuller published her landmark book, *Woman in the Nineteenth Century.* The groundbreaking feminist work advocated for political equality between the sexes and promoted emotional, intellectual, and spiritual fulfillment for women. She encouraged young women to seek independence from the home and family, with education as the vehicle to do so. She argued against strictly domestic roles for women, saying that they should fulfill their potential in whatever ways appealed to them. "Let them be sea-captains, if they will," she wrote. The first edition of the book sold out in two weeks. *Knickerbocker Magazine* called it "a well-reasoned and well-written treatise." *Woman in the Nineteenth Century* was widely influential, inspiring numerous readers as well as the Seneca Falls Women's Convention, the first women's rights convention in the U.S., in 1848.

The present volume is divided into three parts. The first section features Fuller's autobiographical writing, including poetry, journal entries, and letters, from 1833 to 1842. The second section is *Summer on the Lakes*, which she published in 1844 about frontier life in Illinois and Wisconsin. The third section collects Fuller's reviews and essays from the *New-York Daily Tribune* from 1844 to 1846. During this period, she was a literary and cultural critic for the newspaper, making her one of the first professional women in the American press. Collectively, these works give a comprehensive look into Fuller's thinking beyond her magnum opus.

Fuller went to Europe in 1846 and became the first American woman to be a foreign correspondent, reporting for the *Tribune*. She traveled to England, France, and Italy, exchanging ideas with writers and radicals. In 1847, she met the Marchese Giovanni Ossoli, a lieutenant in the Italian Unification Movement. They had a child, Angelo, and apparently got married secretly. They were involved in the Roman revolution in 1848, and Fuller wrote a history of the revolution. In 1850, while attempting to return to the United States, she died in a shipwreck near Fire Island, New York. Fuller, her husband, and her manuscript were never found; only the body of her infant son was recovered.

Contents

TO A. H. B.

On our meeting, on my return from N.Y.

to Boston, August 1835.—   Written Jany 1836

Brief was the meeting,—tear-stained, full of fears
   For future days, and sad thoughts of the past,—
   Thou, seeing thy horizon overcast,
Timid, didst shrink from the dark-coming years;
And I, (though less ill in mine appears,)
   Was haunted by a secret dread of soul,
   That Fate had something written in her scroll
Which soon must ope again the fount of tears;
   Oh could we on the waves have lingered then,
Or in that bark, together borne away,
   Have sought some isle far from the haunts of men,
Ills left behind which cloud the social day,
   What grief I had escaped; yet left untried
   That holy faith by which, now fortified,
   I feel a peace to happiness allied;—
And thou, although for thee my loving heart
Would gladly some Elysium set apart,
From treachery's pestilence, and passion's strife,
Where thou might'st lead a pure untroubled life,
Sustained and fostered by hearts like thy own,
The conflicts which thy friend must brave, unknown,—
Yet I feel deeply, that it may be best
For thee as me, that fire the gold should test,
And that in God's good time we shall know perfect rest!

~

TO THE SAME. A FEVERISH VISION.

After a day of wearying, wasting pain,
   At last my aching eyes I think to close;—
   Hoping to win some moments of repose,
Though I must wake to suffering again.
But what delirious horrors haunt my brain!
   In a deep ghastly pit, bound down I lie,—
   About me flows a stream of crimson dye,
Amid its burning waves I strive in vain;
   Upward I stretch my arms,—aloud I cry
   In frantic anguish,—"raise me, or I die!"
When with soft eyes, beaming the tenderest love,
I see thy dear face, Anna! far above,—
By magnet drawn up to thee I seem,
And for some moments was dispelled the fever's frightful
    dream!—

                      Sept. 1835

∼

                      Journal, 1835

On the evening of the 30th of September, 1835, ever memorable era—my father was seized with cholera and on the 2d of October was a corpse. For the first two days, my grief under this calamity was such as I dare not speak of. But since my father's head is laid in the dust, I feel an awful calm, and am becoming familiar with the thought of being an orphan. I have prayed to God that *Duty* may now be the first object and self sit aside. May I have light and strength to do what is right in the highest sense for my Mother, brothers and sister.

It has been a gloomy week indeed. The children have all been ill, and dearest Mother is overpowered with sorrow, fatigue and anxiety. I suppose she must be ill too. When the children recover I shall endeavor to keep my mind steady by remembering that there is a God, and that grief is but for a season. Grant, Oh Father, that neither the joys and sorrows of this past season shall have visited my heart in vain. Make me wise and strong for the performance of immediate duties, and ripen me, by what means Thou seest best for those which lie beyond.

My father's image follows me constantly, whenever I am in my room he seems to open the door and look on me with a complacent tender smile. What would I not give to have it in my power to make that heart beat once more with joy. The saddest feeling is the remembrance of little things, in which I have fallen short of love and duty. I never sympathized in his liking for this farm, and secretly wondered how a mind which had for thirty years been so widely engaged in the affairs of men could care so much for trees and crops. But now, amidst the beautiful autumn days, I walk over the grounds and look with painful emotions at every little improvement. He had selected a spot to place a seat where I might go to read alone and had asked me to visit it. I contented myself with "where you please, Father," but we never went; what would I not now give, if I had fixed a time, and shown more interest. A day or two since I went there. The tops of the distant blue hills were veiled in delicate autumn haze, soft silence brooded over the landscape, on one side a brook gave to the gently sloping meadow spring-like verdure, on the other a grove—which he had named for me—lay softly glowing in the gorgeous hues of October. It was very sad; may this sorrow give me a higher sense of duty in the relationships which remain!

Journal, July 1833

The occupations of the coming months I have settled. Some duties come first to parents, brothers and sister but these will not consume above one sixth of the time— The family is so small now Mother will have little need of my sewing— We shall probably receive very little company— The visits required of me by civility will be few— When the Farrars return I hope to see them frequently—and E. Woodward I may possibly know if she comes. But I shall not, of free-will look out of door for a moment's pleasure— I shall have no one to stay here any time except Eliz— I love her and she is never in the way— All hopes of travelling I have dismissed— All youthful hopes of every kind I have pushed from my thoughts— I will not, if I can help it, lose an hour in castle-building and repining— Too much of that already! I have now a pursuit of immediate importance to the German language and literature I will give my undivided attention— I have made rapid progress for one quite unassisted— I have always hitherto been too constantly distracted by childish feelings to acquire any thing properly but have snatched a little here and there to feed my restless fancy therewith— Please God now to keep my mind composed, that I may atone it with all that may be conducive hereafter to the best good of others—

Oh! keep me steady in an honorable ambition. Favored by this calm, this obscurity of life I might learn every-thing, did not these feelings lavish away my strength— Let it be no longer thus— Teach me to think justly and act firmly— Stifle in my breast those feelings which pouring forth so aimlessly did indeed water but the desert and offend the sun's clear eye by producing weeds of rank luxuriance. Thou art my only Friend, thou hast not seen fit to interpose one feeling, understanding breast between me and a rude, woful world, vouchsafe then thy protection that I may "hold on in courage of soul."

～

Journal, March 1839

What did Elizabeth's father gain by forcing her young mind—by constraining her attention long after the physical sense was weary—by keeping her, a delicate child up till midnight whenever it suited him?— He did, as he proposed, sharpen her faculties, give her the power of attention, and bestow an intellectual tinge on a being born only to love eagerly and feel keenly— But the time gained then has been lost since fifty times over in the indulgence of a morbid sensibility created by this unnatural taxing of her faculties—her imagination is disordered; she is doomed to nervous horrors through life, her soul is constantly shaken by too aspiring thoughts on subjects she has not strength to comprehend— Had she grown up an unmolested flower by the side of some secret stream she had been a thing all natural life, softness, bloom and fragrance—

What have I gained by my precocity? I have never been happy— my faculties have always been rather intensely in action and produced no harmonious result. I was more robust by nature than E. Therefore the results have been different. But I am confident that I should have been much superior to my present self had sense, intellect, passion been brought out in the natural order. . . .

Many observations in this book give me new light upon myself— From my *own* experience merely I should go great lengths with him— In childhood I was a somnambulist— I was very subject to attacks of delirium— I perceive I had what are now called spectral illusions— For a long time I dreaded excessively going to bed for as soon as I was left alone—huge shapes—usually faces advanced from the corners of the room and pressed upon me growing larger and larger till they seemed about to crush me— Then I would scream and sit up in bed to get out of the way— Sometimes eyes would detach themselves from the faces and come upon me— I had peculiar horror of this. I told these things sometimes but little notice was taken— I thought other children felt the same for I knew they generally dreaded going to bed— Mother seemed ashamed of my sleep-walking and I had an idea something ridiculous was attached to it— I was twice found in convulsions in consequence of dreadful dreams— One of these dreams I shall never forget— I was wading in a sea of blood— I caught at twigs and rocks to save myself: they all streamed blood on me— This fancy was attributed at the time to my incessant reading of Virgil.— When I was about twelve all these things left me—but were succeeded by a determination of the blood to the head— My Father attributed it to my overheating myself, my Mother to an unfortunate cold—both were much mortified to see the fineness of my complexion destroyed— My own vanity was for a time severely wounded but I recovered and made up my mind to be bright and ugly— My father could not be so easily reconciled but was always scolding me for getting my forehead so red when excited.

If Brigham's theory were correct it would be curious to trace the singular traits of mind I exhibited up to my twenty first year to this ugly and very painful flush in the forehead— The summer of that year my forehead and indeed my whole system was pretty fairly exhausted of the vital fluid under the care of Dr. Robbins—Thanks to his medicines, my nerves became calmed, flushes and headaches gradually disappeared— I craved sleep, so long almost impossible to me— My wakefulness had always been troublesome to myself and others— I would now lie down in the middle of the day and sleep for hours....

∼

Journal, c. 1839

The son of the Gods has sold his birthright. He has received therefor one, not merely the fairest, but the sweetest and holiest of earth's daughters. Yet is it not a fit exchange. His pinions droop powerless, he must no longer soar amid the golden stars. No matter, he thinks— I will take her to some green and flowering isle. I will pay the penalty for Adam for the sake of the daughter of Eve. For her I will make the earth fruitful by the sweat of my brow. No longer shall my hands bear the coal to the lips of the inspired singer, no longer my voice modulate its tones to the accompaniment of spheral harmonies. My hands lift the clod of the valley which now dares cling to them with brotherly familiarity. And for my soiling dreary task-work all the day I receive—food.

But the smile with which she greets me at the set of sun, is it not worth all that sun has seen me endure. Can angelic delights surpass those I possess when pacing the shore with her watched by the quiet Moon, we listen to the tide of the world surging up impatiently against the Eden it cannot conquer. Truly, the joys of heaven were gregarious and low in comparison. This alone is exquisite, because exclusive and peculiar.

Ah Seraph—but the winter's frost must nip thy vine. A viper lurks beneath the flowers to sting the foot of thy child, and pale decay must steal over the cheek thou dost adore. In the realm of Ideas all was imperishable. Be blest, while thou canst; —I love thee, fallen Seraph, but thou shouldst not have sold thy birthright.

All for love and the world well lost. That sounds so true. But Genius when it sells itself gives up not only the world but the universe.

Yet does not Love comprehend the universe? The universe is Love: Why should I weary my eye with scanning the parts, when I can clasp the whole this moment to my beating heart?

But if the intellect be repressed, the idea will never be brought out from the feeling. The amaranth wreath will in thy grasp be changed to one of roses, more fragrant, indeed, but withering with a single sun.

Went to bed with pain in the right side of my head. Could not get to sleep for a long time, when I did, dreamt that the Egyptian, who has so often tormented me into the nervous headache, sat by my side and kept alluring a gigantic butterfly who was hovering near to rest upon her finger. He approached, but, declining her skinny fingers, flapped his crimson wings for a moment, then settled on the *left* side of my forehead; I tried in vain to drive him away; he plunged his feet, bristling with feelers, deeper and deeper into my forehead till my pain rose to agony. I awoke with my hand on the left side of my forehead to which the pain had changed. After the usual applications had been made I again fell asleep. Now I was in a room of a large hotel, very ill. On the bed was a pink counterpane, such as was in the little room where I endured so many weeks of nervous headache without complaining to any body. I wandered out, I know not why, and could not find my way back. I went through the usual distresses of going into strange rooms, & at last, in despair and quite exhausted, lay down in an entry. Many persons passed by, some looked scornfully at me, others tried to lift me but I was too heavy and at last was left lying on the floor. I was in great pain in the back. I was wrapt in a long robe, but my feet were bare They seemed growing cold as marble. I thought I must die in this forlorn condition, and tried to resign myself to bear it well. At last a sweet female form approached she sat down by me on the cold, damp, brick floor. I cried, O Amy, and laid my head on her bosom. I wept long and bitterly. She had dark eyes and regular features the face I never saw before, but the feeling I had was the same as when Anna in the fever drew me up out of the pit of blood. It is the true feeling of feminine influence, the same which Goethe wished to illustrate by his tale of the child charming the lion, the influence of benignity, purity and faith. As I have masculine traits, I am naturally often relieved by the women in my imaginary distresses. When I awoke the warmth was gone from the stone + (+ not a tombstone) which had been placed at my feet. They were marble cold, the pain had gone, into the spine and my pillow was drenched with tears.

This dream seems, as mine, from the nature of my illness must be, very illustrative of the influence of the body on the mind when will and understanding are not on the alert to check it. Let those who undervalue the moral powers of will analyze their dreams and see what they become without it.

∼

Journal fragment, 183—?

But I love many a good deal, and see some way into their eventual beauty. I am myself growing better, and shall by and by be a worthy object of love, one that will not anywhere disappoint or need forbearance. Meanwhile I have no fetter on me, no engagement, and as I look on others almost every other, can I fail to feel this great privilege? I have no way tied my hands or feet. And yet the varied calls on my sympathy have been such that I hope not to be made partial, cold or ignorant by this isolation. I have no child, and the woman in me has so craved this experience that it has seemed the want of it must paralyze me. But now as I look on these lovely children of a human birth what slow and neutralizing cares they bring with them to the mother. The children of the muse come quicker, with less pain and disgust, rest these lightly on the bosom. . . .

∼

Second moonlight. A lonely one. A sweeping, voluptuous breeze. A cloud car for the moon. My ridge of rocks and trysting tree. The singing grove. The distant hills and sweeping fields across which the eye of Raphael steals. Sympathy with between Nature and Man.

Thoughts of Makaria and her stellar correspondences But I cannot think of other souls now. Mine is too fresh and living. Understood wreaths of stars and the wandering in the Elysian grove.

My head wrapped in my shawl I would listen to the music of earth then raise it and look straight into the secrets of the heaven. I fail the moon. Thoughts on lunacy. How could Swedenborg think children were in the moon. She makes me understand the attraction Sand finds in un front impassible. I need to go wild when she rose and shriek. No bliss for me. But now Nature suffices me, and often I rest in her centre as in the bosom of God!

Shapes move across the valley. Abandon thyself to second sight. . . .

DISTANT SHOUTS of laughter. Reflexions on kindred. Michel Angelo's Sybils. Where is my tripod? Clearest moon. Heaven without a fleck or mark.

7th   High rapture of solitude. Full moon. Presence of my Daemon. I cannot yet touch its hand. . . .

≈

10 Dec 39

. . . Yet O it seems almost no mortal before me can know such a rapture as mine in the pine wood. Alas that I cannot paint it, only tell the feeling. I envied God, as the last flush of the sun light fell. Then rose the silver bow amid the gorgeous clouds and then again I saw it, a diamond of shivering sparks, trembling in the brook!

≈

Journal, 17 April 1840

Then a woman of tact and brilliancy like me has an undue advantage in conversation with men. They are astonished at our instincts. They do not see where we got our knowledge and while they tramp on in their clumsy way we wheel and fly and dance hither and thither and seize with ready eye all the weak points (like Saladin in the desert). It is quite another thing when we are come to write and without suggestions from another mind to declare the *positive* amount of thought that is in us. Because we seemed to know all they think we can tell all—and finding we can tell so little lose faith in their first opinion of us *which naturally was true.*

Then these gentlemen are surprised that I write no better because I talk so well. But I have served a long apprenticeship to the one, none to the other. I will write well yet, but never I think so well as I talk for then I feel inspired and the means are pleasant; my voice excites me, my pen never.

I shall by no means be discouraged, nor take what they say for gospel, but try to sift from it all the truth & use it. I feel within myself the strength to dispense with all illusions and I will manifest it. I will stand steady and rejoice in the severest probations!

~

Then all earth is sanctified
Upsprings Paradise around.

Then shall come the Eden days
   Guardian watch from seraph eyes,
Angels on the slanting rays
   Voices from the opening skies.

From this spirit land afar
   All disturbing force shall flee,
Sin nor toil nor *hope*, shall mar
   Its immortal unity.

Summer 1840

~

Journal, 1840

It was Thanksgiving day, (Nov., 1831,) and I was obliged to go to church or exceedingly displease my father. I almost always suffered much in church from a feeling of disunion with the hearers and dissent from the preacher; but to-day, more than ever before, the services jarred upon me from their grateful and joyful tone. I was wearied out with mental conflicts, and in a mood of most childish, child-like sadness. I felt within myself great power, and generosity, and tenderness;

but it seemed to me as if they were all unrecognized, and as if it was impossible that they should be used in life. I was only one-and-twenty; the past was worthless, the future hopeless; yet I could not remember ever voluntarily to have done a wrong thing, and my aspiration seemed very high. I looked round the church, and envied all the little children; for I supposed they had parents who protected them, so that they could never know this strange anguish, this dread uncertainty. I knew not, then, that none could have any father but God. I knew not, that I was not the only lonely one, that I was not the selected Oedipus, the special victim of an iron law. I was in haste for all to be over, that I might get into the free air.

I walked away over the fields as fast as I could walk. This was my custom at that time, when I could no longer bear the weight of my feelings, and fix my attention on any pursuit; for I do believe I never voluntarily gave way to these thoughts one moment. The force I exerted I think, even now, greater than I ever knew in any other character. But when I could bear myself no longer, I walked many hours, till the anguish was wearied out, and I returned in a state of prayer. To-day all seemed to have reached its height. It seemed as if I could never return to a world in which I had no place,—to the mockery of humanities. I could not act a part, nor seem to live any longer. It was a sad and sallow day of the late autumn. Slow processions of sad clouds were passing over a cold blue sky; the hues of earth were dull, and gray, and brown, with sickly struggles of late green here and there; sometimes a moaning gust of wind drove late, reluctant leaves across the path;—there was no life else. In the sweetness of my present peace, such days seem to me made to tell man the worst of his lot; but still that November wind can bring a chill of memory.

I paused beside a little stream, which I had envied in the merry fulness of its spring life. It was shrunken, voiceless, choked with withered leaves. I marvelled that it did not quite lose itself in the earth. There was no stay for me, and I went on and on, till I came to where the trees were thick about a little pool, dark and silent. I sat down there. I did not think; all was dark, and cold, and still. Suddenly the sun shone out with that transparent sweetness, like the last smile of a dying lover, which it will use when it has been unkind all a cold autumn day. And, even then, passed into my thought a beam from its true sun, from its native sphere, which has never since departed from me. I remembered how, a little child, I had stopped myself one day on the stairs, and asked, how came I here? How is it that I seem to be this Margaret Fuller? What does it mean? What shall I do about it? I remembered all the times and ways in which the same thought had returned. I saw how long it must be before the soul can learn to act under these limitations of time and space, and human nature; but I saw, also, that it MUST do it,—that it must make all this false true,—and sow new and immortal plants in the garden of God, before it could return again. I saw there was no self; that selfishness was all folly, and the result of circumstance; that it was only because I thought self real that I suffered; that I had only to live in the idea of the ALL, and all was mine. This truth came to me, and I received it unhesitatingly; so that I was for that hour taken up into God. In that true ray most of the relations of earth seemed mere films, phenomena.

My earthly pain at not being recognized never went deep after this hour. I had passed the extreme of passionate sorrow; and all check, all failure, all ignorance, have seemed temporary ever since. When I consider that this will be nine years ago next November, I am astonished that I have not gone on faster since; that I am not yet sufficiently purified to be taken back to God. Still, I did but touch then on the only haven of Insight. You know what I would say. I was dwelling in the ineffable, the unutterable. But the sun of earth set, and it grew dark around; the moment came for me to go. I had never been accustomed to walk alone at night, for my father was very strict on that subject, but now I had not one fear. When I came back, the moon was riding clear above the houses. I went into the churchyard, and there offered a prayer as holy, if not as deeply true, as any I know now; a prayer, which perhaps took form as the guardian angel of my life. If that word in the Bible, Selah, means what gray-headed old men think it does, when they read aloud, it should be written here,—Selah!

Since that day, I have never more been completely engaged in self; but the statue has been emerging, though slowly, from the block. Others may not see the promise even of its pure symmetry, but I do, and am learning to be patient. I shall be all human yet; and then the hour will come to leave humanity, and live always in the pure ray.

This first day I was taken up; but the second time the Holy Ghost descended like a dove. I went out again for a day, but this time it was spring. I walked in the fields of Groton. But I will not describe that day; its music still sounds too sweetly near. Suffice it to say, I gave all into our Father's hands, and was no stern-weaving Fate more, but one elected to obey, and love, and at last know. Since then I have suffered, as I must suffer again, till all the complex be made simple, but I have never been in discord with the grand harmony.

Journal fragment, 1840

I grow more and more what they will call a mystic. Nothing interests me except listening to the secret harmonies of nature. . . .

The oar has fallen from hand, the sail has sent away. I have no means to steer my boat. There shines the polestar, I keep my eye fixed upon it; friendly waves,—will ye not drift me to the needed haven!

If I meet men for a brief time, they check and veil the music, like heavy draperies near an instrument, but if they stay near me long I fill them till they vibrate.

But this music is sweet in my soul to very pain. I cannot alter it, and the hour when I should do so seems afar, yet it swells my heart painfully, thoughts move and push forth from my heart like young birds from the nest, but as yet, if any tries to take wing it falls back into the nest ruffled and trembling with cold.

We mortals live too imperfectly to be happy. While brooding on our birds we famish and our bright plumes fall off. I would brood a beautiful lark into life every night and let it soar with the morning sun. I would let loose whole flights of little birds with every new fleece of snow. I would drop them numerous as hail, gentle as manna, upon the harvest field. There is no need of an Inferno, it will be punishment enough for every fault, if we never become creators!

~

To Caroline Sturgis

8 Sept. 1840

. . . I live, I am—*The carbuncle is found.* And at present the mere sight of my talisman is enough. The hour may come when I wish to charm with it, but not yet. I have no future, as no past. . . .

~

To Caroline Sturgis

26 Sept. 1840

. . . Of the mighty changes in my spiritual life I do not wish to speak, yet surely you cannot be ignorant of them. All has been revealed, all foreshown yet I know it not. Experiment has given place to certainty, pride to obedience, thought to love, and truth is lost in beauty. . . . When we meet you will find me at home. Into that home cold winds may blow, keen lightnings dart their bolts, but I cannot be driven from it more. . . .

～

To Ralph Waldo Emerson

29 Sept. 1840

. . . All things I have given up to the central power, you also; yet, I cannot forbear adding, dear friend. I am now so at home, I know not how again to wander and grope, seeking my place in another Soul. I need to be recognized. After this, I shall be claimed, rather than claim, yet if I speak of facts, it must be as I see them. . . .

～

To Caroline Sturgis

22 Oct. 1840

. . . But I can say very little now, scarce a word that is not absolutely drawn from me at the moment. I cannot plunge into myself enough. I cannot dedicate myself sufficiently. The life that flows in upon me from so many quarters is too beautiful to be checked. I would not check a single pulsation. It all ought to be;—if caused by any apparition of the Divine in me I could bless myself like the holy Mother. But like her I long to be virgin. I would fly from the land of my birth. I would hide myself in night and poverty. Does a star point out the spot. The gifts I must receive, yet for my child, not me. I have no words, wait till he is of age, then hear *him.*

Oh Caroline, my soul swells with the future. The past, I know it not. . . .

～

To William H. Channing

25/28 Oct. 1840

. . . The old religionists did talk about "grace, conversion," and the like, technically, without striving to enter into the idea, till they quite lost sight of it. Undervaluing the intellect, they became slaves of a sect, instead of organs of the Spirit. . . . Yet the time seems now to have come for reinterpreting the old dogmas. I would now preach the Holy Ghost as zealously as they have been preaching Man, and faith instead of the understanding, and mysticism &c. . . .

∾

To William H. Channing

3 Dec. 1840

. . . My brother Edward was born on my birth-day, and they said he should be my child. But he sickened and died just as the bud of his existence showed its first bright hues. He was some weeks wasting away, and I took care of him always half the night. He was a beautiful child, and became very dear to me then. Still in lonely woods the up-turned violets show me the pleading softness of his large blue eyes, in those hours when I would have given worlds to prevent his suffering, and could not I used to carry him about in my arms for hours; it soothed him, and I loved to feel his gentle weight of helpless purity upon my heart, while night listened around. At last, when death came, and the soul took wing like an overtasked bird from his sweet form, I felt what I feel now. Might I free ————, as that angel freed him! . . .

∾

1st Jany 1841

River of beauty flowing through the life
How joyful were thy smiles in plain and vale,
Flower, Star, Swan, graceful tree and golden sands
Decked thy long course in its successive thoughts
It seemed could know no end. Soft spread the meadow
Nobly the tenderness of heavenly blue
And o'er thy mirror the fair clouds were happy
Alike in coming and in vanishing,

And canst thou pause, Oh poem of the world,
    Oh lyre once strung, how canst thou fail a note?
If music be the food of love, play on,
    Love pauses not; how can its accents cease?
    Alas! there was a chasm in the earth,
    Down plunged my stream, astonished, where stern rocks
Repelled its sweetness, and refused its depths,
    Foam blurred its amber clearness, and its tones
Of happy faith are roused to beg and chide
    "Impede me not, my brethren of the Earth,
    Still let me, blissful, deck his gentle breast."
    —But no! the wild cleft opens, wilder still,
    And draws her into a cold silent rush
    Through caverns dark, unvisited, unthought of,
Where never look of love from moon nor star,
    Where never thought of power from nearest Sun,
    Nor bird, nor falling flower with mute caress
Shall cheer the longing waves from weariness
    Of following, following—whither no wave knows.

And yet, they shrink not from thee, solemn cave
    Forbidding, yet inviting this dimmed love
The Suns and Moons which flatter need them not,
    And faithfully have they adorned the vale;
Has now the moment come to live with thee,
    Thou must not be left lonely. Doth the light
The cheerful light refuse to follow—
    Yet music hangs upon the darkened course
Of Echoes silvery plaintive, and, indeed,
    In the faint wooing winning tenderer
Than the full voices of triumphant day;
    And we will dress the hall where they abide
With diamond sheen which asks not to be seen,
    But, conscious of its worth, for centuries
Can wait the flashing torch, unless indeed
    The inmost powers a strange convulsion cause
And give the glorious secrets of sad love,
    Of darkened, chilled, but changeless love to day;
Then shall, perchance, be seen
    From this dim grotto to the crystal heights
    Of those serenest heavens is but a step
        For winged feet elastic.

The pilgrim angels wandered on the plain
Long, long had most been absent from their home,
　　All suffered, and all strove for their return,
Melodia suffered most, much would have striven,
　　Had but her way been clear.
Her heart was large with love, her ear was keen,
Her hand was strong upon the golden wires,
But through her flowed such endless wishing sweetness
As dimmed here eye with tears; she asked a guide,
　　Or else to have that sweetness harmonized,
That she might pause in thought, kneel in the shrine,
　　And see, clear eyed, the Virgin Mother smile.

One day she wandered lonely in the grove,
Lonely she long had been, thus was the best;
　　For other pilgrims saw not why she wept,
And, walking in their paths, she sang to them
　　Of their own hope, but none had ear for hers,
Nor cleared her eye, nor prophesied the song
　　In which the key of all her being lay;
True they were hers, because they were from God,
　　But none her ministrants, companions none,
Their office different, hopeless deep; *less wild*
　　Melodia sometimes felt, but never thought.

And now she sang a song, a full-voiced descant song,
But often lost the key and changed the strain
　　For the key-note was placed in other spheres
　　Whose echo her soul knew, but her ear missed;
When lo! a note sent back, vibration felt,
　　Startled her soul to sudden revelation,
And near her stood her angel and her friend,
　　Receptive, bounteous, radiant, and profound.

　　　Not quite unknown the form;—
For in a marble quarry wandering,
Once her keen voice startled it from the rock;
But she in childish marvel silent grew
And paused to gaze,—as ceased her heavenward song
　　The form drew back into its cradle tomb,
For ages to await the sculptor's thought,
　　Nor could her voluntary song recal,
And haunting hope grew sister to despair.

But now the hour had come;—
And, through the skilful wounds and splintering blows
    Which Nature uses most, loving the most,
Slowly he had come forth, of godlike mould.
The Paria, from Paros' whiteness named
Sepulchral whiteness of the holiest tomb.

How met that music and that purity
They knew not; meetings never can be known
    As separations are; it was; it lived;
It is, and what is known, in being known, is not.

But not a moment could they be detained,
When thus united, from their proper home,
    One marble gleam, one short and lovely note,
The dazzling gate was passed; the robe of primal life put on.

Too soon, too keen! The work of Love is still
To antedate our Fates; this union pure,
    This wedlock of the two Eternities
Meeting in God has for its child a Man.

Close in the bosom of the only Love,
Birds drawn back to the nest, one moment full
    They felt the pulse of the creative heart,
And were the key-note of Concordia,
    They lived the multiple of Unity,
Revolved, the all-embracing Sun and Moon,
    Shed forth in that one look of mutual love,
All stars, flowers, rivers, Angels, Gods and Thoughts,
    And brooding, trembling, hovered into life;
Such was the smile of God which these two angels meant,
    The fullest utterance One has ever made,
The much that calls for more, the light of final shade.

Oh words weak wondrous words! Night listened round
The Spheral Music singing without sound,
    All that was ever lost that instant found,
All that was ever loosed that life-pulse bound,
Speech wedded silence, Death life crowning crowned;
    It is and yet has ceased to be.
    Melodia was again, and being so
Paria had fled into the secret caves

To purify anew a second life
And from the marble centre to the diamond.
　　But she, Melodia!
How can she wait, a voice, which was a life?
　　Oh reassure, Eternal Harmony,
This wandering vestal of herself bereft,
　　And veil in prayers the breast without a heart,
And bind with truth the wound that truth has made,
And calm in faithful death the broken life of Love.

Journal, Jan. 1841

Each moment is an age between me, and the consummation of my existence. I have realized the phenomenal nature of outward action, and can there find refuge and rest never again, only by deepening the fountains of Spirit can I obtain any peace. At present I can only wait as I may. I die daily, yet cannot plunge down to rise again into heaven. I rest with heavenward, though languid eye, with broad and gloomy pinion upon the surface of myself. Seeing thee, Sun, far and bright, though wild, I trust thou will enable me to wait the fertilizing beam. Permit not that I say "Why hast thou forsaken me?"

I wandered in the subterranean recesses, the light was darkness; my feet bled with the sharp stones I could not see to avoid; cliffs pierced my ardent breast; cold and foreign substances slid on either side from my seeking hands. Gleams of light came sometimes only to show me that the path wound on and on. Suddenly a wide blaze, of meteoric light? showed me the cave with its diamond pillars and river path, which had been waiting for ages the seeker who must try the depths as well as scale the heights. I looked around a moment at the glittering walls, then plunged in with brow serene; the waters were cold but I did not shrink, beside they rushed onward with a force I felt, the stern chill and the sudden darkness into which they drew me were nothing—but now they have left me on this unknown lake, how shall I pass the moments, till I am seized and borne once more toward the eternal sea. How —I ask not why is it, but *how* I shall bear it? . . .

My head is very sensitive, and as they described the Spina Christi, I shuddered all over, and could have fainted only at the thought of its pressure on his head. Yet if he had experienced the sufferings of humanity and believed that by "thy will be done" a steady feeling in his breast during these hours of torture from an ungrateful race, he could free them from suffering & sin. I feel how he might have borne it.— It seems to me I might be educated through suffering to the same purity . . .

Return Madonna, for none since thee has been the mother of a perfectly holy child. Why have not all women since been dedicate and pure, then he would not have been left alone. Is there not one, one whose heart is free from idolatry? not one worthy of a miracle? Ah there were buds of promise, yet not one that I know would dare to invoke the Angel, or arm her hand with the palm branch.

∼

Journal, Feb. 1841

I wish I were a man, and then there would be one. I weary in this playground of boys, proud and happy in their balls and marbles. Give me heroes, poets, lawgivers, then.

There are women much less unworthy to love than you, men. The best are so unripe, the wisest, so ignoble, the truest so cold!

Divine Spirit, I pray thee, grow out into our age before I leave it. I pray, I prophesy, I trust, yet I pine.

∼

c. 1840–41

LILLO

New England village. Father a lawyer. Much engrossment in his profession. Upright and kind, but sharp outward and Martinet. Aunts hardened a vulgarized representation of himself. Mother died early. The child's heart pious for the rainbow of beauty and love. The sign of an eternal covenant that the Mother's face affords as she bends over her sobbing child. She stoops to him as the rainbow of the heavens over the earth— Nature always avenges herself and these feelings, if not indulged at their natural season vindicate their claims at another. My anguish at a later day on seeing the Madonna of the chair. At 17 I elected a Mother, but this comes in a later chapter. My first view of society. Gossips that visit my Aunt. Marriage and domestic life made hateful by their profaning talk. My tutor, also a Martinet— His influence. Good and bad. My life is twofold— The Roman chapter & the Garden. What flowers were to me. The little door that opened beneath the vine to the sunset. Objects breathing and growing in the moonlight. Modern European influences. English lady known at 7 years old. Gaze at her in church. Her dress, her hazel eyes and clustering locks. My visit to her. Her harp, and all it gave rise to in my mind. She gives me the bunch of golden flowers which come, she says from Madeira. Greek phantasy Islands of the blest. Meads of Asphodel, and lives passed in playing on golden harps. How my father's library was formed. On the whole how good for me. Elegant extracts, Pope and Spectator on Sunday. I steal the keys quite destitute of moral compunction. First night of Shakspeare. Chapter on Shakspeare. My good thus brought me also Moliere and Cervantes. My bad Lesage and Smollet— Critique— English novelists— State of the body and brain at this too until lecture period—when my father hid the keys. He should have given me active games in their place. What daily contact with boys teaches easily and pleasantly I had to learn afterwards with care and pain at the university and too late for the good influences on my bodily constitution. First influence of society. When I was brought into contact with it. Makes me a coxcomb, or bully, and an intriguer. French period. Frederick the Great. De Retz. Rousseau. My Mother Elect. Arminians. Beauty & truth are the same. The Italian poets. The German philosophers. Many intimacies follow one another. They cultivate the intellect and develope the passions but speak not to the soul. My life is for years social, polite and various, but shallow music raises me in some measure from this. Then comes love, Ella. I give her up to another. Renunciation hallows and clarifies. My life begins to be musical. I am one string on the great harp. I go abroad. Art. A tropical nature Rafaello & Marc ———. Pictures. Goethe. My father's death recals me to N England. Episode of my cousin Annette. Ce n'est que le premier pas que coute. I encounter practical life—I teach. Buy and sell. I know men as citizens. Meet Lillo. The crisis of soul and final & N England life. Transcendentalism. Crudeness of reform—Vulgarity of reformers. Pas encore. Yet Geere saved the Capital. Bettine. The silver time, how it had spoken to me since my childhood. By that I abide. The church, quite set aside. Jesus Christ. Elizabeth's Children. Swedenborg. Lillo. Crisis of my life. My heart breaks. The soul chooses its own. I go to the western forest to think it out. Thou art strong O Bettine. Live in the world and wait for me. I will return.

～

A Credo

Summer 1842

There is a spirit uncontainable and uncontained. —Within it all manifestation is contained, whether of good (accomplishment) or evil (obstruction). To itself its depths are unknown. By living it seeks to know itself. Thus evolving plants, animals, men, suns, stars, angels, and, it is to be presumed an infinity of forms not yet visible in the horizon of this being who now writes.

Its modes of operation are two-fold. First as genius inspires genius,—love love,—angel mother brings forth angel-child. This is the uninterrupted generation or publication of spirit taking upon itself congenial forms.

—Second

Conquering obstruction, finding the like in the unlike. This is a secondary generation, a new dynasty, as virtue for simplicity, faith for oneness, charity for pure love.

Then begins the genesis of Man, as through his consciousness he attests the laws which regulated the divine genesis. The Father is justified in the Son.

The mind of man asks "why was this second development? —Why seeks the divine to exchange best for better, bliss for hope, domesticity for knowledge? We reject the plan in the universe which the Spirit permitted as the condition of conscious life.

We reject it in the childhood of the soul's life. —The cry of infancy is why should we seek God when he is always there, why seek what is ours as soul's through indefinite pilgrimages, and burdensome cultures.

The intellect has no answer to this question, yet as we through faith and purity of deed enter into the nature of the Divine it is answered from our own experience. We understand though we cannot explain the mystery of something gained where all already is.

God we say is Love, if we believe this we must trust him. Whatever has been permitted by the law of being must be *for* good, and only *in time* not *good*. We do trust him and are led forward by experience. Light gives experience of outward life, faith of inward. We then discern however faintly the necessary harmony of the true lives. The moment we have broken through an obstruction, not accidentally but by the aid of Faith we begin to realize why any was permitted. We begin to interpret the Universe and deeper depths are opened with each soul that is convinced. For it would seem that the Divine expressed his meaning to himself more distinctly in man than in the other forms of our sphere, and through him uttered distinctly the Hallelujah which the other forms of nature only intimate.

Whenever man remains imbedded in nature, whether from sensuality or because he is not yet awakened to consciousness, the purpose of the whole remains unfulfilled, hence our displeasure when man is not, in a sense, *above* nature. Yet when he is not so closely bound with all other manifestations, as duly to express their spirit, we are also displeased. He must be at once the highest form of nature and conscious of the meaning she has been striving successively to unfold through those below him. . . .

~

Journal, October 1842

Many things interested me at the time which are not worth writing about, but nothing fixed my attention so much, as a large engraving of Me Recamier in her boudoir. I have so often thought over the intimacy between her and Me de Stael. It is so true that a woman may be in love with a woman, and a man with a man. It is so pleasant to be sure of it because undoubtedly it is the same love that we shall feel when we are angels when we ascend to the only place fit for the Mignon's where

Sie fragen nicht nach Mann und Weib—

It is regulated by the same law as that of love between persons of different sexes, only it is purely intellectual and spiritual, unprofaned by any mixture of lower instincts, undisturbed by any need of consulting temporal interests, its law is the desire of the spirit to realize a whole which makes it seek in another being for what it finds not in itself. Thus the beautiful seeks the strong, and the strong the beautiful, the mute seek the eloquent &c the butterfly settles always on the dark flower. Why did Socrates love Alcibiades?—why did Korner love Schneider? how natural is the love of Wallenstein for Max, that of Me de Stael for de Recamier, mine for Anna Barker[.] I loved Anna for a time I think with as much passion as I was then strong enough to feel— Her face was always gleaming before me, her voice was echoing in my ear, all poetic thoughts clustered round the dear image. This love was a key which unlocked for me many a treasure which I still possess, it was the carbuncle (emblematic gem) which cast light into many of the darkest caverns of human nature. — She loved me, too, though not so much, because her nature was "less high, less grave, less large, less deep" but she loved more tenderly, less passionately[.] She loved me, for I well remember her suffering when she first would feel my faults and knew one part of the exquisite veil rent away, how she wished to stay apart and weep the whole day. Then again that night when she leaned on me and her eyes were such a deep violet blue, so like night, as they never were before, and we both felt such a strange mystic thrill and knew what we had never known before. Now well too can I now account for that desire which I often had to get away from her and be alone with nature, which displeased her so, for she wished to be with me all the time. I do not love her now with passion, for I have exhausted her idea, and she does not stimulate my fancy, she does not represent the Beautiful to me now, she is only one beautiful object. Then she has never had a chance to get a hold on my heart by the thousand links of intimacy, we have been so little together; all was from the elective affinities. But still I love her with a sort of pallid, tender romance and feel towards her as I can to no other woman. I thought of all this as I looked at Me Recamier and had one thought beside which has often come into my mind, but I will not write it down; it is so singular that I have often thought I would never express it in any way; I am sure no human being but myself would understand it—

AUTOBIOGRAPHICAL ROMANCE

Parents

My FATHER was a lawyer and a politician. He was a man largely endowed with that sagacious energy, which the state of New England society, for the last half century, has been so well fitted to develop. His father was a clergyman, settled as pastor in Princeton, Massachusetts, within the bounds of whose parish-farm was Wachuset. His means were small, and the great object of his ambition was to send his sons to college. As a boy, my father was taught to think only of preparing himself for Harvard University, and when there of preparing himself for the profession of Law. As a Lawyer, again, the ends constantly presented were to work for distinction in the community, and for the means of supporting a family. To be an honored citizen, and to have a home on earth, were made the great aims of existence. To open the deeper fountains of the soul, to regard life here as the prophetic entrance to immortality, to develop his spirit to perfection,—motives like these had never been suggested to him, either by fellow-beings or by outward circumstances. The result was a character, in its social aspect, of quite the common sort. A good son and brother, a kind neighbor, an active man of business—in all these outward relations he was but one of a class, which surrounding conditions have made the majority among us. In the more delicate and individual relations, he never approached but two mortals, my mother and myself.

His love for my mother was the green spot on which he stood apart from the common-places of a mere bread-winning, bread-bestowing existence. She was one of those fair and flower-like natures, which sometimes spring up even beside the most dusty highways of life—a creature not to be shaped into a merely useful instrument, but bound by one law with the blue sky, the dew, and the frolic birds. Of all

24

persons whom I have known, she had in her most of the angelic,—of that spontaneous love for every living thing, for man, and beast, and tree, which restores the golden age.

Death in the House

MY EARLIEST recollection is of a death,—the death of a sister, two years younger than myself. Probably there is a sense of childish endearments, such as belong to this tie, mingled with that of loss, of wonder, and mystery; but these last are prominent in memory. I remember coming home and meeting our nursery-maid, her face streaming with tears. That strange sight of tears made an indelible impression. I realize how little I was of stature, in that I looked up to this weeping face;—and it has often seemed since, that—full-grown for the life of this earth, I have looked up just so, at times of threatening, of doubt, and distress, and that just so has some being of the next higher order of existences looked down, aware of a law unknown to me, and tenderly commiserating the pain I must endure in emerging from my ignorance.

She took me by the hand and led me into a still and dark chamber,—then drew aside the curtain and showed me my sister. I see yet that beauty of death! The highest achievements of sculpture are only the reminder of its severe sweetness. Then I remember the house all still and dark,—the people in their black clothes and dreary faces,—the scent of the newly-made coffin,—my being set up in a chair and detained by a gentle hand to hear the clergyman,—the carriages slowly going, the procession slowly doling out their steps to the grave. But I have no remembrance of what I have since been told I did,—insisting, with loud cries, that they should not put the body in the ground. I suppose that my emotion was spent at the time, and so there was nothing to fix that moment in my memory.

I did not then, nor do I now, find any beauty in these ceremonies. What had they to do with the sweet playful child? Her life and death were alike beautiful, but all this sad parade was not. Thus my first experience of life was one of death. She who would have been the companion of my life was severed from me, and I was left alone. This has made a vast difference in my lot. Her character, if that fair face promised right, would have been soft, graceful and lively; it would have tempered mine to a gentler and more gradual course.

Overwork

MY FATHER,—all of whose feelings were now concentred on me,—instructed me himself. The effect of this was so far good that, not passing through the hands of many ignorant and weak persons as so many do at preparatory schools, I was put at once under discipline of considerable severity, and, at the same time, had a more than ordinarily high standard presented to me. My father was a man of business, even in literature; he had been a high scholar at college, and was warmly attached to all he had learned there, both from the pleasure he had derived in the exercise of his faculties and the associated memories of success and good repute. He was, beside, well read in French literature, and in English, a Queen Anne's man. He hoped to make me the heir of all he knew, and of as much more as the income of his profession enabled him to give me means of acquiring. At the very beginning, he made one great mistake, more common, it is to be hoped, in the last generation, than the warnings of physiologists will permit it to be with the next. He thought to gain time, by bringing forward the intellect as early as possible. Thus I had tasks given me, as many and various as the hours would allow, and on subjects beyond my age; with the additional disadvantage of reciting to him in the evening, after he returned from his office. As he was subject to many interruptions, I was often kept up till very late; and as he was a severe teacher, both from his habits of mind and his ambition for me, my feelings were kept on the stretch till the recitations were over. Thus frequently, I was sent to bed several hours too late, with nerves unnaturally stimulated. The consequence was a premature development of the brain, that made me a "youthful prodigy" by day, and by night a victim of spectral illusions, nightmare, and somnambulism, which at the time prevented the harmonious development of my bodily powers and checked my growth, while, later, they induced continual headache, weakness and nervous affections, of all kinds. As these again re-acted on the brain, giving undue force to every thought and every feeling, there was finally produced a state of being both too active and too intense, which wasted my constitution, and will bring me,—even although I have learned to understand and regulate my now morbid temperament,—to a premature grave.

No one understood this subject of health then. No one knew why this child, already kept up so late, was still unwilling to retire. My aunts cried out upon the "spoiled child, the most unreasonable child that ever was,—if brother could but open his eyes to see it,—who was never willing to go to bed." They did not know that, so soon as the light was taken away, she seemed to see colossal faces advancing slowly towards her, the eyes dilating, and each feature swelling loathsomely as they came, till at last, when they were about to close upon her, she started up with a shriek which drove them away, but only to return when she lay down again. They did not know that, when at last she went to sleep, it was to dream of horses trampling over her, and to awake once more in fright, or, as she had just read in her Virgil, of being among trees that dripped with blood, where she walked and walked and could not get out, while the blood became a pool and plashed over her feet, and rose higher and higher, till soon she dreamed it would reach her lips. No wonder the child arose and walked in her sleep, moaning all over the house, till once, when they heard her, and came and waked her, and she told what she had dreamed, her father sharply bid her "leave off thinking of such nonsense, or she would be crazy,"—never knowing that he was himself the cause of all these horrors of the night. Often she dreamed of following to the grave the body of her mother, as she had done that of her sister, and woke to find the pillow drenched in tears. These dreams softened her heart too much, and cast a deep shadow over her young days; for then, and later, the life of dreams,—probably because there was in it less to distract the mind from its own earnestness,—has often seemed to her more real, and been remembered with more interest, than that of waking hours.

Poor child! Far remote in time, in thought, from that period, I look back on these glooms and terrors, wherein I was enveloped, and perceive that I had no natural childhood!

Books

THUS PASSED my first years. My mother was in delicate health, and much absorbed in the care of her younger children. In the house was neither dog nor bird, nor any graceful animated form of existence. I saw no persons who took my fancy, and real life offered no attraction. Thus my already over-excited mind found no relief from without, and was driven for refuge from itself to the world of books. I was taught Latin and English grammar at the same time, and began to read Latin at six years old, after which, for some years, I read it daily. In this branch of study, first by my father, and afterwards by a tutor, I was trained to quite a high degree of precision. I was expected to understand the mechanism of the language thoroughly, and in translating to give the thoughts in as few well-arranged words as possible, and without breaks or hesitation,—for with these my father had absolutely no patience.

Indeed, he demanded accuracy and clearness in everything: you must not speak, unless you can make your meaning perfectly intelligible to the person addressed; must not express a thought, unless you can give a reason for it, if required; must not make a statement, unless sure of all particulars—such were his rules. "But," "if," "unless," "I am mistaken," and "it may be so," were words and phrases excluded from the province where he held sway. Trained to great dexterity in artificial methods, accurate, ready, with entire command of his resources, he had no belief in minds that listen, wait, and receive. He had no conception of the subtle and indirect motions of imagination and feeling. His influence on me was great, and opposed to the natural unfolding of my character, which was fervent, of strong grasp, and disposed to infatuation, and self-forgetfulness. He made the common prose world so present to me, that my natural bias was controlled. I did not go mad, as many would do, at being continually roused from my dreams. I had too much strength to be crushed,—and since I must put on the fetters, could not submit to let them impede my motions. My own world sank deep within, away from the surface of my life; in what I did and said I learned to have reference to other minds. But my true life was only the dearer that it was secluded and veiled over by a thick curtain of available intellect, and that coarse, but wearable stuff woven by the ages,— Common Sense.

In accordance with this discipline in heroic common sense, was the influence of those great Romans, whose thoughts and lives were my daily food during those plastic years. The genius of Rome displayed itself in Character, and scarcely needed an occasional wave of the torch of thought to show its lineaments, so marble strong they gleamed in every light. Who, that has lived with those men, but admires the plain force of fact, of thought passed into action? They take up things with their naked hands. There is just the man, and the block he casts before you,—no divinity, no demon, no unfulfilled aim, but just the man and Rome, and what he did for Rome. Everything turns your attention to what a man can become, not by yielding himself freely to impressions, not by letting nature play freely through him, but by a single thought, an earnest purpose, an indomitable will, by hardihood, self-command, and force of expression. Architecture was the art in which Rome excelled, and this corresponds with the feeling these men of Rome excite. They did not grow,—they built themselves up, or were built up by the fate of Rome, as a temple for Jupiter Stator. The ruined Roman sits among the ruins; he flies to no green garden; he does not look to heaven; if his intent is defeated, if he is less than he meant to be, he lives no more. The names which end in "*us,*" seem to speak with lyric cadence. That measured cadence,—that tramp and march,—which are not stilted, because they indicate real force, yet which seem so when compared with any other language,—make Latin a study in itself of mighty influence. The language alone, without the literature, would give one the *thought* of Rome. Man present in nature, commanding nature too sternly to be inspired by it, standing like the rock amid the sea, or moving like the fire over the land, either impassive, or irresistible; knowing not the soft mediums or fine flights of life, but by the force which he expresses, piercing to the centre.

We are never better understood than when we speak of a "Roman virtue," a "Roman outline." There is somewhat indefinite, somewhat yet unfulfilled in the thought of Greece, of Spain, of modern Italy; but ROME! it stands by itself, a clear Word. The power of will, the dignity of a fixed purpose is what it utters. Every Roman was an emperor. It is well that the infallible church should have been founded on this rock, that the presumptuous Peter should hold the keys, as the conquering Jove did before his thunderbolts, to be seen of all the world. The Apollo tends flocks with Admetus, Christ teaches by the lonely lake, or plucks wheat as he wanders through the fields some Sabbath morning. They never come to this stronghold, they could not have breathed freely where all became stone as soon as spoken, where divine youth found no horizon for its all-promising glance, but every thought put on, before it dared issue to the day in action, its *toga virilis*.

Suckled by this wolf, man gains a different complexion from that which is fed by the Greek honey. He takes a noble bronze in camps and battle-fields; the wrinkles of council well beseem his brow, and the eye cuts its way like the sword. The Eagle should never have been used as a symbol by any other nation: it belonged to Rome

The history of Rome abides in mind, of course, more than the literature. It was degeneracy for a Roman to use the pen; his life was in the day. The "vaunting" of Rome, like that of the North American Indians, is her proper literature. A man rises; he tells who he is, and what he has done; he speaks of his country and her brave men; he knows that a conquering god is there, whose agent is his own right hand; and he should end like the Indian, "I have no more to say."

It never shocks us that the Roman is self-conscious. One wants no universal truths from him, no philosophy, no creation, but only his life, his Roman life felt in every pulse, realized in every gesture. The universal heaven takes in the Roman only to make us feel his individuality the more. The Will, the Resolve of Man!—it has been expressed,—fully expressed!

I steadily loved this ideal in my childhood, and this is the cause, probably, why I have always felt that man must know how to stand firm on the ground, before he can fly. In vain for me are men more, if they are less, than Romans. Dante was far greater than any Roman, yet I feel he was right to take the Mantuan as his guide through hell, and to heaven.

Horace was a great deal to me then, and is so still. Though his words do not abide in memory, his presence does: serene, courtly, of darting hazel eye, a self-sufficient grace, and an appreciation of the world of stern realities, sometimes pathetic, never tragic. He is the natural man of the world; he is what he ought to be, and his darts never fail of their aim. There is a perfume and raciness, too, which makes life a banquet, where the wit sparkles no less that the viands were bought with blood.

Ovid gave me not Rome, nor himself, but a view into the enchanted gardens of the Greek mythology. This path I followed, have been following ever since; and now, life half over, it seems to me, as in my childhood, that every thought of which man is susceptible, is intimated there. In those young years, indeed, I did not see what I now see, but loved to creep from amid the Roman pikes to lie beneath this great vine, and see the smiling and serene shapes go by, woven from the finest fibres of all the elements. I knew not why, at that time,—but I loved to get away from the hum of the forum, and the mailed clang of Roman speech, to these shifting shows of nature, these Gods and Nymphs born of the sunbeam, the wave, the shadows on the hill.

As with Rome I antedated the world of deeds, so I lived in those Greek forms the true faith of a refined and intense childhood. So great was the force of reality with which these forms impressed me, that I prayed earnestly for a sign,—that it would lighten in some particular region of the heavens, or that I might find a bunch of grapes in the path, when I went forth in the morning. But no sign was given, and I was left a waif stranded upon the shores of modern life!

Of the Greek language, I knew only enough to feel that the sounds told the same story as the mythology;—that the law of life in that land was beauty, as in Rome it was a stern composure. I wish I had learned as much of Greece as of Rome,—so freely does the mind play in her sunny waters, where there is no chill, and the restraint is from within out; for these Greeks, in an atmosphere of ample grace, could not be impetuous, or stern, but loved moderation as equable life always must, for it is the law of beauty.

With these books I passed my days. The great amount of study exacted of me soon ceased to be a burden, and reading became a habit and a passion. The force of feeling, which, under other circumstances, might have ripened thought, was turned to learn the thoughts of others. This was not a tame state, for the energies brought out by rapid acquisition gave glow enough. I thought with rapture of the all-accomplished man, him of the many talents, wide resources, clear sight, and omnipotent will. A Caesar seemed great enough. I did not then know that such men impoverish the treasury to build the palace. I kept their statues as belonging to the hall of my ancestors, and loved to conquer obstacles, and fed my youth and strength for their sake.

STILL, though the bias was so great that in earliest years I learned, in these ways, how the world takes hold of a powerful nature, I had yet other experiences. None of these were deeper than what I found in the happiest haunt of my childish years,—our little garden. Our house, though comfortable, was very ugly, and in a neighborhood which I detested,—every dwelling and its appurtenances having a *mesquin* and huddled look. I liked nothing about us except the tall graceful elms before the house, and the dear little garden behind. Our back door opened on a high flight of steps, by which I went down to a green plot, much injured in my ambitious eyes by the presence of the pump and tool-house. This opened into a little garden, full of choice flowers and fruit-trees, which was my mother's delight, and was carefully kept. Here I felt at home. A gate opened thence into the fields,—a wooden gate made of boards, in a high, unpainted board wall, and embowered in the clematis creeper. This gate I used to open to see the sunset heaven; beyond this black frame I did not step, for I liked to look at the deep gold behind it. How exquisitely happy I was in its beauty, and how I loved the silvery wreaths of my protecting vine! I never would pluck one of its flowers at that time, I was so jealous of its beauty, but often since I carry off wreaths of it from the wild-wood, and it stands in nature to my mind as the emblem of domestic love.

Of late I have thankfully felt what I owe to that garden, where the best hours of my lonely childhood were spent. Within the house everything was socially utilitarian; my books told of a proud world, but in another temper were the teachings of the little garden. There my thoughts could lie callow in the nest, and only be fed and kept warm,

not called to fly or sing before the time. I loved to gaze on the roses, the
violets, the lilies, the pinks; my mother's hand had planted them, and
they bloomed for me. I culled the most beautiful. I looked at them on
every side. I kissed them, I pressed them to my bosom with passionate
emotions, such as I have never dared express to any human being. An
ambition swelled my heart to be as beautiful, as perfect as they. I have
not kept my vow. Yet, forgive, ye wild asters, which gleam so sadly
amid the fading grass; forgive me, ye golden autumn flowers, which so
strive to reflect the glories of the departing distant sun; and ye silvery
flowers, whose moonlight eyes I knew so well, forgive! Living and
blooming in your unchecked law, ye know nothing of the blights, the
distortions, which beset the human being; and which at such hours it
would seem that no glories of free agency could ever repay!

THERE WAS, in the house, no apartment appropriated to the purpose
of a library, but there was in my father's room a large closet filled with
books, and to these I had free access when the task-work of the day
was done. Its window overlooked wide fields, gentle slopes, a rich and
smiling country, whose aspect pleased without much occupying the
eye, while a range of blue hills, rising at about twelve miles distance, allured to reverie. "Distant mountains," says Tieck, "excite the fancy, for
beyond them we place the scene of our Paradise." Thus, in the poems
of fairy adventure, we climb the rocky barrier, pass fearless its dragon
caves, and dark pine forests, and find the scene of enchantment in the
vale behind. My hopes were never so definite, but my eye was constantly allured to that distant blue range, and I would sit, lost in fancies,
till tears fell on my cheek. I loved this sadness; but only in later years,
when the realities of life had taught me moderation, did the passionate
emotions excited by seeing them again teach how glorious were the
hopes that swelled my heart while gazing on them in those early days.

Melancholy attends on the best joys of a merely ideal life, else
I should call most happy the hours in the garden, the hours in the
book closet. Here were the best French writers of the last century; for
my father had been more than half a Jacobin, in the time when the
French Republic cast its glare of promise over the world. Here, too,
were the Queen Anne authors, his models, and the English novelists;
but among them I found none that charmed me. Smollet, Fielding,
and the like, deal too broadly with the coarse actualities of life. The
best of their men and women—so merely natural, with the nature
found every day—do not meet our hopes. Sometimes the simple picture, warm with life and the light of the common son, cannot fail to

charm,—as in the wedded love of Fielding's Amelia,—but it is at a later day, when the mind is trained to comparison, that we learn to prize excellence like this as it deserves. Early youth is princelike: it will bend only to "the king, my father." Various kinds of excellence please, and leave their impression, but the most commanding, alone, is duly acknowledged at that all-exacting age.

Three great authors it was my fortune to meet at this important period,—all, though of unequal, yet congenial powers,—all of rich and wide, rather than aspiring genius,—all free to the extent of the horizon their eye took in,—all fresh with impulse, racy with experience; never to be lost sight of, or superseded, but always to be apprehended more and more.

Ever memorable is the day on which I first took a volume of SHAKSPEARE in my hand to read. It was on a Sunday.

—This day was punctiliously set apart in our house. We had family prayers, for which there was no time on other days. Our dinners were different, and our clothes. We went to church. My father put some limitations on my reading, but—bless him for the gentleness which has left me a pleasant feeling for the day!—he did not prescribe what was, but only what was *not,* to be done. And the liberty this left was a large one. "You must not read a novel, or a play;" but all other books, the worst, or the best, were open to me. The distinction was merely technical. The day was pleasing to me, as relieving me from the routine of tasks and recitations; it gave me freer play than usual, and there were fewer things occurred in its course, which reminded me of the divisions of time; still the church-going, where I heard nothing that had any connection with my inward life, and these rules, gave me associations with the day of empty formalities, and arbitrary restrictions; but though the forbidden book or walk always seemed more charming then, I was seldom tempted to disobey.—

This Sunday—I was only eight years old—I took from the bookshelf a volume lettered SHAKSPEARE. It was not the first time I had looked at it, but before I had been deterred from attempting to read, by the broken appearance along the page, and preferred smooth narrative. But this time I held in my hand "Romeo and Juliet" long enough to get my eye fastened to the page. It was a cold winter afternoon. I took the book to the parlor fire, and had there been seated an hour or two, when my father looked up and asked me what I was reading so intently. "Shakspeare," replied the child, merely raising her eye from the page. "Shakspeare,—that won't do; that's no book for Sunday; go put it away and take another." I went as I was bid, but took no other.

Returning to my seat, the unfinished story, the personages to whom
I was but just introduced, thronged and burnt my brain. I could not
bear it long; such a lure it was impossible to resist. I went and brought
the book again. There were several guests present, and I had got half
through the play before I again attracted attention. "What is that child
about that she don't hear a word that's said to her?" quoth my aunt.
"What are you reading?" said my father. "Shakspeare" was again the
reply, in a clear, though somewhat impatient, tone. "How?" said my
father angrily,—then restraining himself before his guests,—"Give me
the book and go directly to bed."

Into my little room no care of his anger followed me. Alone, in the
dark, I thought only of the scene placed by the poet before my eye,
where the free flow of life, sudden and graceful dialogue, and forms,
whether grotesque or fair, seen in the broad lustre of his imagination, gave just what I wanted, and brought home the life I seemed
born to live. My fancies swarmed like bees, as I contrived the rest
of the story;—what all would do, what say, where go. My confinement tortured me. I could not go forth from this prison to ask after
these friends; I could not make my pillow of the dreams about them
which yet I could not forbear to frame. Thus was I absorbed when
my father entered. He felt it right, before going to rest, to reason
with me about my disobedience, shown in a way, as he considered, so
insolent. I listened, but could not feel interested in what he said, nor
turn my mind from what engaged it. He went away really grieved
at my impenitence, and quite at a loss to understand conduct in me
so unusual.

—Often since I have seen the same misunderstanding between parent and child,—the parent thrusting the morale, the discipline, of life
upon the child, when just engrossed by some game of real importance
and great leadings to it. That is only a wooden horse to the father,—
the child was careering to distant scenes of conquest and crusade,
through a country of elsewhere unimagined beauty. None but poets
remember their youth; but the father who does not retain poetical
apprehension of the world, free and splendid as it stretches out before
the child, who cannot read his natural history, and follow out its inti-
mations with reverence, must be a tyrant in his home, and the purest
intentions will not prevent his doing much to cramp him. Each new
child is a new Thought, and has bearings and discernings, which the
Thoughts older in date know not yet, but must learn.—

My attention thus fixed on Shakspeare. I returned to him at every
hour I could command. Here was a counterpoise to my Romans, still

more forcible than the little garden. My author could read the Roman nature too,—read it in the sternness of Coriolanus, and in the varied wealth of Caesar. But he viewed these men of will as only one kind of men; he kept them in their place, and I found that he, who could understand the Roman, yet expressed in Hamlet a deeper thought.

In CERVANTES, I found far less productive talent,—indeed, a far less powerful genius,—but the same wide wisdom, a discernment piercing the shows and symbols of existence, yet rejoicing in them all, both for their own life, and as signs of the unseen reality. Not that Cervantes philosophized,— his genius was too deeply philosophical for that; he took things as they came before him, and saw their actual relations and bearings. Thus the work he produced was of deep meaning, though he might never have expressed that meaning to himself. It was left implied in the whole. A Coleridge comes and calls Don Quixote the pure Reason, and Sancho the Understanding. Cervantes made no such distinctions in his own mind; but he had seen and suffered enough to bring out all his faculties, and to make him comprehend the higher as well as the lower part of our nature. Sancho is too amusing and sagacious to be contemptible; the Don too noble and clear-sighted towards absolute truth, to be ridiculous. And we are pleased to see manifested in this way, how the lower must follow and serve the higher, despite its jeering mistrust and the stubborn realities which break up the plans of this pure-minded champion.

The effect produced on the mind is nowise that described by Byron:—

"Cervantes smiled Spain's chivalry away," &c.

On the contrary, who is not conscious of a sincere reverence for the Don, prancing forth on his gaunt steed? Who would not rather be he than any of the persons who laugh at him?—Yet the one we would wish to be is thyself, Cervantes, unconquerable spirit! gaining flavor and color like wine from every change, while being carried round the world; in whose eye the serene sagacious laughter could not be dimmed by poverty, slavery, or unsuccessful authorship. Thou art to us still more the Man, though less the Genius, than Shakspeare; thou dost not evade our sight, but, holding the lamp to thine own magic shows, dost enjoy them with us.

My third friend was MOLIÈRE, one very much lower, both in range and depth, than the others, but, as far as he goes, of the same character. Nothing secluded or partial is there about his genius,—a man of the world, and a man by himself, as he is. It was, indeed, only the poor social world of Paris that he saw, but he viewed it from the firm foundations of his manhood, and every lightest laugh rings from a clear perception, and teaches life anew.

These men were all alike in this,—they loved the *natural history* of man. Not what he should be, but what he is, was the favorite subject of their thought. Whenever a noble leading opened to the eye new paths of light, they rejoiced; but it was never fancy, but always fact, that inspired them. They loved a thorough penetration of the murkiest dens, and most tangled paths of nature; they did not spin from the desires of their own special natures, but reconstructed the world from materials which they collected on every side. Thus their influence upon me was not to prompt me to follow out thought in myself so much as to detect it everywhere, for each of these men is not only a nature, but a happy interpreter of many natures. They taught me to distrust all invention which is not based on a wide experience. Perhaps, too, they taught me to overvalue an outward experience at the expense of inward growth; but all this I did not appreciate till later.

It will be seen that my youth was not unfriended, since those great minds came to me in kindness. A moment of action in one's self, however, is worth an age of apprehension through others; not that our deeds are better, but that they produce a renewal of our being. I have had more productive moments and of deeper joy, but never hours of more tranquil pleasure than those in which these demi-gods visited me,—and with a smile so familiar, that I imagined the world to be full of such. They did me good, for by them a standard was early given of sight and thought, from which I could never go back, and beneath which I cannot suffer patiently my own life or that of any friend to fall. They did me harm, too, for the child fed with meat instead of milk becomes too soon mature. Expectations and desires were thus early raised, after which I must long toil before they can be realized. How poor the scene around, how tame one's own existence, how meagre and faint every power, with these beings in my mind! Often I must cast them quite aside in order to grow in my small way, and not sink into despair. Certainly I do not wish that instead of these masters I had read baby books, written down to children, and with such ignorant dulness that they blunt the senses and corrupt the tastes of the still plastic human being. But I do wish that I had read no books at all till later,—that I had lived with toys, and played in the open air. Children should not cull the fruits of reflection and observation early, but expand in the sun, and let thoughts come to them. They should not through books antedate their actual experiences, but should take them gradually, as sympathy and interpretation are needed. With me, much of life was devoured in the bud.

First Friend

FOR A FEW MONTHS, this bookish and solitary life was invaded by interest in a living, breathing figure. At church, I used to look around with a feeling of coldness and disdain, which, though I now well understand its causes, seems to my wiser mind as odious as it was unnatural. The puny child sought everywhere for the Roman or Shakspeare figures, and she was met by the shrewd, honest eye, the homely decency, or the smartness of a New England village on Sunday. There was beauty, but I could not see it then; it was not of the kind I longed for. In the next pew sat a family who were my especial aversion. There were five daughters, the eldest not above four-and-twenty,—yet they had the old fairy, knowing look, hard, dry, dwarfed, strangers to the All-Fair,—were working-day residents in this beautiful planet. They looked as if their thoughts had never strayed beyond the jobs of the day, and they were glad of it. Their mother was one of those shrunken, faded patterns of woman who have never done anything to keep smooth the cheek and dignify the brow. The father had a Scotch look of shrewd narrowness, and entire self-complacency. I could not endure this family, whose existence contradicted all my visions; yet I could not forbear looking at them.

As my eye one day was ranging about with its accustomed coldness, and the proudly foolish sense of being in a shroud of thoughts that were not their thoughts, it was arrested by a face most fair, and well-known as it seemed at first glance,—for surely I had met her before and waited for her long. But soon I saw that she was a new apparition foreign to that scene, if not to me. Her dress,—the arrangement of her hair, which had the graceful pliancy of races highly cultivated for long,—the intelligent and full picture of her eye, whose reserve was in its self-possession, not in timidity,—all combined to make up a whole impression, which, though too young to understand, I was well prepared to feel.

How wearisome now appears that thorough-bred *millefleur* beauty, the distilled result of ages of European culture! Give me rather the wild heath on the lonely hill-side, than such a rose-tree from the daintily clipped garden. But, then, I had but tasted the cup, and knew not how little it could satisfy; more, more, was all my cry; continued through years, till I had been at the very fountain. Indeed, it was a ruby-red, a perfumed draught, and I need not abuse the wine because I prefer water, but merely say I have had enough of it. Then, the first sight, the first knowledge of such a person was intoxication.

She was an English lady, who, by a singular chance, was cast upon this region for a few months. Elegant and captivating, her every look and gesture was tuned to a different pitch from anything I had ever known. She was in various ways "accomplished," as it is called, though to what degree I cannot now judge. She painted in oils;—I had never before seen any one use the brush, and days would not have been too long for me to watch the pictures growing beneath her hand. She played the harp; and its tones are still to me the heralds of the promised land I saw before me then. She rose, she looked, she spoke; and the gentle swaying motion she made all through life has gladdened memory, as the stream does the woods and meadows.

As she was often at the house of one of our neighbors, and afterwards at our own, my thoughts were fixed on her with all the force of my nature. It was my first real interest in my kind, and it engrossed me wholly. I had seen her,—I should see her,—and my mind lay steeped in the visions that flowed from this source. My task-work I went through with, as I have done on similar occasions all my life, aided by pride that could not bear to fail, or be questioned. Could I cease from doing the work of the day, and hear the reason sneeringly given,— "Her head is so completely taken up with ———— that she can do nothing"? Impossible.

Should the first love be blighted, they say, the mind loses its sense of eternity. All forms of existence seem fragile, the prison of time real, for a god is dead. Equally true is this of friendship. I thank Heaven that this first feeling was permitted its free flow. The years that lay between the woman and the girl only brought her beauty into perspective, and enabled me to see her as I did the mountains from my window, and made her presence to me a gate of Paradise. That which she was, that which she brought, that which she might have brought, were mine, and over a whole region of new life I ruled proprietor of the soil in my own right.

Her mind was sufficiently unoccupied to delight in my warm devotion. She could not know what it was to me, but the light cast by the flame through so delicate a vase cheered and charmed her. All who saw admired her in their way; but she would lightly turn her head from their hard or oppressive looks, and fix a glance of full-eyed sweetness on the child, who, from a distance, watched all her looks and motions. She did not say much to me—not much to any one; she spoke in her whole being rather than by chosen words. Indeed, her proper speech was dance or song, and what was less expressive did not greatly interest her. But she saw much, having in its perfection the woman's delicate sense for sympathies and attractions. We walked in the fields, alone. Though others were present, her eyes were gliding over all the field and plain for the objects of beauty to which she was of kin. She was not cold to her seeming companions; a sweet courtesy satisfied them, but it hung about her like her mantle that she wore without thinking of it; her thoughts were free, for these civilized beings can really live two lives at the same moment. With them she seemed to be, but her hand was given to the child at her side; others did not observe me, but to her I was the only human presence. Like a guardian spirit she led me through the fields and groves, and every tree, every bird greeted me, and said, what I felt, "She is the first angel of your life."

One time I had been passing the afternoon with her. She had been playing to me on the harp, and I sat listening in happiness almost unbearable. Some guests were announced. She went into another room to receive them, and I took up her book. It was Guy Mannering, then lately published, and the first of Scott's novels I had ever seen. I opened where her mark lay, and read merely with the feeling of continuing our mutual existence by passing my eyes over the same page where hers had been. It was the description of the rocks on the sea-coast where the little Harry Bertram was lost. I had never seen such places, and my mind was vividly stirred to imagine them. The scene rose before me, very unlike reality, doubtless, but majestic and wild. I was the little Harry Bertram, and had lost her,—all I had to lose,—and sought her vainly in long dark caves that had no end, plashing through the water; while the crags beetled above, threatening to fall and crush the poor child. Absorbed in the painful vision, tears rolled down my cheeks. Just then she entered with light step, and full-beaming eye. When she saw me thus, a soft cloud stole over her face, and clothed every feature with a lovelier tenderness than I had seen there before. She did not question, but fixed on me inquiring looks of beautiful love. I laid my head against her shoulder and wept,—dimly feeling that I must lose her and all,—all who spoke to me of the same things,— that the cold wave must rush over me. She waited till my tears were spent, then rising, took from a little box a bunch of golden amaranths or everlasting flowers, and gave them to me. They were very fragrant. "They came," she said, "from Madeira." These flowers stayed with me seventeen years. "Madeira" seemed to me the fortunate isle, apart in the blue ocean from all of ill or dread. Whenever I saw a sail passing

in the distance,—if it bore itself with fulness of beautiful certainty,—
I felt that it was going to Madeira. Those thoughts are all gone now.
No Madeira exists for me now,—no fortunate purple isle,—and all
these hopes and fancies are lifted from the sea into the sky. Yet I thank
the charms that fixed them here so long,—fixed them till perfumes
like those of the golden flowers were drawn from the earth, teaching
me to know my birth-place.

I can tell little else of this time,—indeed, I remember little, except
the state of feeling in which I lived. For I *lived,* and when this is the
case, there is little to tell in the form of thought. We meet—at least
those who are true to their instincts meet—a succession of persons
through our lives, all of whom have some peculiar errand to us. There
is an outer circle, whose existence we perceive, but with whom we
stand in no real relation. They tell us the news, they act on us in the offices of society, they show us kindness and aversion; but their influence
does not penetrate; we are nothing to them, nor they to us, except as
a part of the world's furniture. Another circle, within this, are dear and
near to us. We know them and of what kind they are. They are to us
not mere facts, but intelligible thoughts of the divine mind. We like to
see how they are unfolded; we like to meet them and part from them;
we like their action upon us and the pause that succeeds and enables us
to appreciate its quality. Often we leave them on our path, and return
no more, but we bear them in our memory, tales which have been told,
and whose meaning has been felt.

But yet a nearer group there are, beings born under the same star,
and bound with us in a common destiny. These are not mere ac-
quaintances, mere friends, but, when we meet, are sharers of our very
existence. There is no separation; the same thought is given at the same
moment to both,—indeed, it is born of the meeting, and would not
otherwise have been called into existence at all! These not only know
themselves more, but *are* more for having met, and regions of their being, which would else have laid sealed in cold obstruction, burst into
leaf and bloom and song.

The times of these meetings are fated, nor will either party be able
ever to meet any other person in the same way. Both seem to rise at
a glance into that part of the heavens where the word can be spoken,
by which they are revealed to one another and to themselves. The step
in being thus gained, can never be lost, nor can it be re-trod; for neither party will be again what the other wants. They are no longer fit
to interchange mutual influence, for they do not really need it, and if
they think they do, it is because they weakly pine after a past pleasure.

To this inmost circle of relations but few are admitted, because some prejudice or lack of courage has prevented the many from listening to their instincts the first time they manifested themselves. If the voice is once disregarded it becomes fainter each time, till, at last, it is wholly silenced, and the man lives in this world, a stranger to its real life, deluded like the maniac who fancies he has attained his throne, while in reality he is on a bed of musty straw. Yet, if the voice finds a listener and servant the first time of speaking, it is encouraged to more and more clearness. Thus it was with me,—from no merit of mine, but because I had the good fortune to be free enough to yield to my impressions. Common ties had not bound me; there were no traditionary notions in my mind; I believed in nothing merely because others believed in it; I had taken no feelings on trust. Thus my mind was open to their sway.

This woman came to me, a star from the east, a morning star, and I worshipped her. She too was elevated by that worship, and her fairest self called out. To the mind she brought assurance that there was a region congenial with its tendencies and tastes, a region of elegant culture and intercourse, whose object, fulfilled or not, was to gratify the sense of beauty, not the mere utilities of life. In our relation she was lifted to the top of her being. She had known many celebrities, had roused to passionate desire many hearts, and became afterwards a wife; but I do not believe she ever more truly realized her best self than towards the lonely child whose heaven she was, whose eye she met, and whose possibilities she predicted. "He raised me," said a woman inspired by love, "upon the pedestal of his own high thoughts, and wings came at once, but I did not fly away. I stood there with downcast eyes worthy of his love, for he had made me so."

Thus we do always for those who inspire us to expect from them the best. That which they are able to be, they become, because we demand it of them. "We expect the impossible—and find it."

My English friend went across the sea. She passed into her former life, and into ties that engrossed her days. But she has never ceased to think of me. Her thoughts turn forcibly back to the child who was to her all she saw of the really New World. On the promised coasts she had found only cities, careful men and women, the aims and habits of ordinary life in her own land, without that elegant culture which she, probably, overestimated, because it was her home. But in the mind of the child she found the fresh prairie, the untrodden forests for which she had longed. I saw in her the storied castles, the fair stately parks and the wind laden with tones from the past, which I desired to know. We wrote to one another for many years;—her shallow and delicate epistles did not disenchant me, nor did she fail to see something of the old poetry in my rude characters and stammering speech. But we must never meet again.

When this friend was withdrawn I fell into a profound depression. I knew not how to exert myself, but lay bound hand and foot. Melancholy enfolded me in an atmosphere, as joy had done. This suffering, too, was out of the gradual and natural course. Those who are really children could not know such love, or feel such sorrow. "I am to blame," said my father, "in keeping her at home so long merely to please myself. She needs to be with other girls, needs play and variety. She does not seem to me really sick, but dull rather. She eats nothing, you say. I see she grows thin. She ought to change the scene."

I was indeed *dull*. The books, the garden, had lost all charm. I had the excuse of headache, constantly, for not attending to my lessons. The light of life was set, and every leaf was withered. At such an early age there are no back or side scenes where the mind, weary and sorrowful, may retreat. Older, we realize the width of the world more, and it is not easy to despair on any point. The effort at thought to which we are compelled relieves and affords a dreary retreat, like hiding in a brick-kiln till the shower be over. But then all joy seemed to have departed with my friend, and the emptiness of our house stood revealed. This I had not felt while I every day expected to see or had seen her, or annoyance and dulness were unnoticed or swallowed up in the one thought that clothed my days with beauty. But now she was gone, and I was roused from habits of reading or reverie to feel the fiery temper of the soul, and to learn that it must have vent, that it would not be pacified by shadows, neither meet without consuming what lay around it. I avoided the table as much as possible, took long walks and lay in bed, or on the floor of my room. I complained of my head, and it was not wrong to do so, for a sense of dulness and suffocation, if not pain, was there constantly.

But when it was proposed that I should go to school, that was a remedy I could not listen to with patience for a moment. The peculiarity of my education had separated me entirely from the girls around, except that when they were playing at active games, I would sometimes go out and join them. I liked violent bodily exercise, which always relieved my nerves. But I had no success in associating with them beyond the mere play. Not only I was not their school-mate, but my book-life and lonely habits had given a cold aloofness to my whole expression, and veiled my manner with a hauteur which turned all hearts away. Yet, as this reserve was superficial, and rather ignorance than arrogance, it produced no deep dislike. Besides, the girls supposed me really superior to themselves, and did not hate me for feeling it, but neither did they like me, nor wish to have me with them. Indeed, I had gradually given up all such wishes myself; for they seemed to me rude, tiresome, and childish, as I did to them dull and strange. This experience had been earlier, before I was admitted to any real friendship; but now that I had been lifted into the life of mature years, and into just that atmosphere of European life to which I had before been tending, the thought of sending me to school filled me with disgust.

Yet what could I tell my father of such feelings? I resisted all I could, but in vain. He had no faith in medical aid generally, and justly saw that this was no occasion for its use. He thought I needed change of scene, and to be roused to activity by other children. "I have kept you at home," he said, "because I took such pleasure in teaching you my-self, and besides I knew that you would learn faster with one who is so desirous to aid you. But you will learn fast enough wherever you are, and you ought to be more with others of your own age. I shall soon hear that you are better, I trust."

SUMMER ON THE LAKES

Summer days of busy leisure,
Long summer days of dear-bought pleasure,
You have done your teaching well;
Had the scholar means to tell
How grew the vine of bitter-sweet,
What made the path for truant feet,
Winter nights would quickly pass,
Gazing on the magic glass
O'er which the new-world shadows pass;
But, in fault of wizard spell,
Moderns their tale can only tell
In dull words, with a poor reed
Breaking at each time of need.
But those to whom a hint suffices
Mottoes find for all devices,
See the knights behind their shields,
Through dried grasses, blooming fields.

TO A FRIEND

Some dried grass-tufts from the wide flowery plain,
A muscle shell from the lone fairy shore,
Some antlers from tall woods which never more
To the wild deer a safe retreat can yield,
An eagle's feather which adorned a Brave,
Well-nigh the last of his despairing band,
For such slight gifts wilt thou extend thy hand
When weary hours a brief refreshment crave?
I give you what I can, not what I would,
If my small drinking-cup would hold a flood,
As Scandinavia sung those must contain
With which the giants gods may entertain;
In our dwarf day we drain few drops, and soon must thirst again.

CHAPTER I

Niagara, June 10, 1843

SINCE you are to share with me such foot-notes as may be made on the pages of my life during this summer's wanderings, I should not be quite silent as to this magnificent prologue to the, as yet, unknown drama. Yet I, like others, have little to say where the spectacle is, for once, great enough to fill the whole life, and supersede thought, giving us only its own presence. "It is good to be here," is the best as the simplest expression that occurs to the mind.

We have been here eight days, and I am quite willing to go away. So great a sight soon satisfies, making us content with itself, and with what is less than itself. Our desires, once realized, haunt us again less readily. Having "lived one day" we would depart, and become worthy to live another.

We have not been fortunate in weather, for there cannot be too much, or too warm sunlight for this scene, and the skies have been lowering, with cold, unkind winds. My nerves, too much braced up by such an atmosphere, do not well bear the continual stress of sight and sound. For here there is no escape from the weight of a perpetual creation; all other forms and motions come and go, the tide rises and recedes, the wind, at its mightiest, moves in gales and gusts, but here is really an incessant, an indefatigable motion. Awake or asleep, there is no escape, still this rushing round you and through you. It is in this way I have most felt the grandeur—somewhat eternal, if not infinite.

At times a secondary music rises; the cataract seems to seize its own rhythm and sing it over again, so that the ear and soul are roused by a double vibration. This is some effect of the wind, causing echoes to the thundering anthem. It is very sublime, giving the effect of a spiritual repetition through all the spheres.

When I first came I felt nothing but a quiet satisfaction. I found that drawings, the panorama, &c. had given me a clear notion of the position and proportions of all objects here; I knew where to look for everything, and everything looked as I thought it would.

Long ago, I was looking from a hill-side with a friend at one of the finest sunsets that ever enriched this world. A little cow-boy, trudging along, wondered what we could be gazing at. After spying about some time, he found it could only be the sunset, and looking, too, a moment, he said approvingly "that sun looks well enough;" a speech worthy of Shakspeare's Cloten, or the infant Mercury, up to everything from the cradle, as you please to take it.

Even such a familiarity, worthy of Jonathan, our national hero, in a prince's palace, or "stumping" as he boasts to have done, "up the Vatican stairs, into the Pope's presence, in my old boots," I felt here; it looks really *well enough,* I felt, and was inclined, as you suggested, to give my approbation as to the one object in the world that would not disappoint.

But all great expression, which, on a superficial survey, seems so easy as well as so simple, furnishes, after a while, to the faithful observer its own standard by which to appreciate it. Daily these proportions widened and towered more and more upon my sight, and I got, at last, a proper foreground for these sublime distances. Before coming away, I think I really saw the full wonder of the scene. After awhile it so drew me into itself as to inspire an undefined dread, such as I never knew before, such as may be felt when death is about to usher us into a new existence. The perpetual trampling of the waters seized my senses. I felt that no other sound, however near, could be heard, and would start and look behind me for a foe. I realized the identity of that mood of nature in which these waters were poured down with such absorbing force, with that in which the Indian was shaped on the same soil. For continually upon my mind came, unsought and unwelcome, images, such as never haunted it before, of naked savages stealing behind me with uplifted tomahawks; again and again this illusion recurred, and even after I had thought it over, and tried to shake it off, I could not help starting and looking behind me.

As picture, the Falls can only be seen from the British side. There they are seen in their veils, and at sufficient distance to appreciate the magical effects of these, and the light and shade. From the boat, as you cross, the effects and contrasts are more melodramatic. On the road back from the whirlpool, we saw them as a reduced picture with delight. But what I liked best was to sit on Table Rock, close to the great fall. There all power of observing details, all separate consciousness, was quite lost.

Once, just as I had seated myself there, a man came to take his first look. He walked close up to the fall, and, after looking at it a moment, with an air as if thinking how he could best appropriate it to his own use, he spat into it.

This trait seemed wholly worthy of an age whose love of *utility* is such that the Prince Puckler Muskau suggests the probability of men coming to put the bodies of their dead parents in the fields to fertilize them, and of a country such as Dickens has described; but these will not, I hope, be seen on the historic page to be truly the age or truly the America. A little leaven is leavening the whole mass for other bread.

The whirlpool I like very much. It is seen to advantage after the great falls; it is so sternly solemn. The river cannot look more imperturbable, almost sullen in its marble green, than it does just below the great fall; but the slight circles that mark the hidden vortex, seem to whisper mysteries the thundering voice above could not proclaim,—a meaning as untold as ever.

It is fearful, too, to know, as you look, that whatever has been swallowed by the cataract, is like to rise suddenly to light here, whether uprooted tree, or body of man or bird.

The rapids enchanted me far beyond what I expected; they are so swift that they cease to seem so; you can think only of their beauty. The fountain beyond the Moss Islands, I discovered for myself, and thought it for some time an accidental beauty which it would not do to leave, lest I might never see it again. After I found it permanent, I returned many times to watch the play of its crest. In the little waterfall beyond, nature seems, as she often does, to have made a study for some larger design. She delights in this,—a sketch within a sketch, a dream within a dream. Wherever we see it, the lines of the great buttress in the fragment of stone, the hues of the waterfall, copied in the flowers that star its bordering mosses, we are delighted; for all the lineaments become fluent, and we mould the scene in congenial thought with its genius.

People complain of the buildings at Niagara, and fear to see it further deformed. I cannot sympathize with such an apprehension: the spectacle is capable to swallow up all such objects; they are not seen in the great whole, more than an earthworm in a wide field.

The beautiful wood on Goat Island is full of flowers; many of the fairest love to do homage here. The Wake Robin and May Apple are in bloom now; the former, white, pink, green, purple, copying the rainbow of the fall, and fit to make a garland for its presiding deity when he walks the land, for they are of imperial size, and shaped like stones for a diadem. Of the May Apple, I did not raise one green tent without finding a flower beneath.

And now farewell, Niagara. I have seen thee, and I think all who come here must in some sort see thee; thou art not to be got rid of as easily as the stars. I will be here again beneath some flooding July moon and sun. Owing to the absence of light, I have seen the rainbow only two or three times by day; the lunar bow not at all. However, the imperial presence needs not its crown, though illustrated by it.

General Porter and Jack Downing were not unsuitable figures here. The former heroically planted the bridges by which we cross to Goat Island, and the Wake-Robin-crowned genius has punished his temerity with deafness, which must, I think, have come upon him when he sank the first stone in the rapids. Jack seemed an acute and entertaining representative of Jonathan, come to look at his great water-privilege. He told us all about the Americanisms of the spectacle; that is to say, the battles that have been fought here. It seems strange that men could fight in such a place; but no temple can still the personal griefs and strifes in the breasts of its visitors.

No less strange is the fact that, in this neighborhood, an eagle should be chained for a plaything. When a child, I used often to stand at a window from which I could see an eagle chained in the balcony of a museum. The people used to poke at it with sticks, and my childish heart would swell with indignation as I saw their insults, and the mien with which they were borne by the monarch-bird. Its eye was dull, and its plumage soiled and shabby, yet, in its form and attitude, all the king was visible, though sorrowful and dethroned. I never saw another of the family till, when passing through the Notch of the White Mountains, at that moment striding before us in all the panoply of sunset, the driver shouted, "Look there!" and following with our eyes his upward-pointing finger, we saw, soaring slow in majestic poise above the highest summit, the bird of Jove. It was a glorious sight, yet I know not that I felt more on seeing the bird in all its natural freedom and royalty, than when, imprisoned and insulted, he had filled my early thoughts with the Byronic "silent rages" of misanthropy.

Now, again, I saw him a captive, and addressed by the vulgar with the language they seem to find most appropriate to such occasions—that of thrusts and blows. Silently, his head averted, he ignored their existence, as Plotinus or Sophocles might that of a modern reviewer. Probably, he listened to the voice of the cataract, and felt that congenial powers flowed free, and was consoled, though his own wing was broken.

The story of the Recluse of Niagara interested me a little. It is wonderful that men do not oftener attach their lives to localities of great beauty—that, when once deeply penetrated, they will let themselves so easily be borne away by the general stream of things, to live any where and any how. But there is something ludicrous in being the hermit of a show-place, unlike St. Francis in his mountain-bed, where none but the stars and rising sun ever saw him.

There is also a "guide to the falls," who wears his title labeled on his hat; otherwise, indeed, one might as soon think of asking for a gentleman usher to point out the moon. Yet why should we wonder at such, either, when we have Commentaries on Shakspeare, and Harmonies of the Gospels?

And now you have the little all I have to write. Can it interest you? To one who has enjoyed the full life of any scene, of any hour, what thoughts can be recorded about it, seem like the commas and semicolons in the paragraph, mere stops. Yet I suppose it is not so to the absent. At least, I have read things written about Niagara, music, and the like, that interested *me*. Once I was moved by Mr. Greenwood's remark, that he could not realize this marvel till, opening his eyes the next morning after he had seen it, his doubt as to the possibility of its being still there, taught him what he had experienced. I remember this now with pleasure, though, or because, it is exactly the opposite to what I myself felt. For all greatness affects different minds, each in "its own particular kind," and the variations of testimony mark the truth of feeling.

I will add a brief narrative of the experience of another here, as being much better than anything I could write, because more simple and individual.

"Now that I have left this 'Earth-wonder,' and the emotions it excited are past, it seems not so much like profanation to analyze my feelings, to recall minutely and accurately the effect of this manifestation of the Eternal. But one should go to such a scene prepared to yield entirely to its influences, to forget one's little self and one's little mind. To see a miserable worm creep to the brink of this falling world of waters, and watch the trembling of its own petty bosom, and fancy that this is made alone to act upon him excites—derision?—No,—pity."

As I rode up to the neighborhood of the falls, a solemn awe imperceptibly stole over me, and the deep sound of the ever-hurrying rapids prepared my mind for the lofty emotions to be experienced. When

I reached the hotel, I felt a strange indifference about seeing the aspiration of my life's hopes. I lounged about the rooms, read the stage bills upon the walls, looked over the register, and, finding the name of an acquaintance, sent to see if he was still there. What this hesitation arose from, I know not; perhaps it was a feeling of my unworthiness to enter this temple which nature has erected to its God.

At last, slowly and thoughtfully I walked down to the bridge leading to Goat Island, and when I stood upon this frail support, and saw a quarter of a mile of tumbling, rushing rapids, and heard their everlasting roar, my emotions overpowered me, a choaking sensation rose to my throat, a thrill rushed through my veins, "my blood ran rippling to my fingers' ends." This was the climax of the effect which the falls produced upon me—neither the American nor the British fall moved me as did these rapids. For the magnificence, the sublimity of the latter I was prepared by descriptions and by paintings. When I arrived in sight of them I merely felt, "ah, yes, here is the fall, just as I have seen it in picture." When I arrived at the terrapin bridge, I expected to be overwhelmed, to retire trembling from this giddy eminence, and gaze with unlimited wonder and awe upon the immense mass rolling on and on, but, somehow or other, I thought only of comparing the effect on my mind with what I had read and heard. I looked for a short time, and then with almost a feeling of disappointment, turned to go to the other points of view to see if I was not mistaken in not feeling any surpassing emotion at this sight. But from the foot of Biddle's stairs, and the middle of the river, and from below the table rock, it was still "barren, barren all." And, provoked with my stupidity in feeling most moved in the wrong place, I turned away to the hotel, determined to set off for Buffalo that afternoon. But the stage did not go, and, after nightfall, as there was a splendid moon, I went down to the bridge, and leaned over the parapet, where the boiling rapids came down in their might. It was grand, and it was also gorgeous; the yellow rays of the moon made the broken waves appear like auburn tresses twining around the black rocks. But they did not inspire me as before. I felt a foreboding of a mightier emotion to rise up and swallow all others, and I passed on to the terrapin bridge. Everything was changed, the misty apparition had taken off its many-colored crown which it had worn by day, and a bow of silvery white spanned its summit. The moonlight gave a poetical indefiniteness to the distant parts of the waters, and while the rapids were glancing in her beams, the river below the falls was black as night, save where the reflection of the sky gave it the appearance of a shield of blued steel. No gaping tourists loitered, eyeing with their glasses, or sketching on cards the hoary locks of the ancient river god. All tended to harmonize with the natural grandeur of the scene. I gazed long. I saw how here mutability and unchangeableness were united. I surveyed the conspiring waters rushing against the rocky ledge to overthrow it at one mad plunge, till, like toppling ambition, o'erleaping themselves, they fall on t'other side, expanding into foam ere they reach the deep channel where they creep submissively away.

Then arose in my breast a genuine admiration, and a humble adoration of the Being who was the architect of this and of all. Happy were the first discoverers of Niagara, those who could come unawares upon this view and upon that, whose feelings were entirely their own. With what gusto does Father Hennepin describe "this great downfall of water," "this vast and prodigious cadence of water, which falls down after a surprising and astonishing manner, insomuch that the universe does not afford its parallel. 'Tis true Italy and Swedeland boast of some such things, but we may well say that they be sorry patterns when compared with this of which we do now speak."

CHAPTER II

THE LAKES

SCENE, STEAMBOAT—*About to leave Buffalo—Baggage coming on board—Passengers bustling for their berths—Little boys persecuting everybody with their newspapers and pamphlets—J., S. and M. huddled up in a forlorn corner, behind a large trunk—A heavy rain falling.*

M.   Water, water everywhere. After Niagara one would like a dry strip of existence. And at any rate it is quite enough for me to have it under foot without having it over head in this way.

J.   Ah, do not abuse the gentle element. It is hardly possible to have too much of it, and indeed, if I were obliged to choose amid the four, it would be the one in which I could bear confinement best.

S.   You would make a pretty Undine, to be sure!

J.   Nay, I only offered myself as a Triton, a boisterous Triton of the sounding shell. You, M. I suppose, would be a salamander, rather.

M.   No! that is too equivocal a position, whether in modern mythology, or Hoffman's tales. I should choose to be a gnome.

J.   That choice savors of the pride that apes humility.

M.   By no means; the gnomes are the most important of all the elemental tribes. Is it not they who make the money?

J.   And are accordingly a dark, mean, scoffing, ———

M.   You talk as if you had always lived in that wild unprofitable element you are so fond of, where all things glitter, and nothing is gold; all show and no substance. My people work in the secret, and their works praise them in the open light; they remain in the dark because only there such marvels could be bred. You call them mean. They do not spend their energies on their own growth, or their own play, but to feed the veins of mother earth with permanent splendors, very different from what she shows on the surface.

Think of passing a life, not merely in heaping together, but making gold. Of all dreams, that of the alchymist is the most poetical, for he looked at the finest symbol. Gold, says one of our friends, is the hidden light of the earth, it crowns the mineral, as wine the vegetable order, being the last expression of vital energy.

J.   Have you paid for your passage?

M.   Yes! and in gold, not in shells or pebbles.

J.   No really wise gnome would scoff at the water, the beautiful water. "The spirit of man is like the water."

S.   Yes, and like the air and fire, no less.

J.   Yes, but not like the earth, this low-minded creature's chosen dwelling.

M.   The earth is spirit made fruitful,—life. And its heart-beats are told in gold and wine.

J.   Oh! it is shocking to hear such sentiments in these times. I thought that Bacchic energy of yours was long since repressed.

M.   No! I have only learned to mix water with my wine, and stamp upon my gold the heads of kings, or the hieroglyphics of worship. But since I have learnt to mix with water, let's hear what you have to say in praise of your favorite.

J.   From water Venus was born, what more would you have? It is the mother of Beauty, the girdle of earth, and the marriage of nations.

S.   Without any of that high-flown poetry, it is enough, I think, that it is the great artist, turning all objects that approach it to picture.

J.   True, no object that touches it, whether it be the cart that ploughs the wave for sea-weed, or the boat or plank that rides upon it, but is brought at once from the demesne of coarse utilities into that of picture. All trades, all callings, become picturesque by the water's side, or on the water. The soil, the slovenliness is washed out of every calling by its touch. All river-crafts, sea-crafts, are picturesque, are poetical. Their very slang is poetry.

M.   The reasons for that are complex.

J.   The reason is, that there can be no plodding, groping words and motions, on my water as there are on your earth. There is no time, no chance for them where all moves so rapidly, though so smoothly, everything connected with water must be like itself, forcible, but clear. That is why sea-slang is so poetical; there is a word for everything and every act, and a thing and an act for every word. Seamen must speak quick and bold, but also with utmost precision. They cannot reef and brace other than in a Homeric dialect—therefore,—(Steamboat bell rings.) But I must say a quick good-by.

M. What, going, going back to earth after all this talk upon the other side. Well, that is nowise Homeric, but truly modern.

J. is borne off without time for any reply, but a laugh—at himself, of course.

S. and M. retire to their state-rooms to forget the wet, the chill and steamboat smell in their just-bought new world of novels.

Next day, when we stopped at Cleveland, the storm was just clearing up; ascending the bluff, we had one of the finest views of the lake that could have been wished. The varying depths of these lakes give to their surface a great variety of coloring, and beneath this wild sky and changeful lights, the waters presented kaleidoscopic varieties of hues, rich, but mournful. I admire these bluffs of red, crumbling earth. Here land and water meet under very different auspices from those of the rock-bound coast to which I have been accustomed. There they meet tenderly to challenge, and proudly to refuse, though not in fact repel. But here they meet to mingle, are always rushing together, and changing places; a new creation takes place beneath the eye.

The weather grew gradually clearer, but not bright; yet we could see the shore and appreciate the extent of these noble waters.

Coming up the river St. Clair, we saw Indians for the first time. They were camped out on the bank. It was twilight, and their blanketed forms, in listless groups or stealing along the bank, with a lounge and a stride so different in its wildness from the rudeness of the white settler, gave me the first feeling that I really approached the West.

The people on the boat were almost all New Englanders, seeking their fortunes. They had brought with them their habits of calculation, their cautious manners, their love of polemics. It grieved me to hear these immigrants who were to be the fathers of a new race, all, from the old man down to the little girl, talking not of what they should do, but of what they should get in the new scene. It was to them a prospect, not of the unfolding nobler energies, but of more ease, and larger accumulation. It wearied me, too, to hear Trinity and Unity discussed in the poor, narrow doctrinal way on these free waters; but that will soon cease, there is not time for this clash of opinions in the West, where the clash of material interests is so noisy. They will need the spirit of religion more than ever to guide them, but will find less time than before for its doctrine. This change was to me, who am tired of the war of words on these subjects, and believe it only sows the wind to reap the whirlwind, refreshing, but I argue nothing from it; there is nothing real in the freedom of thought at the West, it is from the position of men's lives, not the state of their minds. So soon as they have time, unless they grow better meanwhile, they will cavil and criticise, and judge other men by their own standard, and outrage the law of love every way, just as they do with us.

We reached Mackinaw the evening of the third day, but, to my great disappointment, it was too late and too rainy to go ashore. The beauty of the island, though seen under the most unfavorable circumstances, did not disappoint my expectations. But I shall see it to more purpose on my return.

As the day has passed dully, a cold rain preventing us from keeping out in the air, my thoughts have been dwelling on a story told when we were off Detroit, this morning, by a fellow passenger, and whose moral beauty touched me profoundly.

Some years ago, said Mrs. L., my father and mother stopped to dine at Detroit. A short time before dinner my father met in the hall Captain P., a friend of his youthful days. He had loved P. extremely, as did many who knew him, and had not been surprised to hear of the distinction and popular esteem which his wide knowledge, talents, and noble temper commanded, as he went onward in the world. P. was every way fitted to succeed; his aims were high, but not too high for his powers, suggested by an instinct of his own capacities, not by an ideal standard drawn from culture. Though steadfast in his course, it was not to overrun others, his wise self-possession was no less for them than himself. He was thoroughly the gentleman, gentle because manly, and was a striking instance that where there is strength for sincere courtesy, there is no need of other adaptation to the character of others, to make one's way freely and gracefully through the crowd.

My father was delighted to see him, and after a shortly parley in the hall—"We will dine together," he cried, "then we shall have time to tell all our stories."

P. hesitated a moment, then said, "My wife is with me."

"And mine with me," said my father, "that's well; they, too, will have an opportunity of getting acquainted and can entertain one another, if they get tired of our college stories."

P. acquiesced, with a grave bow, and shortly after they all met in the dining-room. My father was much surprised at the appearance of Mrs. P. He had heard that his friend married abroad, but nothing further, and he was not prepared to see the calm, dignified P. with a woman on his arm, still handsome, indeed, but whose coarse and imperious expression showed as low habits of mind as her exaggerated dress and gesture did of education. Nor could there be a greater contrast to my mother, who, though understanding her claims and place with the certainty of a lady, was soft and retiring in an uncommon degree.

However, there was no time to wonder or fancy; they sat down, and P. engaged in conversation, without much vivacity, but with his usual ease. The first quarter of an hour passed well enough. But soon it was observable that Mrs. P. was drinking glass after glass of wine, to an extent few gentlemen did, even then, and soon that she was actually excited by it. Before this, her manner had been brusque, if not contemptuous towards her new acquaintance; now it became, towards my mother especially, quite rude. Presently she took up some slight remark made by my mother, which, though it did not naturally mean anything of the sort, could be twisted into some reflection upon England, and made it a handle, first of vulgar sarcasm, and then, upon my mother's defending herself with some surprise and gentle dignity, hurled upon her a volley of abuse, beyond Billingsgate.

My mother, confounded, feeling scenes and ideas presented to her mind equally new and painful, sat trembling; she knew not what to do, tears rushed into her eyes. My father, no less distressed, yet unwilling to outrage the feelings of his friend by doing or saying what his indignation prompted, turned an appealing look on P.

Never, as he often said, was the painful expression of that sight effaced from his mind. It haunted his dreams and disturbed his waking thoughts. P. sat with his head bent forward, and his eyes cast down, pale, but calm, with a fixed expression, not merely of patient woe, but of patient shame, which it would not have been thought possible for that noble countenance to wear, "yet," said my father, "it became him. At other times he was handsome, but then beautiful, though of a beauty saddened and abashed. For a spiritual light borrowed from the worldly perfection of his mien that illustration by contrast, which the penitence of the Magdalen does from the glowing earthliness of her charms."

Seeing that he preserved silence, while Mrs. P. grew still more exasperated, my father rose and led his wife to her own room. Half an hour had passed, in painful and wondering surmises, when a gentle knock was heard at the door, and P. entered equipped for a journey. "We are just going," he said, and holding out his hand, but without looking at them, "Forgive."

They each took his hand, and silently pressed it, then he went without a word more.

Some time passed and they heard now and then of P., as he passed from one army station to another, with his uncongenial companion, who became, it was said, constantly more degraded. Whoever mentioned having seen them, wondered at the chance which had yoked him to such a woman, but yet more at the silent fortitude with which he bore it. Many blamed him for enduring it, apparently without efforts to check her; others answered that he had probably made such at an earlier period, and finding them unavailing, had resigned himself to despair, and was too delicate to meet the scandal that, with such a resistance as such a woman could offer, must attend a formal separation.

But my father, who was not in such haste to come to conclusions, and substitute some plausible explanation for the truth, found something in the look of P. at that trying moment to which none of these explanations offered a key. There was in it, he felt, a fortitude, but not the fortitude of the hero, a religious submission, above the penitent, if not enkindled with the enthusiasm of the martyr.

I have said that my father was not of those who are ready to substitute specious explanations for truth, and those who are thus abstinent rarely lay their hand on a thread without making it a clue. Such an one, like the dexterous weaver, lets not one color go, till he finds that which matches it in the pattern; he keeps on weaving, but chooses his shades, and my father found at last what he wanted to make out the pattern for himself. He met a lady who had been intimate with both himself and P. in early days, and finding she had seen the latter abroad, asked if she knew the circumstances of the marriage. "The circumstances of the act I know," she said, "which sealed the misery of our friend, though as much in the dark as any one about the motives that led to it."

We were quite intimate with P. in London, and he was our most delightful companion. He was then in the full flower of the varied accomplishments, which set off his fine manners and dignified character, joined, towards those he loved, with a certain soft willingness which gives the desirable chivalry to a man. None was more clear of choice where his personal affections were not touched, but where they were, it cost him pain to say no, on the slightest occasion. I have thought this must have had some connexion with the mystery of his misfortunes.

One day he called on me, and, without any preface, asked if I would be present next day at his marriage. I was so surprised, and so unpleasantly surprised, that I did not at first answer a word. We had been on terms so familiar, that I thought I knew all about him, yet had never dreamed of his having an attachment, and, though I had never inquired on the subject, yet this reserve, where perfect openness had been supposed, and really, on my side, existed, seemed to me a kind of treachery. Then it is never pleasant to know that a heart, on which we have some claim, is to be given to another. We cannot tell how it will affect our own relations with a person; it may strengthen or it may swallow up other affections; the crisis is hazardous, and our first thought, on such an occasion, is too often for ourselves, at least, mine was. Seeing me silent, he repeated his question.

To whom, said I, are you to be married?

That, he replied, I cannot tell you. He was a moment silent, then continued with an impassive look of cold self-possession, that affected me with strange sadness.

"The name of the person you will hear, of course, at the time, but more I cannot tell you. I need, however, the presence, not only of legal, but of respectable and friendly witnesses. I have hoped you and your husband would do me this kindness. Will you?"

Something in his manner made it impossible to refuse. I answered before I knew I was going to speak, "We will," and he left me.

I will not weary you with telling how I harassed myself and my husband, who was, however, scarce less interested, with doubts and conjectures. Suffice it that, next morning, P. came and took us in a carriage to a distant church. We had just entered the porch when a cart, such as fruit and vegetables are brought to market in, drove up, containing an elderly woman and a young girl. P. assisted them to alight, and advanced with the girl to the altar.

The girl was neatly dressed and quite handsome, yet something in her expression displeased me the moment I looked upon her. Meanwhile the ceremony was going on, and, at its close, P. introduced us to the bride, and we all went to the door.

Good-by, Fanny, said the elderly woman. The new-made Mrs. P. replied without any token of affection or emotion. The woman got into the cart and drove away.

From that time I saw but little of P. or his wife. I took our mutual friends to see her, and they were civil to her for his sake. Curiosity was very much excited, but entirely baffled; no one, of course, dared speak to P. on the subject, and no other means could be found of solving the riddle.

He treated his wife with grave and kind politeness, but it was always obvious that they had nothing in common between them. Her manners and tastes were not at that time gross, but her character showed itself hard and material. She was fond of riding, and spent much time so. Her style in this, and in dress, seemed the opposite of P.'s; but he indulged all her wishes, while, for himself, he plunged into his own pursuits.

For a time he seemed, if not happy, not positively unhappy; but, after a few years, Mrs. P. fell into the habit of drinking, and then such scenes as you witnessed grew frequent. I have often heard of them, and always that P. sat, as you describe him, his head bowed down and perfectly silent all through, whatever might be done or whoever be present, and always his aspect has inspired such sympathy that no person has questioned him or resented her insults, but merely got out of the way, so soon as possible.

Hard and long penance, said my father, after some minutes musing, for an hour of passion, probably for his only error.

Is that your explanation? said the lady. O, improbable. P. might err, but not be led beyond himself.

I know his cool gray eye and calm complexion seemed to say so, but a different story is told by the lip that could tremble, and showed what flashes might pierce those deep blue heavens; and when these over intellectual beings do swerve aside, it is to fall down a precipice, for their narrow path lies over such. But he was not one to sin without making a brave atonement, and that it had become a holy one, was written on that downcast brow.

The fourth day on these waters, the weather was milder and brighter, so that we could now see them to some purpose. At night was clear moon, and, for the first time, from the upper deck, I saw one of the great steamboats come majestically up. It was glowing with lights, looking many-eyed and sagacious; in its heavy motion it seemed a dowager queen, and this motion, with its solemn pulse, and determined sweep, becomes these smooth waters, especially at night, as much as the dip of the sailship the long billows of the ocean.

But it was not so soon that I learned to appreciate the lake scenery; it was only after a daily and careless familiarity that I entered into its beauty, for nature always refuses to be seen by being stared at. Like Bonaparte, she discharges her face of all expression when she catches the eye of impertinent curiosity fixed on her. But he who has gone to sleep in childish ease on her lap, or leaned an aching brow upon her breast, seeking there comfort with full trust as from a mother, will see all a mother's beauty in the look she bends upon him. Later, I felt that I had really seen these regions, and shall speak of them again.

In the afternoon we went on shore at the Manitou islands, where the boat stops to wood. No one lives here except woodcutters for the steamboats. I had thought of such a position, from its mixture of profound solitude with service to the great world, as possessing an ideal beauty. I think so still, after seeing the woodcutters and their slovenly huts.

In times of slower growth, man did not enter a situation without a certain preparation or adaptedness to it. He drew from it, if not to the poetical extent, at least, in some proportion, its moral and its meaning. The woodcutter did not cut down so many trees a day, that the hamadryads had not time to make their plaints heard; the shepherd tended his sheep, and did no jobs or chores the while; the idyl had a chance to grow up, and modulate his oaten pipe. But now the poet must be at the whole expense of the poetry in describing one of these positions; the worker is a true Midas to the gold he makes. The poet must describe, as the painter sketches Irish peasant girls and Danish fishwives, adding the beauty, and leaving out the dirt.

I come to the west prepared for the distaste I must experience at its mushroom growth. I know that where "go ahead" is the only motto, the village cannot grow into the gentle proportions that successive lives, and the gradations of experience involuntarily give. In older countries the house of the son grew from that of the father, as naturally as new joints on a bough. And the cathedral crowned the whole as naturally as the leafy summit the tree. This cannot be here. The march of peaceful is scarce less wanton than that of warlike invasion. The old landmarks are broken down, and the land, for a season, bears none, except of the rudeness of conquest and the needs of the day, whose bivouac fires blacken the sweetest forest glades. I have come prepared to see all this, to dislike it, but not with stupid narrowness to distrust or defame. On the contrary, while I will not be so obliging as to confound ugliness with beauty, discord with harmony, and laud and be contented with all I meet, when it conflicts with my best desires and tastes, I trust by reverent faith to woo the mighty meaning of the scene, perhaps to foresee the law by which a new order, a new poetry is to be evoked from this chaos, and with a curiosity as ardent, but not so selfish as that of Macbeth, to call up the apparitions of future kings from the strange ingredients of the witch's caldron. Thus, I will not grieve that all the noble trees are gone already from this island to feed this caldron, but believe it will have Medea's virtue, and reproduce them in the form of new intellectual growths, since centuries cannot again adorn the land with such.

On this most beautiful beach of smooth white pebbles, interspersed with agates and cornelians, for those who know how to find them, we stepped, not like the Indian, with some humble offering, which, if no better than an arrow-head or a little parched corn, would, he judged, please the Manitou, who looks only at the spirit in which it is offered. Our visit was so far for a religious purpose that one of our party went to inquire the fate of some Unitarian tracts left among the wood-cutters a year or two before. But the old Manitou, though, daunted like his children by the approach of the fire-ships which he probably considered demons of a new dynasty, he had suffered his woods to be felled to feed their pride, had been less patient of an encroachment, which did not to him seem so authorized by the law of the strongest, and had scattered those leaves as carelessly as the others of that year.

But S. and I, like other emigrants, went not to give, but to get, to rifle the wood of flowers for the service of the fire-ship. We returned with a rich booty, among which was the uva ursi, whose leaves the Indians smoke, with the kinnick-kinnick, and which had then just put forth its highly-finished little blossoms, as pretty as those of the blueberry.

Passing along still further, I thought it would be well if the crowds assembled to stare from the various landings were still confined to the kinnick-kinnick, for almost all had tobacco written on their faces, their cheeks rounded with plugs, their eyes dull with its fumes. We reached Chicago on the evening of the sixth day, having been out five days and a half, a rather longer passage than usual at a favorable season of the year.

Chicago, June 20

There can be no two places in the world more completely thoroughfares than this place and Buffalo. They are the two correspondent valves that open and shut all the time, as the life-blood rushes from east to west, and back again from west to east.

Since it is their office thus to be the doors, and let in and out, it would be unfair to expect from them much character of their own. To make the best provisions for the transmission of produce is their office, and the people who live there are such as are suited for this; active, complaisant, inventive, business people. There are no provisions for the student or idler; to know what the place can give, you should be at work with the rest, the mere traveller will not find it profitable to loiter there as I did.

Since circumstances made it necessary for me so to do, I read all the books I could find about the new region, which now began to become real to me. All the books about the Indians, a paltry collection, truly, yet which furnished material for many thoughts. The most narrow-minded and awkward recital still bears some lineaments of the great features of this nature, and the races of men that illustrated them.

Catlin's book is far the best. I was afterwards assured by those acquainted with the regions he describes, that he is not to be depended on for the accuracy of his facts, and, indeed, it is obvious, without the aid of such assertions, that he sometimes yields to the temptation of making out a story. They admitted, however, what from my feelings I was sure of, that he is true to the spirit of the scene, and that a far better view can be got from him than from any source at present existing, of the Indian tribes of the far west, and of the country where their inheritance lay.

Murray's travels I read, and was charmed by their accuracy and clear broad tone. He is the only Englishman that seems to have traversed these regions, as man, simply, not as John Bull. He deserves to belong to an aristocracy, for he showed his title to it more when left without a guide in the wilderness, than he can at the court of Victoria. He has, himself, no poetic force at description, but it is easy to make images from his hints. Yet we believe the Indian cannot be looked at truly except by a poetic eye. The Pawnees, no doubt, are such as he describes them, filthy in their habits, and treacherous in their character, but some would have seen, and seen truly, more beauty and dignity than he does with all his manliness and fairness of mind. However, his one fine old man is enough to redeem the rest, and is perhaps the relic of a better day, a Phocion among the Pawnees.

Schoolcraft's Algic Researches is a valuable book, though a worse use could hardly have been made of such fine material. Had the mythological or hunting stories of the Indians been written down exactly as they were received from the lips of the narrators, the collection could not have been surpassed in interest, both for the wild charm they carry with them, and the light they throw on a peculiar modification of life and mind. As it is, though the incidents have an air of originality and pertinence to the occasion, that gives us confidence that they have not been altered, the phraseology in which they were expressed has been entirely set aside, and the flimsy graces, common to the style of annuals and souvenirs, substituted for the Spartan brevity and sinewy grasp of Indian speech. We can just guess what might have been there, as we can detect the fine proportions of the Brave whom the bad taste of some white patron has arranged in frock-coat, hat, and pantaloons.

The few stories Mrs. Jameson wrote out, though to these also a sentimental air has been given, offend much less in that way than is common in this book. What would we give for a completely faithful version of some among them. Yet with all these drawbacks we cannot doubt from internal evidence that they truly ascribe to the Indian a delicacy of sentiment and of fancy that justifies Cooper in such inventions as his Uncas. It is a white man's view of a savage hero, who would be far finer in his natural proportions; still, through a masquerade figure, it implies the truth.

Irving's books I also read, some for the first, some for the second time, with increased interest, now that I was to meet such people as he received his materials from. Though the books are pleasing from their grace and luminous arrangement, yet, with the exception of the Tour to the Prairies, they have a stereotype, second-hand air. They lack the breath, the glow, the charming minute traits of living presence. His scenery is only fit to be glanced at from dioramic distance; his Indians are academic figures only. He would have made the best of pictures, if he could have used his own eyes for studies and sketches; as it is, his success is wonderful, but inadequate.

McKenney's Tour to the Lakes is the dullest of books, yet faithful and quiet, and gives some facts not to be met with elsewhere.

I also read a collection of Indian anecdotes and speeches, the worst compiled and arranged book possible, yet not without clues of some value. All these books I read in anticipation of a canoe-voyage on Lake Superior as far as the Pictured Rocks, and, though I was afterwards compelled to give up this project, they aided me in judging of what I afterwards saw and heard of the Indians.

In Chicago I first saw the beautiful prairie flowers. They were in their glory the first ten days we were there—

"The golden and the flame-like flowers."

The flame-like flower I was taught afterwards, by an Indian girl, to call "Wickapee;" and she told me, too, that its splendors had a useful side, for it was used by the Indians as a remedy for an illness to which they were subject.

Beside these brilliant flowers, which gemmed and gilt the grass in a sunny afternoon's drive near the blue lake, between the low oakwood and the narrow beach, stimulated, whether sensuously by the optic nerve, unused to so much gold and crimson with such tender green, or symbolically through some meaning dimly seen in the flowers, I enjoyed a sort of fairyland exultation never felt before, and the first drive amid the flowers gave me anticipation of the beauty of the prairies.

At first, the prairie seemed to speak of the very desolation of dullness. After sweeping over the vast monotony of the lakes to come to this monotony of land, with all around a limitless horizon,—to walk, and walk, and run, but never climb, oh! it was too dreary for any but a Hollander to bear. How the eye greeted the approach of a sail, or the smoke of a steamboat; it seemed that any thing so animated must come from a better land, where mountains gave religion to the scene.

The only thing I liked at first to do, was to trace with slow and unexpecting step the narrow margin of the lake. Sometimes a heavy swell gave it expression; at others, only its varied coloring, which I found more admirable every day, and which gave it an air of mirage instead of the vastness of ocean. Then there was a grandeur in the feeling that I might continue that walk, if I had any seven-leagued mode of conveyance to save fatigue, for hundreds of miles without an obstacle and without a change.

But after I had rode out, and seen the flowers and seen the sun set with that calmness seen only in the prairies, and the cattle winding slowly home to their homes in the "island groves"—peacefulest of sights—I began to love because I began to know the scene, and shrank no longer from "the encircling vastness."

It is always thus with the new form of life; we must learn to look at it by its own standard. At first, no doubt my accustomed eye kept saying, if the mind did not, What! no distant mountains? what, no valleys? But after a while I would ascend the roof of the house where we lived, and pass many hours, needing no sight but the moon reigning in the heavens, or starlight falling upon the lake, till all the lights were out in the island grove of men beneath my feet, and felt nearer heaven that there was nothing but this lovely, still reception on the earth; no towering mountains, no deep tree-shadows, nothing but plain earth and water bathed in light.

Sunset, as seen from that place, presented most generally, low-lying, flaky clouds, of the softest serenity, "like," said S., "the Buddhist tracts."

One night a star shot madly from its sphere, and it had a fair chance to be seen, but that serenity could not be astonished.

Yes! it was a peculiar beauty of those sunsets and moonlights on the levels of Chicago which Chamouny or the Trosachs could not make me forget.

Notwithstanding all the attractions I thus found out by degrees on the flat shores of the lake, I was delighted when I found myself really on my way into the country for an excursion of two or three weeks. We set forth in a strong wagon, almost as large, and with the look of those used elsewhere for transporting caravans of wild beasts, loaded with every thing we might want, in case nobody would give it to us—for buying and selling were no longer to be counted on—with a pair of strong horses, able and willing to force their way through mud holes and amid stumps, and a guide, equally admirable as marshal and companion, who knew by heart the country and its history, both natural and artificial, and whose clear hunter's eye needed neither road nor goal to guide it to all the spots where beauty best loves to dwell.

Add to this the finest weather, and such country as I had never seen, even in my dreams, although these dreams had been haunted by wishes for just such an one, and you may judge whether years of dullness might not, by these bright days, be redeemed, and a sweetness be shed over all thoughts of the West.

The first day brought us through woods rich in the moccasin flower and lupine, and plains whose soft expanse was continually touched with expression by the slow moving clouds which

> "Sweep over with their shadows, and beneath
> The surface rolls and fluctuates to the eye;
> Dark hollows seem to glide along and chase
>   The sunny ridges,"

to the banks of the Fox river, a sweet and graceful stream. We reached Geneva just in time to escape being drenched by a violent thunder shower, whose rise and disappearance threw expression into all the features of the scene.

Geneva reminds me of a New England village, as indeed there, and in the neighborhood, are many New Englanders of an excellent stamp, generous, intelligent, discreet, and seeking to win from life its true values. Such are much wanted, and seem like points of light among the swarms of settlers, whose aims are sordid, whose habits thoughtless and slovenly.

With great pleasure we heard, with his attentive and affectionate congregation, the Unitarian clergyman, Mr. Conant, and afterward visited him in his house, where almost everything bore traces of his own handy-work or that of his father. He is just such a teacher as is wanted in this region, familiar enough with the habits of those he addresses to come home to their experience and their wants; earnest and enlightened enough to draw the important inferences from the life of every day.

A day or two we remained here, and passed some happy hours in the woods that fringe the stream, where the gentlemen found a rich booty of fish.

Next day, travelling along the river's banks, was an uninterrupted pleasure. We closed our drive in the afternoon at the house of an English gentleman, who has gratified, as few men do, the common wish to pass the evening of an active day amid the quiet influences of country life. He showed us a bookcase filled with books about this country; these he had collected for years, and become so familiar with the localities that, on coming here at last, he sought and found, at once, the very spot he wanted, and where he is as content as he hoped to be, thus realizing Wordsworth's description of the wise man, who "sees what he foresaw."

A wood surrounds the house, through which paths are cut in every direction. It is, for this new country, a large and handsome dwelling; but round it are its barns and farm yard, with cattle and poultry. These, however, in the framework of wood, have a very picturesque and pleasing effect. There is that mixture of culture and rudeness in the aspect of things as gives a feeling of freedom, not of confusion.

I wish it were possible to give some idea of this scene as viewed by the earliest freshness of dewy dawn. This habitation of man seemed like a nest in the grass, so thoroughly were the buildings and all the objects of human care harmonized with what was natural. The tall trees bent and whispered all around, as if to hail with sheltering love the men who had come to dwell among them.

The young ladies were musicians, and spoke French fluently, having been educated in a convent. Here in the prairie, they had learned to take care of the milk-room, and kill the rattlesnakes that assailed their poultry yard. Beneath the shade of heavy curtains you looked out from the high and large windows to see Norwegian peasants at work in their national dress. In the wood grew, not only the flowers I had before seen, and wealth of tall, wild roses, but the splendid blue spider-wort, that ornament of our gardens. Beautiful children strayed there, who were soon to leave these civilized regions for some really wild and western place, a post in the buffalo country. Their no less beautiful mother was of Welsh descent, and the eldest child bore the name of Gwynthleon. Perhaps there she will meet with some young descendants of Madoc, to be her friends; at any rate, her looks may retain that sweet, wild beauty, that is soon made to vanish from eyes which look too much on shops and streets, and the vulgarities of city "parties."

Next day we crossed the river. We ladies crossed on a little foot-bridge, from which we could look down the stream, and see the wagon pass over at the ford. A black thunder cloud was coming up. The sky and waters heavy with expectation. The motion of the wagon, with its white cover, and the laboring horses, gave just the due inter-est to the picture, because it seemed as if they would not have time to cross before the storm came on. However, they did get across, and we were a mile or two on our way before the violent shower obliged us to take refuge in a solitary house upon the prairie. In this country it is as pleasant to stop as to go on, to lose your way as to find it, for the variety in the population gives you a chance for fresh entertainment in every hut, and the luxuriant beauty makes every path attractive. In this house we found a family "quite above the common," but, I grieve to say, not above false pride, for the father, ashamed of being caught barefoot, told us a story of a man, one of the richest men, he said, in one of the eastern cities, who went barefoot, from choice and taste.

Near the door grew a Provence rose, then in blossom. Other families we saw had brought with them and planted the locust. It was pleasant to see their old home loves, brought into connection with their new splendors. Wherever there were traces of this tenderness of feeling, only too rare among Americans, other things bore signs also of pros-perity and intelligence, as if the ordering mind of man had some idea of home beyond a mere shelter, beneath which to eat and sleep.

No heaven need wear a lovelier aspect than earth did this after-noon, after the clearing up of the shower. We traversed the blooming plain, unmarked by any road, only the friendly track of wheels which tracked, not broke the grass. Our stations were not from town to town, but from grove to grove. These groves first floated like blue islands in the distance. As we drew nearer, they seemed fair parks, and the little log houses on the edge, with their curling smokes, harmonized beauti-fully with them.

One of these groves, Ross's grove, we reached just at sunset. It was of the noblest trees I saw during this journey, for the trees generally were not large or lofty, but only of fair proportions. Here they were large enough to form with their clear stems pillars for grand cathedral aisles. There was space enough for crimson light to stream through upon the floor of water which the shower had left. As we slowly plashed through. I thought I was never in a better place for vespers.

That night we rested, or rather tarried at a grove some miles be-yond, and there partook of the miseries so often jocosely portrayed, of bedchambers for twelve, a milk dish for universal handbasin, and expectations that you would use and lend your "hankercher" for a towel. But this was the only night, thanks to the hospitality of private families, that we passed thus, and it was well that we had this bit of experience, else might we have pronounced all Trollopian records of the kind to be inventions of pure malice.

With us was a young lady who showed herself to have been bathed in the Britannic fluid, wittily described by a late French writer, by the impossibility she experienced of accommodating herself to the indecorums of the scene. We ladies were to sleep in the bar-room, from which its drinking visiters could be ejected only at a late hour. The outer door had no fastening to prevent their return. However, our host kindly requested we would call him, if they did, as he had "conquered them for us," and would do so again. We had also rather hard couches; (mine was the supper table,) but we yankees, born to rove, were altogether too much fatigued to stand upon trifles, and slept as sweetly as we would in the "bigly bower" of any baroness. But I think England sat up all night, wrapped in her blanket shawl, and with a neat lace cap upon her head; so that she would have looked perfectly the lady, if any one had come in; shuddering and listening. I know that she was very ill next day, in requital. She watched, as her parent country watches the seas, that nobody may do wrong in any case, and deserved to have met some interruption, she was so well prepared. However, there was none, other than from the nearness of some twenty sets of powerful lungs, which would not leave the night to a deadly stillness. In this house we had, if not good beds, yet good tea, good bread, and wild strawberries, and were entertained with most free communications of opinion and history from our hosts. Neither shall any of us have a right to say again that we cannot find any who may be willing to hear all we may have to say. "A's fish that comes to the net," should be painted on the sign at Papaw grove.

CHAPTER III

IN THE AFTERNOON of this day we reached the Rock river, in whose neighborhood we proposed to make some stay, and crossed at Dixon's ferry.

This beautiful stream flows full and wide over a bed of rocks, traversing a distance of near two hundred miles, to reach the Mississippi. Great part of the country along its banks is the finest region of Illinois, and the scene of some of the latest romance of Indian warfare. To these beautiful regions Black Hawk returned with his band "to pass the summer," when he drew upon himself the warfare in which he was finally vanquished. No wonder he could not resist the longing, unwise though its indulgence might be, to return in summer to this home of beauty.

Of Illinois, in general, it has often been remarked that it bears the character of country which has been inhabited by a nation skilled like the English in all the ornamental arts of life, especially in landscape gardening. That the villas and castles seem to have been burnt, the enclosures taken down, but the velvet lawns, the flower gardens, the stately parks, scattered at graceful intervals by the decorous hand of art, the frequent deer, and the peaceful herd of cattle that make picture of the plain, all suggest more of the masterly mind of man, than the prodigal, but careless, motherly love of nature. Especially is this true of the Rock river country. The river flows sometimes through these parks and lawns, then betwixt high bluffs, whose grassy ridges are covered with fine trees, or broken with crumbling stone, that easily assumes the forms of buttress, arch and clustered columns. Along the face of such crumbling rocks, swallows' nests are clustered, thick as cities, and eagles and deer do not disdain their summits. One morning, out in the boat along the base of these rocks, it was amusing, and affecting too, to see these swallows put their heads out to look at us. There was something very hospitable about it, as if man had never shown himself a tyrant near them. What a morning that was! Every sight is worth twice as much by the early morning light. We borrow something of the spirit of the hour to look upon them.

The first place where we stopped was one of singular beauty, a beauty of soft, luxuriant wildness. It was on the bend of the river, a place chosen by an Irish gentleman, whose absenteeship seems of the wisest kind, since for a sum which would have been but a drop of water to the thirsty fever of his native land, he commands a residence which has all that is desirable, in its independence, its beautiful retirement, and means of benefit to others.

His park, his deer-chase, he found already prepared; he had only to make an avenue through it. This brought us by a drive, which in the heat of noon seemed long, though afterwards, in the cool of morning and evening, delightful, to the house. This is, for that part of the world, a large and commodious dwelling. Near it stands the log-cabin where its master lived while it was building, a very ornamental accessory.

In front of the house was a lawn, adorned by the most graceful trees. A few of these had been taken out to give a full view of the river, gliding through banks such as I have described. On this bend the bank is high and bold, so from the house or the lawn the view was very rich and commanding. But if you descended a ravine at the side to the water's edge, you found there a long walk on the narrow shore, with a wall above of the richest hanging wood, in which they said the deer lay hid. I never saw one, but often fancied that I heard them rustling, at daybreak, by these bright clear waters, stretching out in such smiling promise, where no sound broke the deep and blissful seclusion, unless now and then this rustling, or the plash of some fish a little gayer than the others; it seemed not necessary to have any better heaven, or fuller expression of love and freedom than in the mood of nature here.

Then, leaving the bank, you would walk far and far through long grassy paths, full of the most brilliant, also the most delicate flowers. The brilliant are more common on the prairie, but both kinds loved this place.

Amid the grass of the lawn, with a profusion of wild strawberries, we greeted also a familiar love, the Scottish harebell, the gentlest, and most touching form of the flower-world.

The master of the house was absent, but with a kindness beyond thanks had offered us a resting place there. Here we were taken care of by a deputy, who would, for his youth, have been assigned the place of a page in former times, but in the young west, it seems he was old enough for a steward. Whatever be called his function, he did the honors of the place so much in harmony with it, as to leave the guests free to imagine themselves in Elysium. And the three days passed here were days of unalloyed, spotless happiness.

There was a peculiar charm in coming here, where the choice of location, and the unobtrusive good taste of all the arrangements, showed such intelligent appreciation of the spirit of the scene, after seeing so many dwellings of the new settlers, which showed plainly that they had no thought beyond satisfying the grossest material wants. Sometimes they looked attractive, the little brown houses, the natural architecture of the country, in the edge of the timber. But almost always when you came near, the slovenliness of the dwelling and the rude way in which objects around it were treated, when so little care would have presented a charming whole, were very repulsive. Seeing the traces of the Indians, who chose the most beautiful sites for their dwellings, and whose habits do not break in on that aspect of nature under which they were born, we feel as if they were the rightful lords of a beauty they forbore to deform. But most of these settlers do not see it at all; it breathes, it speaks in vain to those who are rushing into its sphere. Their progress is Gothic, not Roman, and their mode of cultivation will, in the course of twenty, perhaps ten, years, obliterate the natural expression of the country.

This is inevitable, fatal; we must not complain, but look forward to a good result. Still, in travelling through this country, I could not but be struck with the force of a symbol. Wherever the hog comes, the rattlesnake disappears; the omnivorous traveller, safe in its stupidity, willingly and easily makes a meal of the most dangerous of reptiles, and one whom the Indian looks on with a mystic awe. Even so the white settler pursues the Indian, and is victor in the chase. But I shall say more upon the subject by-and-by.

While we were here we had one grand thunder storm, which added new glory to the scene.

One beautiful feature was the return of the pigeons every afternoon to their home. Every afternoon they came sweeping across the lawn, positively in clouds, and with a swiftness and softness of winged motion, more beautiful than anything of the kind I ever knew. Had I been a musician, such as Mendelssohn, I felt that I could have improvised a music quite peculiar, from the sound they made, which should have indicated all the beauty over which their wings bore them. I will here insert a few lines left at this house, on parting, which feebly indicate some of the features.

Familiar to the childish mind were tales
   Of rock-girt isles amid a desert sea,
Where unexpected stretch the flowery vales
   To soothe the shipwrecked sailor's misery.
Fainting, he lay upon a sandy shore,
And fancied that all hope of life was o'er;
But let him patient climb the frowning wall,
Within, the orange glows beneath the palm tree tall,
And all that Eden boasted waits his call.

Almost these tales seem realized to-day,
When the long dullness of the sultry way,
Where "independent" settlers' careless cheer
Made us indeed feel we were "strangers" here,
Is cheered by sudden sight of this fair spot,
On which "improvement" yet has made no blot,
But Nature all-astonished stands, to find
Her plan protected by the human mind.

Blest be the kindly genius of the scene;
   The river, bending in unbroken grace,
The stately thickets, with their pathways green,
   Fair lonely trees, each in its fittest place.
Those thickets haunted by the deer and fawn;
Those cloudlike flights of birds across the lawn;
The gentlest breezes here delight to blow,
And sun and shower and star are emulous to deck the show
Wondering, as Crusoe, we survey the land;
Happier than Crusoe we, a friendly band;
Blest be the hand that reared this friendly home,
The heart and mind of him to whom we owe
Hours of pure peace such as few mortals know;
May he find such, should he be led to roam;
Be tended by such ministering sprites—
Enjoy such gaily childish days, such hopeful nights!
And yet, amid the goods to mortals given,
To give those goods again is most like heaven.

                   Hazelwood, Rock River, 30 June 1843

    The only really rustic feature was of the many coops of poultry near the house, which I understood it to be one of the chief pleasures of the master to feed.

Leaving this place, we proceeded a day's journey along the beautiful stream, to a little town named Oregon. We called at a cabin, from whose door looked out one of those faces which, once seen, are never forgotten; young, yet touched with many traces of feeling, not only possible, but endured; spirited, too, like the gleam of a finely tempered blade. It was a face that suggested a history, and many histories, but whose scene would have been in courts and camps. At this moment their circles are dull for want of that life which is waning unexcited in this solitary recess.

The master of the house proposed to show us a "short cut," by which we might, to especial advantage, pursue our journey. This proved to be almost perpendicular down a hill, studded with young trees and stumps. From these he proposed, with a hospitality of service worthy an Oriental, to free our wheels whenever they should get entangled, also, to be himself the drag, to prevent our too rapid descent. Such generosity deserved trust; however, we women could not be persuaded to render it. We got out and admired, from afar, the process. Left by our guide—and prop! we found ourselves in a wide field, where, by playful quips and turns, an endless "creek," seemed to divert itself with our attempts to cross it. Failing in this, the next best was to whirl down a steep bank, which feat our charioteer performed with an air not unlike that of Rhesus, had he but been as suitably furnished with chariot and steeds!

At last, after wasting some two or three hours on the "short cut," we got out by following an Indian trail,—Black Hawk's! How fair the scene through which it led! How could they let themselves be conquered, with such a country to fight for!

Afterwards, in the wide prairie, we saw a lively picture of nonchalance, (to speak in the fashion of dear Ireland.) There, in the wide sunny field, with neither tree nor umbrella above his head, sat a pedler, with his pack, waiting apparently for customers. He was not disappointed. We bought, what hold in regard to the human world, as unmarked, as mysterious, and as important an existence, as the infusoria to the natural, to wit, pins. This incident would have delighted those modern sages, who, in imitation of the sitting philosophers of ancient Ind, prefer silence to speech, waiting to going, and scornfully smile in answer to the motions of earnest life,

> "Of itself will nothing come,
> That ye must still be seeking?"

However, it seemed to me to-day, as formerly on these sublime occasions, obvious that nothing would come, unless something would go; now, if we had been as sublimely still as the pedler, his pins would have tarried in the pack, and his pockets sustained an aching void of pence!

Passing through one of the fine, park-like woods, almost clear from underbrush and carpeted with thick grasses and flowers, we met, (for it was Sunday,) a little congregation just returning from their service, which had been performed in a rude house in its midst. It had a sweet and peaceful air, as if such words and thoughts were very dear to them. The parents had with them all their little children; but we saw no old people; that charm was wanting, which exists in such scenes in older settlements, of seeing the silver bent in reverence beside the flaxen head.

At Oregon, the beauty of the scene was of even a more sumptuous character than at our former "stopping place." Here swelled the river in its boldest course, interspersed by halcyon isles on which nature had lavished all her prodigality in tree, vine, and flower, banked by noble bluffs, three hundred feet high, their sharp ridges as exquisitely definite as the edge of a shell; their summits adorned with those same beautiful trees, and with buttresses of rich rock, crested with old hemlocks, which wore a touching and antique grace amid the softer and more luxuriant vegetation. Lofty natural mounds rose amidst the rest, with the same lovely and sweeping outline, showing everywhere the plastic power of water,—water, mother of beauty, which, by its sweet and eager flow, had left such lineaments as human genius never dreamt of.

Not far from the river was a high crag, called the Pine Rock, which looks out, as our guide observed, like a helmet above the brow of the country. It seems as if the water left here and there a vestige of forms and materials that preceded its course, just to set off its new and richer designs.

The aspect of this country was to me enchanting, beyond any I have ever seen, from its fullness of expression, its bold and impassioned sweetness. Here the flood of emotion has passed over and marked everywhere its course by a smile. The fragments of rock touch it with a wildness and liberality which give just the needed relief. I should never be tired here, though I have elsewhere seen country of more secret and alluring charms, better calculated to stimulate and suggest. Here the eye and heart are filled.

How happy the Indians must have been here! It is not long since they were driven away, and the ground, above and below, is full of their traces.

"The earth is full of men."

You have only to turn up the sod to find arrowheads and Indian pottery. On an island, belonging to our host, and nearly opposite his house, they loved to stay, and, no doubt, enjoyed its lavish beauty as much as the myriad wild pigeons that now haunt its flower-filled shades. Here are still the marks of their tomahawks, the troughs in which they prepared their corn, their caches.

A little way down the river is the site of an ancient Indian village, with its regularly arranged mounds. As usual, they had chosen with the finest taste. It was one of those soft shadowy afternoons when we went there, when nature seems ready to weep, not from grief, but from an overfull heart. Two prattling, lovely little girls, and an African boy, with glittering eye and ready grin, made our party gay; but all were still as we entered their little inlet and trod those flowery paths. They may blacken Indian life as they will, talk of its dirt, its brutality, I will ever believe that the men who chose that dwelling-place were able to feel emotions of noble happiness as they returned to it, and so were the women that received them. Neither were the children sad or dull, who lived so familiarly with the deer and the birds, and swam that clear wave in the shadow of the Seven Sisters. The whole scene suggested to me a Greek splendor, a Greek sweetness, and I can believe that an Indian brave, accustomed to ramble in such paths, and be bathed by such sunbeams, might be mistaken for Apollo, as Apollo was for him by West. Two of the boldest bluffs are called the Deer's Walk, (not because deer do not walk there,) and the Eagle's Nest. The latter I visited one glorious morning; it was that of the fourth of July, and certainly I think I had never felt so happy that I was born in America. Woe to all country folks that never saw this spot, never swept an enraptured gaze over the prospect that stretched beneath. I do believe Rome and Florence are suburbs compared to this capital of nature's art.

The bluff was decked with great bunches of a scarlet variety of the milkweed, like cut coral, and all starred with a mysterious-looking dark flower, whose cup rose lonely on a tall stem. This had, for two or three days, disputed the ground with the lupine and phlox. My companions disliked, I liked it.

Here I thought of, or rather saw, what the Greek expresses under the form of Jove's darling, Ganymede, and the following stanzas took form.

GANYMEDE TO HIS EAGLE,

Suggested by a Work of Thorwaldsen's.

Composed on the height called the Eagle's Nest, Oregon. Rock River, 4 July 1843.

Upon the rocky mountain stood the boy,
  A goblet of pure water in his hand,
His face and form spoke him one made for joy,
  A willing servant to sweet love's command,
But a strange pain was written on his brow,
And thrilled throughout his silver accents now—

"My bird," he cries, "my destined brother friend,
  O whither fleets to-day thy wayward flight?
Hast thou forgotten that I here attend,
  From the full noon until this sad twilight?
A hundred times, at least, from the clear spring,
  Since the full noon o'er hill and valley glowed,
I've filled the vase which our Olympian king
  Upon my care for thy sole use bestowed;
That at the moment when thou should'st descend,
A pure refreshment might thy thirst attend.

Hast thou forgotten earth, forgotten me,
  Thy fellow bondsman in a royal cause,
Who, from the sadness of infinity,
  Only with thee can know that peaceful pause
In which we catch the flowing strain of love,
Which binds our dim fates to the throne of Jove?

Before I saw thee, I was like the May,
  Longing for summer that must mar its bloom,
Or like the morning star that calls the day,
  Whose glories to its promise are the tomb;
And as the eager fountain rises higher
  To throw itself more strongly back to earth,

Still, as more sweet and full rose my desire,
    More fondly it reverted to its birth,
For, what the rosebud seeks tells not the rose,
The meaning foretold by the boy the man cannot disclose.

I was all Spring, for in my being dwelt
    Eternal youth, where flowers are the fruit,
Full feeling was the thought of what was felt,
    Its music was the meaning of the lute;
But heaven and earth such life will still deny,
For earth, divorced from heaven, still asks the question *Why?*

Upon the highest mountains my young feet
    Ached, that no pinions from their lightness grew,
My starlike eyes the stars would fondly greet,
    Yet win no greeting from the circling blue;
Fair, self-subsistent each in its own sphere,
    They had no care that there was none for me;
Alike to them that I was far or near,
    Alike to them, time and eternity.

But, from the violet of lower air,
    Sometimes an answer to my wishing came,
Those lightning births my nature seemed to share,
    They told the secrets of its fiery frame,
The sudden messengers of hate and love,
The thunderbolts that arm the hand of Jove,
And strike sometimes the sacred spire, and strike the sacred
grove.

Come in a moment, in a moment gone,
They answered me, then left me still more lone,
They told me that the thought which ruled the world,
As yet no sail upon its course had furled,
That the creation was but just begun,
New leaves still leaving from the primal one,
But spoke not of the goal to which *my* rapid wheels would run.

Still, still my eyes, though tearfully, I strained
To the far future which my heart contained,
And no dull doubt my proper hope profaned.

At last, O bliss, thy living form I spied,
    Then a mere speck upon a distant sky,

Yet my keen glance discerned its noble pride,
    And the full answer of that sun-filled eye;
I knew it was the wing that must upbear
My earthlier form into the realms of air.

Thou knowest how we gained that beauteous height,
Where dwells the monarch of the sons of light,
Thou knowest he declared us two to be
The chosen servants of his ministry,
Thou as his messenger, a sacred sign
Of conquest, or with omen more benign,
To give its due weight to the righteous cause,
To express the verdict of Olympian laws.

And I to wait upon the lonely spring,
    Which slakes the thirst of bards to whom 'tis given
The destined dues of hopes divine to sing,
    And weave the needed chain to bind to heaven
Only from such could be obtained a draught
For him who in his early home from Jove's own cup has
quaffed.

To wait, to wait, but not to wait too long,
Till heavy grows the burthen of a song;
O bird! too long has thou been gone to-day,
My feet are weary of their frequent way,
The spell that opes the spring my tongue no more
can say.

If soon thou com'st not, night will fall around,
My head with a sad slumber will be bound,
And the pure draught be spilt upon the ground.

Remember that I am not yet divine,
Long years of service to the fatal Nine
Are yet to make a Delphian vigor mine.

O, make them not too hard, thou bird of Jove,
Answer the stripling's hope, confirm his love,
Receive the service in which he delights,
And bear him often to the serene heights,
Where hands that were so prompt in serving thee,
Shall be allowed the highest ministry,
And Rapture live with bright Fidelity.

The afternoon was spent in a very different manner. The family, whose guests we were, possessed a gay and graceful hospitality that gave zest to each moment. They possessed that rare politeness which, while fertile in pleasant expedients to vary the enjoyment of a friend, leaves him perfectly free the moment he wishes to be so. With such hosts, pleasure may be combined with repose. They lived on the bank opposite the town, and, as their house was full, we slept in the town, and passed three days with them, passing to and fro morning and evening in their boats. (To one of these, called the Fairy, in which a sweet little daughter of the house moved about lighter than any Scotch Ellen ever sung, I should indite a poem, if I had not been guilty of rhyme on the very last page.) At morning this was very pleasant; at evening; I confess I was generally too tired with the excitements of the day to think it so.

Their house—a double log cabin—was, to my eye, the model of a Western villa. Nature had laid out before it grounds which could not be improved. Within, female taste had veiled every rudeness—availed itself of every sylvan grace.

In this charming abode what laughter, what sweet thoughts, what pleasing fancies, did we not enjoy! May such never desert those who reared it and made us so kindly welcome to all its pleasures!

Fragments of city life were dexterously crumbled into the dish prepared for general entertainment. Ice creams followed the dinner drawn by the gentlemen from the river, and music and fireworks wound up the evening of days spent on the Eagle's Nest. Now they had prepared a little fleet to pass over to the Fourth of July celebration, which some queer drumming and fifing, from the opposite bank, had announced to be "on hand."

We found the free and independent citizens there collected beneath the trees, among whom many a round Irish visage dimpled at the usual puffs of Ameriky.

The orator was a New Englander, and the speech smacked loudly of Boston, but was received with much applause, and followed by a plentiful dinner, provided by and for the Sovereign People, to which Hail Columbia served as grace.

Returning, the gay flotilla hailed the little flag which the children had raised from a log-cabin, prettier than any president ever saw, and drank the health of their country and all mankind, with a clear conscience.

Dance and song wound up the day. I know not when the mere local habitation has seemed to me to afford so fair a chance of happiness as this. To a person of unspoiled tastes, the beauty alone would afford stimulus enough. But with it would be naturally associated all kinds of wild sports, experiments, and the studies of natural history. In these regards, the poet, the sportsman, the naturalist, would alike rejoice in this wide range of untouched loveliness.

Then, with a very little money, a ducal estate may be purchased, and by a very little more, and moderate labor, a family be maintained upon it with raiment, food and shelter. The luxurious and minute comforts of a city life are not yet to be had without effort disproportionate to their value. But, where there is so great a counterpoise, cannot these be given up once for all? If the houses are imperfectly built, they can afford immense fires and plenty of covering; if they are small, who cares?— with such fields to roam in. In winter, it may be borne; in summer, is of no consequence. With plenty of fish, and game, and wheat, can they not dispense with a baker to bring "muffins hot" every morning to the door for their breakfast?

Here a man need not take a small slice from the landscape, and fence it in from the obtrusions of an uncongenial neighbor, and there cut down his fancies to miniature improvements which a chicken could run over in ten minutes. He may have water and wood and land enough, to dread no incursions on his prospect from some chance Vandal that may enter his neighborhood. He need not painfully economise and manage how he may use it all; he can afford to leave some of it wild, and to carry out his own plans without obliterating those of nature.

Here, whole families might live together, if they would. The sons might return from their pilgrimages to settle near the parent hearth; the daughters might find room near their mother. Those painful separations, which already desecrate and desolate the Atlantic coast, are not enforced here by the stern need of seeking bread; and where they are voluntary, it is no matter. To me, too, used to the feelings which haunt a society of struggling men, it was delightful to look upon a scene where nature still wore her motherly smile and seemed to promise room not only for those favored or cursed with the qualities best adapting for the strifes of competition, but for the delicate, the thoughtful, even the indolent or eccentric. She did not say, Fight or starve; nor even, Work or cease to exist; but, merely showing that the apple was a finer fruit than the wild crab, gave both room to grow in the garden.

A pleasant society is formed of the families who live along the banks of this stream upon farms. They are from various parts of the world, and have much to communicate to one another. Many have cultivated minds and refined manners, all a varied experience, while they have in common the interests of a new country and a new life. They must traverse some space to get at one another, but the journey is through scenes that make it a separate pleasure. They must bear inconveniences to stay in one another's houses; but these, to the well-disposed, are only a source of amusement and adventure.

The great drawback upon the lives of these settlers, at present, is the unfitness of the women for their new lot. It has generally been the choice of the men, and the women follow, as women will, doing their best for affection's sake, but too often in heartsickness and weariness. Beside it frequently not being a choice or conviction of their own minds that it is best to be here, their part is the hardest, and they are least fitted for it. The men can find assistance in field labor, and recreation with the gun and fishing-rod. Their bodily strength is greater, and enables them to bear and enjoy both these forms of life.

The women can rarely find any aid in domestic labor. All its various and careful tasks must often be performed, sick or well, by the mother and daughters, to whom a city education has imparted neither the strength nor skill now demanded.

The wives of the poorer settlers, having more hard work to do than before, very frequently become slatterns; but the ladies, accustomed to a refined neatness, feel that they cannot degrade themselves by its absence, and struggle under every disadvantage to keep up the necessary routine of small arrangements.

With all these disadvantages for work, their resources for pleasure are fewer. When they can leave the housework, they have not learnt to ride, to drive, to row, alone. Their culture has too generally been that given to women to make them "the ornaments of society." They can dance, but not draw; talk French, but know nothing of the language of flowers; neither in childhood were allowed to cultivate them, lest they should tan their complexions. Accustomed to the pavement of Broadway, they dare not tread the wildwood paths for fear of rattlesnakes!

Seeing much of this joylessness, and inaptitude, both of body and mind, for a lot which would be full of blessings for those prepared for it, we could not but look with deep interest on the little girls, and hope they would grow up with the strength of body, dexterity, simple tastes, and resources that would fit them to enjoy and refine the western farmer's life.

But they have a great deal to war with in the habits of thought acquired by their mothers from their own early life. Everywhere the fatal spirit of imitation, of reference to European standards, penetrates, and threatens to blight whatever of original growth might adorn the soil.

If the little girls grow up strong, resolute, able to exert their faculties, their mothers mourn over their want of fashionable delicacy. Are they gay, enterprising, ready to fly about in the various ways that teach them so much, these ladies lament that "they cannot go to school, where they might learn to be quiet." They lament the want of "education" for their daughters, as if the thousand needs which call out their young energies, and the language of nature around, yielded no education.

Their grand ambition for their children, is to send them to school in some eastern city, the measure most likely to make them useless and unhappy at home. I earnestly hope that, ere long, the existence of good schools near themselves, planned by persons of sufficient thought to meet the wants of the place and time, instead of copying New York or Boston, will correct this mania. Instruction the children want to enable them to profit by the great natural advantages of their position; but methods copied from the education of some English Lady Augusta, are as ill suited to the daughter of an Illinois farmer, as satin shoes to climb the Indian mounds. An elegance she would diffuse around her, if her mind were opened to appreciate elegance; it might be of a kind new, original, enchanting, as different from that of the city belle as that of the prairie torchflower from the shopworn article that touches the cheek of that lady within her bonnet.

To a girl really skilled to make home beautiful and comfortable, with bodily strength to enjoy plenty of exercise, the woods, the streams, a few studies, music, and the sincere and familiar intercourse, far more easily to be met here than elsewhere, would afford happiness enough. Her eyes would not grow dim, nor her cheeks sunken, in the absence of parties, morning visits, and milliner's shops.

As to music, I wish I could see in such places the guitar rather than the piano, and good vocal more than instrumental music.

The piano many carry with them, because it is the fashionable instrument in the eastern cities. Even there, it is so merely from the habit of imitating Europe, for not one in a thousand is willing to give the labor requisite to ensure any valuable use of the instrument.

But, out here, where the ladies have so much less leisure, it is still less desirable. Add to this, they never know how to tune their own instruments, and as persons seldom visit them who can do so, these pianos are constantly out of tune, and would spoil the ear of one who began by having any.

The guitar, or some portable instrument which requires less practice, and could be kept in tune by themselves, would be far more desirable for most of these ladies. It would give all they want as a household companion to fill up the gaps of life with a pleasant stimulus or solace, and be sufficient accompaniment to the voice in social meetings.

Singing in parts is the most delightful family amusement, and those who are constantly together can learn to sing in perfect accord. All the practice it needs, after some good elementary instruction, is such as meetings by summer twilight, and evening firelight naturally suggest. And, as music is an universal language, we cannot but think a fine Italian duet would be as much at home in the log cabin as one of Mrs. Gore's novels.

The sixth July we left this beautiful place. It was one of those rich days of bright sunlight, varied by the purple shadows of large sweeping clouds. Many a backward look we cast, and left the heart behind.

Our journey to-day was no less delightful than before, still all new, boundless, limitless. Kinmont says, that limits are sacred; that the Greeks were in the right to worship a god of limits. I say, that what is limitless is alone divine, that there was neither wall nor road in Eden, that those who walked there lost and found their way just as we did, and that all the gain from the Fall was that we had a wagon to ride in. I do not think, either, that even the horses doubted whether this last was any advantage.

Everywhere the rattlesnake-weed grows in profusion. The antidote survives the bane. Soon the coarser plantain, the "white man's footstep," shall take its place.

We saw also the compass plant, and the western tea plant. Of some of the brightest flowers an Indian girl afterwards told me the medicinal virtues. I doubt not those students of the soil knew a use to every fair emblem, on which we could only look to admire its hues and shape.

After noon we were ferried by a girl, (unfortunately not of the most picturesque appearance) across the Kishwaukie, the most graceful stream, and on whose bosom rested many full-blown water-lilies, twice as large as any of ours. I was told that, *en revanche,* they were scentless, but I still regret that I could not get at one of them to try.

Query, did the lilied fragrance which, in the miraculous times, accompanied visions of saints and angels, proceed from water or garden lilies?

Kishwaukie is, according to tradition, the scene of a famous battle, and its many grassy mounds contain the bones of the valiant. On these waved thickly the mysterious purple flower, of which I have spoken before. I think it springs from the blood of the Indians, as the hyacinth did from that of Apollo's darling.

The ladies of our host's family at Oregon, when they first went there, after all the pains and plagues of building and settling, found their first pastime in opening one of these mounds, in which they found, I think, three of the departed, seated in the Indian fashion.

One of these same ladies, as she was making bread one winter morning, saw from the window a deer directly before the house. She ran out, with her hands covered with dough, calling the others, and they caught him bodily before he had time to escape.

Here (at Kishwaukie) we received a visit from a ragged and barefoot, but bright-eyed gentleman, who seemed to be the intellectual loafer, the walking Will's coffeehouse of the place. He told us many charming snake stories; among others, of himself having seen seventeen young ones reenter the mother snake, on the intrusion of a visiter.

This night we reached Belvidere, a flourishing town in Boon county, where was the tomb, now despoiled, of Big Thunder. In this later day we felt happy to find a really good hotel.

From this place, by two days of very leisurely and devious journeying, we reached Chicago, and thus ended a journey, which one at least of the party might have wished unending.

I have not been particularly anxious to give the geography of the scene, inasmuch as it seemed to me no route, nor series of stations, but a garden interspersed with cottages, groves and flowery lawns, through which a stately river ran. I had no guidebook, kept no diary, do not know how many miles we travelled each day, nor how many in all. What I got from the journey was the poetic impression of the country at large; it is all I have aimed to communicate.

The narrative might have been made much more interesting, as life was at the time, by many piquant anecdotes and tales drawn from private life. But here courtesy restrains the pen, for I know those who received the stranger with such frank kindness would feel ill requited by its becoming the means of fixing many spy-glasses, even though the scrutiny might be one of admiring interest, upon their private homes.

For many of these, too, I was indebted to a friend, whose property they more lawfully are. This friend was one of those rare beings who are equally at home in nature and with man. He knew a tale of all that ran and swam, and flew, or only grew, possessing that extensive familiarity with things which shows equal sweetness of sympathy and playful penetration. Most refreshing to me was his unstudied lore, the unwritten poetry which common life presents to a strong and gentle mind. It was a great contrast to the subtleties of analysis, the philosophic strainings of which I had seen too much. But I will not attempt to transplant it. May it profit others as it did me in the region where it was born, where it belongs. The evening of our return to

Chicago the sunset was of a splendor and calmness beyond any we saw at the West. The twilight that succeeded was equally beautiful; soft, pathetic, but just so calm. When afterwards I learned this was the evening of Allston's death, it seemed to me as if this glorious pageant was not without connection with that event; at least, it inspired similar emotions,—a heavenly gate closing a path adorned with shows well worthy Paradise.

> Farewell, ye soft and sumptuous solitudes!
> Ye fairy distances, ye lordly woods,
> Haunted by paths like those that Poussin knew,
> When after his all gazers eyes he drew;
> I go,—and if I never more may steep
> An eager heart in your enchantments deep,
> Yet ever to itself that heart may say,
> Be not exacting; thou hast lived one day;
> Hast looked on that which matches with thy mood,
> Impassioned sweetness of full being's flood,
> Where nothing checked the bold yet gentle wave,
> Where nought repelled the lavish love that gave.
> A tender blessing lingers o'er the scene,
> Like some young mother's thought, fond, yet serene,
> And through its life new-born our lives have been.
> Once more farewell,—a sad, a sweet farewell;
> And, if I never must behold you more,
> In other worlds I will not cease to tell
> The rosary I here have numbered o'er;
> And bright-haired Hope will lend a gladdened ear,
> And Love will free him from the grasp of Fear,
> And Gorgon critics, while the tale they hear,
> Shall dew their stony glances with a tear,
> If I but catch one echo from your spell;—
> And so farewell,—a grateful, sad farewell!

CHAPTER IV

Chicago Again

CHICAGO had become interesting to me now, that I knew it as the portal to so fair a scene. I had become interested in the land, in the people, and looked sorrowfully on the lake on which I must soon embark, to leave behind what I had just begun to enjoy.

Now was the time to see the lake. The July moon was near its full, and night after night it rose in a cloudless sky above this majestic sea. The heat was excessive, so that there was no enjoyment of life, except in the night, but then the air was of that delicious temperature, worthy of orange groves. However, they were not wanted;—nothing was, as that full light fell on the faintly rippling waters which then seemed boundless.

A poem received shortly after, from a friend in Massachusetts, seemed to say that the July moon shone there not less splendid, and may claim insertion here.

TRIFORMIS

I

So pure her forehead's dazzling white;
     So swift and clear her radiant eyes,
Within the treasure of whose light
     Lay undeveloped destinies,—
Of thoughts repressed such hidden store
     Was hinted by each flitting smile,
I could but wonder and adore,
     Far off, in awe, I gazed the while.

87

I gazed at her, as at the moon,
   Hanging in lustrous twilight skies,
Whose virgin crescent, sinking soon,
   Peeps through the leaves before it flies.
Untouched Diana, flitting dim,
   While sings the wood its evening hymn.

II

Again we met. O joyful meeting!
   Her radiance now was all for me,
Like kindly airs her kindly greeting,
   So full, so musical, so free.
Within romantic forest aisles,
   Within romantic paths we walked,
I bathed me in her sister smiles,
   I breathed her beauty as we talked.

So full-orbed Cynthia walks the skies,
   Filling the earth with melodies,
Even so she condescends to kiss
   Drowsy Endymions, coarse and dull,
Or fills our waking souls with bliss,
   Making long nights too beautiful.

III

O fair, but fickle lady-moon,
   Why must thy full form ever wane?
O love! O friendship! why so soon
   Must your sweet light recede again?
I wake me in the dead of night,
   And start,—for through the misty gloom
Red Hecate stares—a boding sight!—
   Looks in, but never fills my room.

Thou music of my boyhood's hour!
   Thou shining light on manhood's way!
No more dost thou fair influence shower
   To move my soul by night or day.
O strange! that while in hall and street
   Thy hand I touch, thy grace I meet,

Such miles of polar ice should part
   The slightest touch of mind and heart!
But all thy love has waned, and so
   I gladly let thy beauty go.

Now that I am borrowing, I will also give a letter received at this time, and extracts from others from an earlier traveller, and in a different region of the country from that I saw, which, I think, in different ways, admirably descriptive of the country.

"And you, too, love the Prairies, flying voyager of a summer hour; but *I* have only there owned the wild forest, the wide-spread meadows; there only built my house, and seen the livelong day the thoughtful shadows of the great clouds color, with all-transient browns, the untrampled floor of grass; there has Spring pranked the long smooth reaches with those golden flowers, whereby became the fields a sea too golden to o'erlast the heats. Yes! and with many a yellow bell she gilded our unbounded path, that sank in the light swells of the varied surface, skirted the untilled barrens, nor shunned the steep banks of rivers darting merrily on. There has the white snow frolicsomely strown itself, till all that vast, outstretched distance glittered like a mirror in which only the heavens were reflected, and among these drifts our steps have been curbed. Ah! many days of precious weather are on the Prairies!

"You have then found, after many a weary hour, when Time has locked your temples as in a circle of heated metal, some cool, sweet, swift-gliding moments, the iron ring of necessity ungirt, and the fevered pulses at rest. You have also found this where fresh nature suffers no ravage, amid those bowers of wild-wood, those dream-like, bee-sung, murmuring and musical plains, swimming under their hazy distances, as if there, in that warm and deep back ground, stood the fairy castle of our hopes, with its fountains, its pictures, its many mystical figures in repose. Ever could we rove over those sunny distances, breathing that modulated wind, eyeing those so well-blended, imaginative, yet thoughtful surfaces, and above us wide—wide a horizon effortless and superb as a young divinity.

"I was a prisoner where you glide, the summer's pensioned guest, and my chains were the past and the future, darkness and blowing sand. There, very weary, I received from the distance a sweet emblem of an incorruptible, lofty and pervasive nature, but was I less weary? I was a prisoner, and you, plains, were my prison bars.

"Yet never, O never, beautiful plains, had I any feeling for you but profoundest gratitude, for indeed ye are only fair, grand and majestic, while I had scarcely a right there. Now, ye stand in that past day, grateful images of unshattered repose, simple in your tranquillity, strong in your self-possession, yet ever musical and springing as the footsteps of a child.

"Ah! that to some poet, whose lyre had never lost a string, to whom mortality, kinder than is her custom, had vouchsafed a day whose down had been untouched,—that to him these plains might enter, and flow forth in airy song. And you, forests, under whose symmetrical shields of dark green the colors of the fawns move, like the waters of the river under its spears,—its cimeters of flag, where, in gleaming circles of steel, the breasts of the wood-pigeons flash in the playful sunbeam, and many sounds, many notes of no earthly music, come over the well-relieved glades,—should not your depth pass into that poet's heart,—in your depths should he not fuse his own?"

The other letters show the painter's eye, as this the poet's heart.

Springfield, Illinois, May 20, 1840

"Yesterday morning I left Griggsville, my knapsack at my back, pursued my journey all day on foot, and found so new and great delight in this charming country, that I must needs tell you about it. Do you remember our saying once, that we never found the trees tall enough, the fields green enough. Well, the trees are for once tall, and fair to look upon, and one unvarying carpet of the tenderest green covers these marvellous fields, that spread out their smooth sod for miles and miles, till they even reach the horizon. But, to begin my day's journey. Griggsville is situated on the west side of the Illinois river, on a high prairie; between it and the river is a long range of bluffs which reaches a hundred miles north and south, then a wide river bottom, and then the river. It was a mild, showery morning, and I directed my steps toward the bluffs. They are covered with forest, not like our forests, tangled and impassable, but where the trees stand fair and apart from one another, so that you might ride every where about on horseback, and the tops of the hills are generally bald, and covered with green turf, like our pastures. Indeed, the whole country reminds me perpetually of one that has been carefully cultivated by a civilized people, who had been suddenly removed from the earth, with all the works of their hands, and the land given again into nature's keeping. The solitudes are not savage; they have not that dreary, stony loneliness that used to affect me in our own country; they never repel; there are no lonely heights, no isolated spots, but all is gentle, mild, inviting,—all is accessible. In following this winding, hilly road for four or five miles, I think I counted at least a dozen new kinds of wild flowers, not timid, retiring little plants like ours, but bold flowers of rich colors, covering the ground in abundance. One very common flower resembles our cardinal flower, though not of so deep a color, another is very like rocket or phlox, but smaller and of various colors, white, blue and purple. Beautiful white lupines I find too, violets white and purple. The vines and parasites are magnificent. I followed on this road till I came to the prairie which skirts the river, and this, of all the beauties of this region, is the most peculiar and wonderful. Imagine a vast and gently-swelling pasture of the brightest green grass, stretching away from you on every side, behind, toward these hills I have described, in all other directions, to a belt of tall trees, all growing up with noble proportions, from the generous soil. It is an unimagined picture of abundance and peace. Somewhere about, you are sure to see a huge herd of cattle, often white, and generally brightly marked, grazing. All looks like the work of man's hand, but you see no vestige of man, save perhaps an almost imperceptible hut on the edge of the prairie. Reaching the river, I ferried myself across, and then crossed over to take the Jacksonville railroad, but, finding there was no train, passed the night at a farm house." And here may find its place this converse between the solitary old man and the young traveller.

SOLITARY

My son, with weariness thou seemest spent,
And toiling on the dusty road all day,
Weary and pale, yet with inconstant step,
Hither and thither turning,—seekest thou
To find aught lost, or what dark care pursues thee?
If thou art weary, rest, if hungry, eat.

TRAVELLER

Oh rather, father, let me ask of thee
What is it I do seek, what thing I lack?
These many days I've left my father's hall,
Forth driven by insatiable desire,
That, like the wind, now gently murmuring,
Enticed me forward with its own sweet voice
Through many-leaved woods, and valleys deep,

Yet ever fled before me. Then with sound
Stronger than hurrying tempest, seizing me,
Forced me to fly its power. Forward still,
Bound by enchanted ties, I seek its source.
Sometimes it is a something I have lost,
Known long since, before I bent my steps
Toward this beautiful broad plane of earth.
Sometimes it is a spirit yet unknown,
In whose dim-imaged features seem to smile
The dear delight of these high-mansioned thoughts,
That sometimes visit me. Like unto mine
Her lineaments appear, but beautiful,
As of a sister in a far-off world,
Waiting to welcome me. And when I think
To reach and clasp the figure, it is gone,
And some ill-omened ghastly vision comes
To bid beware, and not too curiously
Demand the secrets of that distant world,
Whose shadow haunts me.—On the waves below
But now I gazed, warmed with the setting sun,
Who sent his golden streamers to my feet,
It seemed a pathway to a world beyond,
And I looked round, if that my spirit beckoned
That I might follow it.

SOLITARY

Dreams all, my son. Yes, even so I dreamed
And even so was thwarted. You must learn
To dream another long and troublous dream,
The dream of life. And you shall think you wake,
And think the shadows substance, love and hate,
Exchange and barter, joy, and weep, and dance,
And this too shall be dream.

TRAVELLER

Oh who can say
Where lies the boundary? What solid things
That daily mock our senses, shall dissolve
Before the might within, while shadowy forms

Freeze into stark reality, defying
The force and will of man. These forms I see,
They may go with me through eternity,
And bless or curse with ceaseless company,
While yonder man, that I met yesternight,
Where is he now? He passed before my eyes,
He is gone, but these stay with me ever.

That night the young man rested with the old,
And, grave or gay, in laughter or in tears,
They wore the night in converse. Morning came,
The dreamer took his solitary way;
And, as he pressed that old man's hand, he sighed,
Must this too be a dream?

Afterwards, of the rolling prairie. "There was one of twenty miles in extent, not flat, but high and rolling, so that when you arrived at a high part, by gentle ascents, the view was beyond measure grand; as far as the eye could reach, nothing but the green, rolling plain, and at a vast distance, groves, all looking gentle and cultivated, yet all uninhabited. I think it would impress you, as it does me, that these scenes are truly sublime. I have a sensation of vastness which I have sought in vain among high mountains. Mountains crowd one sensation on another, till all is excitement, all is surprise, wonder, enchantment. Here is neither enchantment or disappointment, but expectation fully realized. I have always had an attachment for a plain. The Roman Campagna is a prairie. Peoria is in a most lovely situation. In fact I am so delighted that I am as full of superlatives as the Italian language. I could, however, find fault enough, if you ask what I dislike."

But no one did ask; it is not worth while where there is so much to admire. Yet the following is a good statement of the shadow side.

"As to the boasts about the rapid progress here, give me rather the firm fibre of a slow and knotty growth. I could not help thinking as much when I was talking to E. the other day, whom I met on board the boat. He quarrelled with Boston for its slowness; said it was a bad place for a young man. He could not make himself felt, could not see the effects of his exertions as he could here.—To be sure he could not. Here he comes, like a yankee farmer, with all the knowledge that our hard soil and laborious cultivation could give him, and what wonder if he is surprised at the work of his own hands, when he comes to such a soil as this. But he feeds not so many mouths, though he tills more acres. The plants he raises have not so exquisite a form, the vegetables so fine a flavor. His cultivation becomes more negligent, he is not so good a farmer. Is not this a true view? It strikes me continually. The traces of a man's hand in a new country are rarely productive of beauty. It is a cutting down of forest trees to make zigzag fences."

The most picturesque objects to be seen from Chicago on the inland side were the lines of Hoosier wagons. These rude farmers, the large first product of the soil, travel leisurely along, sleeping in their wagons by night, eating only what they bring with them. In the town they observe the same plan, and trouble no luxurious hotel for board and lodging. In the town they look like foreign peasantry, and contrast well with the many Germans, Dutch, and Irish. In the country it is very pretty to see them prepared to "camp out" at night, their horses taken out of harness, and they lounging under the trees, enjoying the evening meal.

On the lake side it is fine to see the great boats come panting in from their rapid and marvellous journey. Especially at night the motion of their lights is very majestic.

When the favorite boats, the Great Western and Illinois, are going out, the town is thronged with people from the south and farther west, to go in them. These moonlight nights I would hear the French rippling and fluttering familiarly amid the rude ups and downs of the Hoosier dialect.

At the hotel table were daily to be seen new faces, and new stories to be learned. And any one who has a large acquaintance may be pretty sure of meeting some of them here in the course of a few days.

Among those whom I met was Mrs. Z., the aunt of an old school-mate, to whom I impatiently hastened, as soon as the meal was over, to demand news of Mariana. The answer startled me. Mariana, so full of life, was dead. That form, the most rich in energy and coloring of any I had ever seen, had faded from the earth. The circle of youthful associations had given way in the part, that seemed the strongest. What I now learned of the story of this life, and what was by myself remembered, may be bound together in this slight sketch.

At the boarding-school to which I was too early sent, a fond, a proud, and timid child, I saw among the ranks of the gay and graceful, bright or earnest girls, only one who interested my fancy or touched my young heart; and this was Mariana. She was, on the father's side, of Spanish Creole blood, but had been sent to the Atlantic coast, to receive a school education under the care of her aunt, Mrs. Z.

This lady had kept her mostly at home with herself, and Mariana had gone from her house to a dayschool; but the aunt, being absent for a time in Europe, she had now been unfortunately committed for some time to the mercies of a boarding-school.

A strange bird she proved there,—a lonely swallow that could not make for itself a summer. At first, her schoolmates were captivated with her ways; her love of wild dances and sudden song, her freaks of passion and of wit. She was always new, always surprising, and, for a time, charming.

But, after awhile, they tired of her. She could never be depended on to join in their plans, yet she expected them to follow out hers with their whole strength. She was very loving, even infatuated in her own affections, and exacted from those who had professed any love for her, the devotion she was willing to bestow.

Yet there was a vein of haughty caprice in her character; a love of solitude, which made her at times wish to retire entirely, and at these times she would expect to be thoroughly understood, and let alone, yet to be welcomed back when she returned. She did not thwart others in their humors, but she never doubted of great indulgence from them.

Some singular habits she had which, when new, charmed, but, after acquaintance, displeased her companions. She had by nature the same habit and power of excitement that is described in the spinning dervishes of the East. Like them, she would spin until all around her were giddy, while her own brain, instead of being disturbed, was excited to great action. Pausing, she would declaim verse of others or her own; act many parts, with strange catch-words and burdens that seemed to act with mystical power on her own fancy, sometimes stimulating her to convulse the hearer with laughter, sometimes to melt him to tears. When her power began to languish, she would spin again till fired to recommence her singular drama, into which she wove figures from the scenes of her earlier childhood, her companions, and the dignitaries she sometimes saw, with fantasies unknown to life, unknown to heaven or earth.

This excitement, as may be supposed, was not good for her. It oftenest came on in the evening, and often spoiled her sleep. She would wake in the night, and cheat her restlessness by inventions that teazed, while they sometimes diverted her companions.

She was also a sleep-walker; and this one trait of her case did somewhat alarm her guardians, who, otherwise, showed the same profound stupidity as to this peculiar being, usual in the overseers of the young. They consulted a physician, who said she would outgrow it, and prescribed a milk diet.

Meantime, the fever of this ardent and too early stimulated nature was constantly increased by the restraints and narrow routine of the boarding school. She was always devising means to break in upon it. She had a taste which would have seemed ludicrous to her mates, if they had not felt some awe of her, from a touch of genius and power that never left her, for costume and fancy dresses, always some sash twisted about her, some drapery, something odd in the arrangement of her hair and dress, so that the methodical preceptress dared not let her go out without a careful scrutiny and remodelling, whose soberizing effects generally disappeared the moment she was in the free air.

At last, a vent for her was found in private theatricals. Play followed play, and in these and the rehearsals she found entertainment congenial with her. The principal parts, as a matter of course, fell to her lot; most of the good suggestions and arrangements came from her, and for a time she ruled masterly and shone triumphant.

During these performances the girls had heightened their natural bloom with artificial red; this was delightful to them—it was something so out of the way. But Mariana, after the plays were over, kept her carmine saucer on the dressing-table, and put on her blushes regularly as the morning.

When stared and jeered at, she at first said she did it because she thought it made her look prettier; but, after a while, she became quite petulant about it,—would make no reply to any joke, but merely kept on doing it.

This irritated the girls, as all eccentricity does the world in general, more than vice or malignity. They talked it over among themselves, till they got wrought up to a desire of punishing, once for all, this sometimes amusing, but so often provoking nonconformist.

Having obtained the leave of the mistress, they laid, with great glee, a plan one evening, which was to be carried into execution next day at dinner.

Among Mariana's irregularities was a great aversion to the mealtime ceremonial. So long, so tiresome she found it, to be seated at a certain moment, to wait while each one was served at so large a table, and one where there was scarcely any conversation; from day to day it became more heavy to her to sit there, or go there at all. Often as possible she excused herself on the ever-convenient plea of headache, and was hardly ever ready when the dinnerbell rang.

To-day it found her on the balcony, lost in gazing on the beautiful prospect. I have heard her say afterwards, she had rarely in her life been so happy,—and she was one with whom happiness was a still rapture. It was one of the most blessed summer days; the shadows of great white clouds empurpled the distant hills for a few moments only to leave them more golden; the tall grass of the wide fields waved in the softest breeze. Pure blue were the heavens, and the same hue of pure content-ment was in the heart of Mariana.

Suddenly on her bright mood jarred the dinner bell. At first rose her usual thought, I will not, cannot go; and then the *must,* which daily life can always enforce, even upon the butterflies and birds, came, and she walked reluctantly to her room. She merely changed her dress, and never thought of adding the artificial rose to her cheek.

When she took her seat in the dining-hall, and was asked if she would be helped, raising her eyes, she saw the person who asked her was deeply rouged, with a bright glaring spot, perfectly round, in either cheek. She looked at the next, same apparition! She then slowly passed her eyes down the whole line, and saw the same, with a sup-pressed smile distorting every countenance. Catching the design at once, she deliberately looked along her own side of the table, at every schoolmate in turn; every one had joined in the trick. The teachers strove to be grave, but she saw they enjoyed the joke. The servants could not suppress a titter.

When Warren Hastings stood at the bar of Westminster Hall—when the Methodist preacher walked through a line of men, each of whom greeted him with a brickbat or a rotten egg, they had some preparation for the crisis, and it might not be very difficult to meet it with an im-passive brow. Our little girl was quite unprepared to find herself in the midst of a world which despised her, and triumphed in her disgrace.

She had ruled, like a queen, in the midst of her companions; she had shed her animation through their lives, and loaded them with prodigal favors, nor once suspected that a powerful favorite might not be loved. Now, she felt that she had been but a dangerous plaything in the hands of those whose hearts she never had doubted.

Yet, the occasion found her equal to it, for Mariana had the kind of spirit, which, in a better cause, had made the Roman matron truly say of her death-wound, "It is not painful, Poetus." She did not blench—she did not change countenance. She swallowed her dinner with apparent composure. She made remarks to those near her, as if she had no eyes.

The wrath of the foe of course rose higher, and the moment they were freed from the restraints of the dining-room, they all ran off, gaily calling, and sarcastically laughing, with backward glances, at Mariana, left alone.

She went alone to her room, locked the door, and threw herself on the floor in strong convulsions. These had sometimes threatened her life, as a child, but of later years, she had outgrown them. School–hours came, and she was not there. A little girl, sent to her door, could get no answer. The teachers became alarmed, and broke it open. Bitter was their penitence and that of her companions at the state in which they found her. For some hours, terrible anxiety was felt; but, at last, nature, exhausted, relieved herself by a deep slumber.

From this Mariana rose an altered being. She made no reply to the expressions of sorrow from her companions, none to the grave and kind, but undiscerning comments of her teacher. She did not name the source of her anguish, and its poisoned dart sank deeply in. It was this thought which stung her so. What, not one, not a single one, in the hour of trial, to take my part, not one who refused to take part against me. Past words of love, and caresses, little heeded at the time, rose to her memory, and gave fuel to her distempered thoughts. Beyond the sense of universal perfidy, of burning resentment, she could not get. And Mariana, born for love, now hated all the world.

The change, however, which these feelings made in her conduct and appearance bore no such construction to the careless observer. Her gay freaks were quite gone, her wildness, her invention. Her dress was uniform, her manner much subdued. Her chief interest seemed now to lie in her studies, and in music. Her companions she never sought, but they, partly from uneasy remorseful feelings, partly that they really liked her much better now that she did not oppress and puzzle them, sought her continually. And here the black shadow comes upon her life, the only stain upon the history of Mariana.

They talked to her, as girls, having few topics, naturally do, of one another. And the demon rose within her, and spontaneously, without design, generally without words of positive falsehood, she became a genius of discord among them. She fanned those flames of envy and jealousy which a wise, true word from a third will often quench forever; by a glance, or a seemingly light reply, she planted the seeds of dissension, till there was scarce a peaceful affection, or sincere intimacy in the circle where she lived, and could not but rule, for she was one whose nature was to that of the others as fire to clay.

It was at this time that I came to the school, and first saw Mariana. Me she charmed at once, for I was a sentimental child, who, in my early ill health, had been indulged in reading novels, till I had no eyes for the common greens and browns of life. The heroine of one of these, "The Bandit's Bride," I immediately saw in Mariana. Surely the

Bandit's Bride had just such hair, and such strange, lively ways, and such a sudden flush of the eye. The Bandit's Bride, too, was born to be "misunderstood" by all but her lover. But Mariana, I was determined, should be more fortunate, for, until her lover appeared, I myself would be the wise and delicate being who could understand her.

It was not, however, easy to approach her for this purpose. Did I offer to run and fetch her handkerchief, she was obliged to go to her room, and would rather do it herself. She did not like to have people turn over for her the leaves of the music book as she played. Did I approach my stool to her feet, she moved away, as if to give me room. The bunch of wild flowers which I timidly laid beside her plate was left there.

After some weeks my desire to attract her notice really preyed upon me, and one day meeting her alone in the entry, I fell upon my knees, and kissing her hand, cried, "O Mariana, do let me love you, and try to love me a little." But my idol snatched away her hand, and, laughing more wildly than the Bandit's Bride was ever described to have done, ran into her room. After that day her manner to me was not only cold, but repulsive; I felt myself scorned, and became very unhappy.

Perhaps four months had passed thus, when, one afternoon, it became obvious that something more than common was brewing. Dismay and mystery were written in many faces of the older girls; much whispering was going on in corners.

In the evening, after prayers, the principal bade us stay; and, in a grave, sad voice, summoned forth Mariana to answer charges to be made against her.

Mariana came forward, and leaned against the chimney-piece. Eight of the older girls came forward, and preferred against her charges, alas, too well-founded, of calumny and falsehood.

My heart sank within me, as one after the other brought up their proofs, and I saw they were too strong to be resisted. I could not bear the thought of this second disgrace of my shining favorite. The first had been whispered to me, though the girls did not like to talk about it. I must confess, such is the charm of strength to softer natures, that neither of these crises could deprive Mariana of hers in my eyes.

At first, she defended herself with self-possession and eloquence. But when she found she could no more resist the truth, she suddenly threw herself down, dashing her head, with all her force, against the iron hearth, on which a fire was burning, and was taken up senseless.

The affright of those present was great. Now that they had perhaps killed her, they reflected it would have been as well, if they had taken warning from the former occasion, and approached very carefully a nature so capable of any extreme. After awhile she revived, with a faint groan, amid the sobs of her companions. I was on my knees by the bed, and held her cold hand. One of those most aggrieved took it from me to beg her pardon, and say it was impossible not to love her. She made no reply.

Neither that night, nor for several days, could a word be obtained from her, nor would she touch food; but, when it was presented to her, or any one drew near for any cause, she merely turned away her head, and gave no sign. The teacher saw that some terrible nervous affection had fallen upon her, that she grew more and more feverish. She knew not what to do.

Meanwhile a new revolution had taken place in the mind of the passionate, but nobly-tempered child. All these months nothing but the sense of injury had rankled in her heart. She had gone on in one mood, doing what the demon prompted, without scruple and without fear.

But, at the moment of detection, the tide ebbed, and the bottom of her soul lay revealed to her eye. How black, how stained and sad. Strange, strange that she had not seen before the baseness and cruelty of falsehood, the loveliness of truth. Now, amid the wreck, uprose the moral nature which never before had attained the ascendant. "But," she thought, "too late, sin is revealed to me in all its deformity, and, sin-defiled, I will not, cannot live. The mainspring of life is broken."

And thus passed slowly by her hours in that black despair of which only youth is capable. In older years men suffer more dull pain, as each sorrow that comes drops its leaden weight into the past, and, similar features of character bringing similar results, draws up a heavy burden buried in those depths. But only youth has energy, with fixed unwinking gaze, to contemplate grief, to hold it in the arms and to the heart, like a child which makes it wretched, yet is indubitably its own.

The lady who took charge of this sad child had never well understood her before, but had always looked on her with great tenderness. And now love seemed, when all around were in greatest distress, fearing to call in medical aid, fearing to do without it, to teach her where the only balm was to be found that could have healed this wounded spirit.

One night she came in, bringing a calming draught. Mariana was sitting, as usual, her hair loose, her dress the same robe they had put on her at first, her eyes fixed vacantly upon the whited wall. To the proffers and entreaties of her nurse she made no reply.

The lady burst into tears, but Mariana did not seem even to observe it.

The lady then said, "O my child, do not despair, do not think that one great fault can mar a whole life. Let me trust you, let me tell you the griefs of my sad life. I will tell to you, Mariana, what I never expected to impart to any one."

And so she told her tale: it was one of pain, of shame, borne, not for herself, but for one near and dear as herself. Mariana knew the lady, knew the pride and reserve of her nature; she had often admired to see how the cheek, lovely, but no longer young, mantled with the deepest blush of youth, and the blue eyes were cast down at any little emotion. She had understood the proud sensibility of the character. She fixed her eyes on those now raised to hers, bright with fast falling tears. She heard the story to the end, and then, without saying a word, stretched out her hand for the cup.

She returned to life, but it was as one who has passed through the valley of death. The heart of stone was quite broken in her. The fiery life fallen from flame to coal. When her strength was a little restored, she had all her companions summoned, and said to them; "I deserved to die, but a generous trust has called me back to life. I will be worthy of it, nor ever betray the truth, or resent injury more. Can you forgive the past?"

And they not only forgave, but, with love and earnest tears, clasped in their arms the returning sister. They vied with one another in offices of humble love to the humbled one; and, let it be recorded as an instance of the pure honor of which young hearts are capable, that these facts, known to forty persons, never, so far as I know, transpired beyond those walls.

It was not long after this that Mariana was summoned home. She went thither a wonderfully instructed being, though in ways those who had sent her forth to learn little dreamed of.

Never was forgotten the vow of the returning prodigal. Mariana could not resent, could not play false. The terrible crisis, which she so early passed through, probably prevented the world from hearing much of her. A wild fire was tamed in that hour of penitence at the boarding school, such as has oftentimes wrapped court and camp in its destructive glow.

But great were the perils she had yet to undergo, for she was one of those barks which easily get beyond soundings, and ride not lightly on the plunging billow.

Her return to her native climate seconded the effects of inward revolutions. The cool airs of the north had exasperated nerves too susceptible for their tension. Those of the south restored her to a more soft and indolent state. Energy gave place to feeling, turbulence to intensity of character.

At this time love was the natural guest, and he came to her under a form that might have deluded one less ready for delusion.

Sylvain was a person well proportioned to her lot in years, family, and fortune. His personal beauty was not great, but of a noble character. Repose marked his slow gesture, and the steady gaze of his large brown eye, but it was a repose that would give way to a blaze of energy when the occasion called. In his stature, expression, and heavy coloring, he might not unfitly be represented by the great magnolias that inhabit the forests of that climate. His voice, like everything about him, was rich and soft, rather than sweet or delicate.

Mariana no sooner knew him than she loved, and her love, lovely as she was, soon excited his. But, oh! it is a curse to woman to love first, or most. In so doing she reverses the natural relations, and her heart can never, never be satisfied with what ensues.

Mariana loved first, and loved most, for she had most force and variety to love with. Sylvain seemed, at first, to take her to himself, as the deep southern night might some fair star. But it proved not so.

Mariana was a very intellectual being, and she needed companionship. This she could only have with Sylvain, in the paths of passion and action. Thoughts he had none, and little delicacy of sentiment. The gifts she loved to prepare of such for him, he took with a sweet, but indolent smile; he held them lightly, and soon they fell from his grasp. He loved to have her near him, to feel the glow and fragrance of her nature, but cared not to explore the little secret paths whence that fragrance was collected.

Mariana knew not this for a long time. Loving so much, she imagined all the rest, and, where she felt a blank, always hoped that further communion would fill it up. When she found this could never be; that there was absolutely a whole province of her being to which nothing in his answered, she was too deeply in love to leave him. Often after passing hours together, beneath the southern moon, when, amid the sweet intoxication of mutual love, she still felt the desolation of solitude, and a repression of her finer powers, she had asked herself, can I give him up? But the heart always passionately answered, no! I may be miserable with him, but I cannot live without him.

And the last miserable feeling of these conflicts was, that if the lover, soon to be the bosom friend, could have dreamed of these conflicts, he would have laughed, or else been angry, even enough to give her up.

Ah weakness of the strong. Of these strong only where strength is weakness. Like others she had the decisions of life to make, before she had light by which to make them. Let none condemn her. Those who have not erred as fatally, should thank the guardian angel who gave them more time to prepare for judgment, but blame no children who thought at arm's length to find the moon. Mariana, with a heart capable of highest Eros, gave it to one who knew love only as a flower or plaything, and bound her heartstrings to one who parted his as lightly as the ripe fruit leaves the bough. The sequel could not fail. Many console themselves for the one great mistake with their children, with the world. This was not possible to Mariana. A few months of domestic life she still was almost happy. But Sylvain then grew tired. He wanted business and the world; of these she had no knowledge, for them no faculties. He wanted in her the head of his house; she to make her heart his home. No compromise was possible between natures of such unequal poise, and which had met only on one or two points. Through all its stages she

"felt
The agonizing sense
Of seeing love from passion melt
Into indifference;
The fearful shame that, day by day,
Burns onward, still to burn,
To have thrown her precious heart away,
And met this black return,"

till death at last closed the scene. Not that she died of one downright blow on the heart. That is not the way such cases proceed. I cannot detail all the symptoms, for I was not there to watch them, and aunt Z. was neither so faithful an observer or narrator as I have shown myself in the school-day passages; but, generally, they were as follows.

Sylvain wanted to go into the world, or let it into his house. Mariana consented; but, with an unsatisfied heart, and no lightness of character, she played her part ill there. The sort of talent and facility she had displayed in early days, were not the least like what is called out in the social world by the desire to please and to shine. Her excitement had been muse-like, that of the improvisatrice, whose kindling fancy seeks to create an atmosphere round it, and makes the chain through which to set free its electric sparks. That had been a time of wild and exuberant life. After her character became more tender and

concentrated, strong affection or a pure enthusiasm might still have
called out beautiful talents in her. But in the first she was utterly disappointed. The second was not roused within her thought. She did not
expand into various life, and remained unequal; sometimes too pas-
sive, sometimes too ardent, and not sufficiently occupied with what
occupied those around her to come on the same level with them and
embellish their hours.

Thus she lost ground daily with her husband, who, comparing
her with the careless shining dames of society, wondered why he had
found her so charming in solitude.

· At intervals, when they were left alone, Mariana wanted to open her
heart, to tell the thoughts of her mind. She was so conscious of secret
riches within herself, that sometimes it seemed, could she but reveal a
glimpse of them to the eye of Sylvain, he would be attracted near her
again, and take a path where they could walk hand in hand. Sylvain, in
these intervals, wanted an indolent repose. His home was his castle. He
wanted no scenes too exciting there. Light jousts and plays were well
enough, but no grave encounters. He liked to lounge, to sing, to read,
to sleep. In fine, Sylvain became the kind, but preoccupied husband,
Mariana, the solitary and wretched wife. He was off continually, with
his male companions, on excursions or affairs of pleasure. At home
Mariana found that neither her books nor music would console her.

She was of too strong a nature to yield without a struggle to so dull a
fiend as despair. She looked into other hearts, seeking whether she could
there find such home as an orphan asylum may afford. This she did
rather because the chance came to her, and it seemed unfit not to seize
the proffered plank, than in hope, for she was not one to double her
stakes, but rather with Cassandra power to discern early the sure course
of the game. And Cassandra whispered that she was one of those.

"Whom men love not, but yet regret,"

And so it proved. Just as in her childish days, though in a different
form, it happened betwixt her and these companions. She could not
be content to receive them quietly, but was stimulated to throw herself
too much into the tie, into the hour, till she filled it too full for them.
Like Fortunio, who sought to do homage to his friends by building a
fire of cinnamon, not knowing that its perfume would be too strong
for their endurance, so did Mariana. What she wanted to tell, they did
not wish to hear; a little had pleased, so much overpowered, and they
preferred the free air of the street, even, to the cinnamon perfume of
her palace.

However, this did not signify; had they staid, it would not have availed her! It was a nobler road, a higher aim she needed now; this did not become clear to her.

She lost her appetite, she fell sick, had fever. Sylvain was alarmed, nursed her tenderly; she grew better. Then his care ceased, he saw not the mind's disease, but left her to rise into health and recover the tone of her spirits, as she might. More solitary than ever, she tried to raise herself, but she knew not yet enough. The weight laid upon her young life was a little too heavy for it. One long day she passed alone, and the thoughts and presages came too thick for her strength. She knew not what to do with them, relapsed into fever, and died.

Notwithstanding this weakness, I must ever think of her as a fine sample of womanhood, born to shed light and life on some palace home. Had she known more of God and the universe, she would not have given way where so many have conquered. But peace be with her; she now, perhaps, has entered into a larger freedom, which is knowledge. With her died a great interest in life to me. Since her I have never seen a Bandit's Bride. She, indeed, turned out to be only a merchant's.—Sylvain is married again to a fair and laughing girl, who will not die, probably, till their marriage grows a "golden marriage."

Aunt Z. had with her some papers of Mariana's, which faintly shadow forth the thoughts that engaged her in the last days. One of these seems to have been written when some faint gleam had been thrown across the path, only to make its darkness more visible. It seems to have been suggested by remembrance of the beautiful ballad, *Helen of Kirconnel Lee,* which once she loved to recite, and in tones that would not have sent a chill to the heart from which it came.

> "Death
> Opens her sweet white arms, and whispers Peace;
> Come, say thy sorrows in this bosom! This
> Will never close against thee, and my heart,
> Though cold, cannot be colder much than man's,"

> "I wish I were where Helen lies,"
> A lover in the times of old,
> Thus vents his grief in lonely sighs,
> And hot tears from a bosom cold.

> But, mourner for thy martyred love,
> Could'st thou but know what hearts must feel,

Where no sweet recollections move,
Whose tears a desert fount reveal.

When "in thy arms lyred Helen fell,"
She died, sad man, she died for thee,
    Nor could the films of death dispel
Her loving eye's sweet radiancy.

Thou wert beloved, and she had loved,
Till death alone the whole could tell,
    Death every shade of doubt removed,
And steeped the star in its cold well.

On some fond breast the parting soul
Relies,—earth has no more to give;
    Who wholly loves has known the whole,
The wholly loved doth truly live.

But some, sad outcasts from this prize,
Wither down to a lonely grave,
    All hearts their hidden love despise,
And leave them to the whelming wave.

They heart to heart have never pressed,
Nor hands in holy pledge have given,
    By father's love were ne'er caressed,
Nor in a mother's eye saw heaven.

A flowerless and fruitless tree,
A dried up stream, a mateless bird,
    They live, yet never living be,
They die, their music all unheard.

I wish I were where Helen lies,
For there I could not be alone;
    But now, when this dull body dies,
The spirit still will make its moan.

Love passed me by, nor touched my brow;
Life would not yield one perfect boon;
    And all too late it calls me now,
O all too late, and all too soon.

If thou couldst the dark riddle read
Which leaves this dart within my breast,

Then might I think thou lov'st indeed,
Then were the whole to thee confest.

Father, they will not take me home,
To the poor child no heart is free;
In sleet and snow all night I roam;
Father,—was this decreed by thee?

I will not try another door,
To seek what I have never found;
Now, till the very last is o'er,
Upon the earth I'll wander round.

I will not hear the treacherous call
That bids me stay and rest awhile,
For I have found that, one and all,
They seek me for a prey and spoil.

They are not bad, I know it well;
I know they know not what they do;
They are the tools of the dread spell
Which the lost lover must pursue.

In temples sometimes she may rest,
In lonely groves, away from men,
There bend the head, by heats distrest,
Nor be by blows awoke again.

Nature is kind, and God is kind,
And, if she had not had a heart,
Only that great discerning mind,
She might have acted well her part.

But oh this thirst, that none can still,
Save those unfounden waters free;
The angel of my life should fill
And soothe me to Eternity!

It marks the defect in the position of woman that one like Mariana should have found reason to write thus. To a man of equal power, equal sincerity, no more!—many resources would have presented themselves. He would not have needed to seek, he would have been called by life, and not permitted to be quite wrecked through the affections only.

But such women as Mariana are often lost, unless they meet some man of sufficiently great soul to prize them.

Van Artevelde's Elena, though in her individual nature unlike my Mariana, is like her in a mind whose large impulses are disproportioned to the persons and occasions she meets, and which carry her beyond those reserves which mark the appointed lot of woman. But, when she met Van Artevelde, he was too great not to revere her rare nature, without regard to the stains and errors of its past history; great enough to receive her entirely and make a new life for her; man enough to be a lover! But as such men come not so often as once an age, their presence should not be absolutely needed to sustain life.

At Chicago I read again Philip Van Artevelde, and certain passages in it will always be in my mind associated with the deep sound of the lake, as heard in the night. I used to read a short time at night, and then open the blind to look out. The moon would be full upon the lake, and the calm breath, pure light, and the deep voice harmonized well with the thought of the Flemish hero. When will this country have such a man? It is what she needs; no thin Idealist, no coarse Realist, but a man whose eye reads the heavens while his feet step firmly on the ground, and his hands are strong and dexterous for the use of human implements. A man religious, virtuous and—sagacious; a man of universal sympathies, but self-possessed; a man who knows the region of emotion, though he is not its slave; a man to whom this world is no mere spectacle, or fleeting shadow, but a great solemn game to be played with good heed, for its stakes are of eternal value, yet who, if his own play be true, heeds not what he loses by the falsehood of others. A man who hives from the past, yet knows that its honey can but moderately avail him; whose comprehensive eye scans the present, neither infatuated by its golden lures, nor chilled by its many ventures; who possesses prescience, as the wise man must, but not so far as to be driven mad to-day by the gift which discerns to-morrow. When there is such a man for America, the thought which urges her on will be expressed.

Now that I am about to leave Illinois, feelings of regret and admiration come over me, as in parting with a friend whom we have not had the good sense to prize and study, while hours of association, never perhaps to return, were granted. I have fixed my attention almost exclusively on the picturesque beauty of this region; it was so new, so inspiring. But I ought to have been more interested in the housekeeping of this magnificent state, in the education she is giving her children, in their prospects.

Illinois is, at present, a by-word of reproach among the nations, for the careless, prodigal course, by which, in early youth, she has endangered her honor. But you cannot look about you there, without seeing that there are resources abundant to retrieve, and soon to retrieve, far greater errors, if they are only directed with wisdom.

Might the simple maxim, that honesty is the best policy be laid to heart! Might a sense of the true aims of life elevate the tone of politics and trade, till public and private honor become identical! Might the western man in that crowded and exciting life which develops his faculties so fully for to-day, not forget that better part which could not be taken from him! Might the western woman take that interest and acquire that light for the education of the children, for which she alone has leisure!

This is indeed the great problem of the place and time. If the next generation be well prepared for their work, ambitious of good and skilful to achieve it, the children of the present settlers may be leaven enough for the mass constantly increasing by emigration. And how much is this needed where those rude foreigners can so little understand the best interests of the land they seek for bread and shelter. It would be a happiness to aid in this good work, and interweave the white and golden threads into the fate of Illinois. It would be a work worthy the devotion of any mind.

In the little that I saw, was a large proportion of intelligence, activity, and kind feeling; but, if there was much serious laying to heart of the true purposes of life, it did not appear in the tone of conversation.

Having before me the Illinois guide-book, I find there mentioned, as a "visionary," one of the men I should think of as able to be a truly valuable settler in a new and great country—Morris Birkbeck, of England. Since my return, I have read his journey to, and letters from, Illinois. I see nothing promised there that will not surely belong to the man who knows how to seek for it.

Mr. Birkbeck was an enlightened philanthropist, the rather that he did not wish to sacrifice himself to his fellow men, but to benefit them with all he had, and was, and wished. He thought all the creatures of a divine love ought to be happy and ought to be good, and that his own soul and his own life were not less precious than those of others; indeed, that to keep these healthy, was his only means of a healthy influence.

But his aims were altogether generous. Freedom, the liberty of law, not license; not indolence, work for himself and children and all men, but under genial and poetic influences;—these were his aims. How different from those of the new settlers in general! And into his mind so long ago shone steadily the two thoughts, now so prevalent in thinking and aspiring minds, of "Resist not evil," and "Every man his own priest, and the heart the only true church."

He has lost credit for sagacity from accidental circumstances. It does not appear that his position was ill chosen, or his means disproportioned to his ends, had he been sustained by funds from England, as he had a right to expect. But through the profligacy of a near relative, commissioned to collect these dues, he was disappointed of them, and his paper protested and credit destroyed in our cities, before he became aware of his danger.

Still, though more slowly and with more difficulty, he might have succeeded in his designs. The English farmer might have made the English settlement a model for good methods and good aims to all that region, had not death prematurely cut short his plans.

I have wished to say these few words, because the veneration with which I have been inspired for his character by those who knew him well, makes me impatient of this careless blame being passed from mouth to mouth and book to book. Success is no test of a man's endeavor, and Illinois will yet, I hope, regard this man, who knew so well what *ought* to be, as one of her true patriarchs, the Abraham of a promised land.

He was one too much before his time to be soon valued; but the time is growing up to him, and will understand his mild philanthropy and clear, large views.

I subjoin the account of his death, given me by a friend, as expressing, in fair picture, the character of the man.

"Mr. Birkbeck was returning from the seat of government, whither he had been on public business, and was accompanied by his son Bradford, a youth of sixteen or eighteen. It was necessary to cross a ford, which was rendered difficult by the swelling of the stream. Mr. B.'s horse was unwilling to plunge into the water, so his son offered to go first, and he followed. Bradford's horse had just gained footing on the opposite shore, when he looked back and perceived his father was dismounted, struggling in the water, and carried down by the current.

"Mr. Birkbeck could not swim; Bradford could; so he dismounted, and plunged into the stream to save his father. He got to him before he sank, held him up above water, and told him to take hold of his collar, and he would swim ashore with him. Mr. B. did so, and Bradford exerted all his strength to stem the current and reach the shore at a point where they could land; but, encumbered by his own clothing and his father's weight, he made no progress; and when Mr. B. perceived this, he, with his characteristic calmness and resolution, gave up his hold of his son, and, motioning to him to save himself, resigned himself to his fate. His son reached the shore, but was too much overwhelmed by his loss to leave it. He was found by some travellers, many hours after, seated on the margin of the stream, with his head in his hands, stupefied with grief.

"The body was found, and on the countenance was the sweetest smile; and Bradford said, 'just so he smiled upon me when he let go and pushed me away from him.'"

Many men can choose the right and best on a great occasion, but not many can, with such ready and serene decision, lay aside even life, when it is right and best. This little narrative touched my imagination in very early youth, and often has come up, in lonely vision, that face, serenely smiling above the current which bore him away to another realm of being.

CHAPTER V

Wisconsin

A TERRITORY, not yet a state; still, nearer the acorn than we were.

It was very pleasant coming up. These large and elegant boats are so well arranged that every excursion may be a party of pleasure. There are many fair shows to see on the lake and its shores, almost always new and agreeable persons on board, pretty children playing about, ladies singing, (and if not very well, there is room to keep out of the way.) You may see a great deal here of Life, in the London sense, if you know a few people; or if you do not, and have the tact to look about you without seeming to stare.

We came to Milwaukie, where we were to pass a fortnight or more.

This place is most beautifully situated. A little river, with romantic banks, passes up through the town. The bank of the lake is here a bold bluff, eighty feet in height. From its summit, you enjoyed a noble outlook on the lake. A little narrow path wound along the edge of the lake below. I liked this walk much. Above me this high wall of rich earth, garlanded on its crest with trees, the long ripples of the lake coming up to my feet. Here, standing in the shadow, I could appreciate better its magnificent changes of color, which are the chief beauties of the lake-waters; but these are indescribable.

It was fine to ascend into the lighthouse, above this bluff, and watch from thence the thunder-clouds which so frequently rose over the lake, or the great boats coming in. Approaching the Milwaukie pier, they made a bend, and seemed to do obeisance in the heavy style of some dowager duchess entering a circle she wishes to treat with especial respect.

These boats come in and out every day, and still afford a cause for general excitement. The people swarm down to greet them, to receive and send away their packages and letters. To me they seemed such mighty messengers, to give, by their noble motion, such an idea of the power and fullness of life, that they were worthy to carry despatches from king to king. It must be very pleasant for those who have an active share in carrying on the affairs of this great and growing world to see them come in. It must be very pleasant to those who have dearly loved friends at the next station. To those who have neither business nor friends, it sometimes gives a desolating sense of insignificance.

The town promises to be, some time, a fine one, as it is so well situated; and they have good building material—a yellow brick, very pleasing to the eye. It seems to grow before you, and has indeed but just emerged from the thickets of oak and wild roses. A few steps will take you into the thickets, and certainly I never saw so many wild roses, or of so beautiful a red. Of such a color were the first red ones the world ever saw, when, says the legend, Venus flying to the assistance of Adonis, the rosebushes kept catching her to make her stay, and the drops of blood the thorns drew from her feet, as she tore herself away, fell on the white roses, and turned them this beautiful red.

I will here insert, though with no excuse, except that it came to memory at the time, this description of Titian's Venus and Adonis.

"This picture has that perfect balance of lines and forms that it would, (as was said of all Raphael's) 'seen at any distance have the air of an ornamental design.' It also tells its story at the first glance, though, like all beautiful works, it gains by study.

"On one side slumbers the little God of Love, as an emblem, I suppose, that only the love of man is worth embodying, for surely Cytherea's is awake enough. The quiver of Cupid, suspended to a tree, gives sportive grace to the scene which softens the tragedy of a breaking tie. The dogs of Adonis pull upon his hand; he can scarce forbear to burst from the detaining arms of Beauty herself, yet he waits a moment to coax her—to make an unmeaning promise. 'A moment, a moment, my love, and I will return; a moment only.' Adonis is not beautiful, except in his expression of eager youth. The Queen of Beauty does not choose Apollo. Venus herself is very beautiful; especially the body is lovely as can be; and the soft, imploring look, gives a conjugal delicacy to the face which purifies the whole picture. This Venus is not as fresh, as moving and breathing as Shakspeare's, yet lovelier to the mind if not to the sense. 'T is difficult to look at this picture without indignation, because it is, in one respect, so true. Why must women always try to detain and restrain what they love? Foolish beauty; let him go; it is thy tenderness that has spoiled him. Be less lovely—less feminine;

abandon thy fancy forgiving thyself wholly; cease to love so well, and any Hercules will spin among thy maids, if thou wilt. But let him go this time; thou canst not keep him. Sit there, by thyself, on that bank, and, instead of thinking how soon he will come back, think how thou may'st love him no better than he does thee, for the time has come."

It was soon after this moment that the poor Queen, hearing the frightened hounds, apprehended the rash huntsman's danger, and, flying through the woods, gave their hue to the red roses.

To return from the Grecian isles to Milwaukie. One day, walking along the river's bank in search of a waterfall to be seen from one ravine, we heard tones from a band of music, and saw a gay troop shooting at a mark, on the opposite bank. Between every shot the band played; the effect was very pretty.

On this walk we found two of the oldest and most gnarled hemlocks that ever afforded study for a painter. They were the only ones we saw; they seemed the veterans of a former race.

At Milwaukie, as at Chicago, are many pleasant people, drawn together from all parts of the world. A resident here would find great piquancy in the associations,—those he met having such dissimilar histories and topics. And several persons I saw evidently transplanted from the most refined circles to be met in this country. There are lures enough in the West for people of all kinds;—the enthusiast and the cunning man; the naturalist, and the lover who needs to be rich for the sake of her he loves.

The torrent of emigration swells very strongly towards this place. During the fine weather, the poor refugees arrive daily, in their national dresses, all travel-soiled and worn. The night they pass in rude shantees, in a particular quarter of the town, then walk off into the country—the mothers carrying their infants, the fathers leading the little children by the hand, seeking a home where their hands may maintain them.

One morning we set off in their track, and travelled a day's journey into this country,—fair, yet not, in that part which I saw, comparable, in my eyes, to the Rock River region. It alternates rich fields, proper for grain, with oak openings, as they are called; bold, various and beautiful were the features of the scene, but I saw not those majestic sweeps, those boundless distances, those heavenly fields; it was not the same world.

Neither did we travel in the same delightful manner. We were now in a nice carriage, which must not go off the road, for fear of breakage, with a regular coachman, whose chief care was not to tire his horses, and who had no taste for entering fields in pursuit of wild flowers, or tempting some strange wood path in search of whatever might befall. It was pleasant, but almost as tame as New England.

But charming indeed was the place where we stopped. It was in the vicinity of a chain of lakes, and on the bank of the loveliest little stream, called the Bark river, which flowed in rapid amber brightness, through fields, and dells, and stately knolls, of most idylic beauty.

The little log cabin where we slept, with its flower garden in front, disturbed the scene no more than a stray lock on the fair cheek. The hospitality of that house I may well call princely; it was the boundless hospitality of the heart, which, if it has no Aladdin's lamp to create a palace for the guest, does him still higher service by the freedom of its bounty up to the very last drop of its powers.

Sweet were the sunsets seen in the valley of this stream, though here, and, I grieve to say, no less near the Rock River, the fiend, who has ever liberty to tempt the happy in this world, appeared in the shape of mosquitoes, and allowed us no bodily to enjoy our mental peace.

One day we ladies gave, under the guidance of our host, to visiting all the beauties of the adjacent lakes—Nomabbin, Silver, and Pine Lakes. On the shore of Nomabbin had formerly been one of the finest Indian villages. Our host said that, one day, as he was lying there beneath the bank, he saw a tall Indian standing at gaze on the knoll. He lay a long time, curious to see how long the figure would maintain its statue-like absorption. But, at last, his patience yielded, and, in moving, he made a slight noise. The Indian saw him, gave a wild, snorting sound of indignation and pain, and strode away.

What feelings must consume their heart at such moments! I scarcely see how they can forbear to shoot the white man where he stands.

But the power of fate is with the white man, and the Indian feels it. This same gentleman told of his travelling through the wilderness with an Indian guide. He had with him a bottle of spirit which he meant to give him in small quantities, but the Indian, once excited, wanted the whole at once. I would not, said Mr. —, give it him, for I thought if he got really drunk, there was an end to his services as a guide. But he persisted, and at last tried to take it from me. I was not armed; he was, and twice as strong as I. But I knew an Indian could not resist the look of a white man, and I fixed my eye steadily on his. He bore it for a moment, then his eye fell; he let go the bottle. I took his gun and threw it to a distance. After a few moments' pause, I told him to go and fetch it, and left it in his hands. From that moment he was quite obedient, even servile, all the rest of the way.

This gentleman, though in other respects of most kindly and liberal heart, showed the aversion that the white man soon learns to feel for the Indian on whom he encroaches, the aversion of the injurer for him he has degraded. After telling the anecdote of his seeing the Indian gazing at the seat of his former home,

"A thing for human feelings the most trying,"

and which, one would think, would have awakened soft compassion—almost remorse—in the present owner of that fair hill, which contained for the exile the bones of his dead, the ashes of his hopes,—he observed, "They cannot be prevented from straggling back here to their old haunts. I wish they could. They ought not to be permitted to drive away *our* game." OUR game—just heavens!

The same gentleman showed, on a slight occasion, the true spirit of the sportsman, or, perhaps I might say of Man, when engaged in any kind of chase. Showing us some antlers, he said, "This one belonged to a majestic creature. But this other was the beauty. I had been lying a long time at watch, when at last I heard them come crackling along. I lifted my head cautiously, as they burst through the trees. The first was a magnificent fellow; but then I saw coming one, the prettiest, the most graceful I ever beheld—there was something so soft and beseeching in its look. I chose him at once; took aim, and shot him dead. You see the antlers are not very large; it was young, but the prettiest creature!"

In the course of this morning's drive, we visited the gentlemen on their fishing party. They hailed us gaily, and rowed ashore to show us what fine booty they had. No disappointment there, no dull work. On the beautiful point of land from which we first saw them, lived a contented woman, the only one I heard of out there. She was English, and said she had seen so much suffering in her own country that the hardships of this seemed as nothing to her. But the others—even our sweet and gentle hostess—found their labors disproportioned to their strength, if not to their patience; and, while their husbands and brothers enjoyed the country in hunting or fishing, they found themselves confined to a comfortless and laborious indoor life. But it need not be so long.

This afternoon, driving about on the banks of these lakes, we found the scene all of one kind of loveliness; wide, graceful woods, and then these fine sheets of water, with fine points of land jutting out boldly into them. It was lovely, but not striking or peculiar.

All woods suggest pictures. The European forest, with its long glades and green sunny dells, naturally suggested the figures of armed knight on his proud steed, or maiden, decked in gold and pearl, pricking along them on a snow white palfrey. The green dells, of weary Palmer sleeping there beside the spring with his head upon his wallet. Our minds, familiar with such figures, people with them the New England woods, wherever the sunlight falls down a longer than usual cart-track, wherever a cleared spot has lain still enough for the trees to look friendly, with their exposed sides cultivated by the light, and the grass to look velvet warm, and be embroidered with flowers. These western woods suggest a different kind of ballad. The Indian legends have, often, an air of the wildest solitude, as has the one Mr. Lowell has put into verse, in his late volume. But I did not see those wild woods; only such as suggest little romances of love and sorrow, like this:

> A maiden sat beneath the tree,
> Tear-bedewed her pale cheeks be,
> And she sigheth heavily.
>
> From forth the wood into the light,
> A hunter strides with carol light,
> And a glance so bold and bright.
>
> He careless stopped and eyed the maid;
> "Why weepest thou?" he gently said,
> "I love thee well; be not afraid."
>
> He takes her hand, and leads her on;
> She should have waited there alone,
> For he was not her chosen one.
>
> He leans her head upon his breast,
> She knew 't was not her home of rest,
> But ah! she had been sore distrest.
>
> The sacred stars looked sadly down;
> The parting moon appeared to frown,
> To see thus dimmed the diamond crown.
>
> Then from the thicket starts a deer,
> The huntsman, seizing on his spear,
> Cries, "Maiden, wait thou for me here."
>
> She sees him vanish into night,
> She starts from sleep in deep affright,
> For it was not her own true knight.

Though but in dream Gunhilda failed;
Though but a fancied ill assailed,
Though she but fancied fault bewailed.

Yet thought of day makes dream of night:
She is not worthy of the knight,
The inmost altar burns not bright.

If loneliness thou canst not bear,
Cannot the dragon's venom dare,
Of the pure meed thou shouldst despair.

Now sadder that lone maiden sighs,
Far bitterer tears profane her eyes,
Crushed in the dust her heart's flower lies.

On the bank of Silver Lake we saw an Indian encampment. A shower threatened us, but we resolved to try if we could not visit it before it came on. We crossed a wide field on foot, and found them amid the trees on a shelving bank; just as we reached them the rain began to fall in torrents, with frequent thunder claps, and we had to take refuge in their lodges. These were very small, being for temporary use, and we crowded the occupants much, among whom were several sick, on the damp ground, or with only a ragged mat between them and it. But they showed all the gentle courtesy which marks them towards the stranger, who stands in any need; though it was obvious that the visit, which inconvenienced them, could only have been caused by the most impertinent curiosity, they made us as comfortable as their extreme poverty permitted. They seemed to think we would not like to touch them: a sick girl in the lodge where I was, persisted in moving so as to give me the dry place; a woman with the sweet melancholy eye of the race, kept off the children and wet dogs from even the hem of my garment.

Without, their fires smouldered, and black kettles, hung over them on sticks, smoked and seethed in the rain. An old theatrical looking Indian stood with arms folded, looking up to the heavens, from which the rain dashed and the thunder reverberated; his air was French-Roman, that is, more romanesque than Roman. The Indian ponies, much excited, kept careering through the wood, around the encampment, and now and then halting suddenly, would thrust in their intelligent, though amazed, phizzes, as if to ask their masters when this awful pother would cease, and then, after a moment, rush and trample off again.

At last we got off, well wetted, but with a picturesque scene for memory. At a house where we stopped to get dry, they told us that this wandering band (of Pottawattamies,) who had returned on a visit, either from homesickness, or need of relief, were extremely destitute. The women had been there to see if they could barter their head bands with which they club their hair behind into a form not unlike a Grecian knot, for food. They seemed, indeed, to have neither food, utensils, clothes, nor bedding; nothing but the ground, the sky, and their own strength. Little wonder if they drove off the game!

Part of the same band I had seen in Milwaukie, on a begging dance. The effect of this was wild and grotesque. They wore much paint and feather head-dresses. "Indians without paint are poor coots," said a gentleman who had been a great deal with, and really liked, them; and I like the effect of the paint on them; it reminds of the gay fantasies of nature. With them in Milwaukie, was a chief, the finest Indian figure I saw, more than six feet in height, erect, and of a sullen, but grand gait and gesture. He wore a deep red blanket, which fell in large folds from his shoulders to his feet, did not join in the dance, but slowly strode about through the streets, a fine sight, not a French-Roman, but a real Roman. He looked unhappy, but listlessly unhappy, as if he felt it was of no use to strive or resist.

While in the neighborhood of these lakes, we visited also a foreign settlement of great interest. Here were minds, it seemed, to "comprehend the trusts," of their new life; and if they can only stand true to them, will derive and bestow great benefits therefrom.

But sad and sickening to the enthusiast who comes to these shores, hoping the tranquil enjoyment of intellectual blessings, and the pure happiness of mutual love, must be a part of the scene that he encounters at first. He has escaped from the heartlessness of courts, to encounter the vulgarity of a mob; he has secured solitude, but it is a lonely, a deserted solitude. Amid the abundance of nature he cannot, from petty, but insuperable obstacles, procure, for a long time, comforts, or a home.

But let him come sufficiently armed with patience to learn the new spells which the new dragons require, (and this can only be done on the spot,) he will not finally be disappointed of the promised treasure; the mob will resolve itself into men, yet crude, but of good dispositions, and capable of good character; the solitude will become sufficiently enlivened and home grow up at last from the rich sod.

In this transition state we found one of these homes. As we approached it seemed the very Eden which earth might still afford to a pair willing to give up the hackneyed pleasures of the world, for a better and more intimate communion with one another and with beauty: the wild road led through wide beautiful woods, to the wilder and more beautiful shores of the finest lake we saw. On its waters, glittering in the morning sun, a few Indians were paddling to and fro in their light canoes. On one of those fair knolls I have so often mentioned, stood the cottage, beneath trees which stooped as if they yet felt brotherhood with its roof tree. Flowers waved, birds fluttered round, all had the sweetness of a happy seclusion; all invited on entrance to cry, All hail ye happy ones! to those who inhabited it.

But on entrance to those evidently rich in personal beauty, talents, love, and courage, the aspect of things was rather sad. Sickness had been with them, death, care, and labor; these had not yet blighted them, but had turned their gay smiles grave. It seemed that hope and joy had given place to resolution. How much, too, was there in them, worthless in this place, which would have been so valuable elsewhere. Refined graces, cultivated powers, shine in vain before field laborers, as laborers are in this present world; you might as well cultivate heliotropes to present to an ox. Oxen and heliotropes are both good, but not for one another.

With them were some of the old means of enjoyment, the books, the pencil, the guitar; but where the wash-tub and the axe are so constantly in requisition, there is not much time and pliancy of hand for these.

In the inner room the master of the house was seated; he had been sitting there long, for he had injured his foot on ship-board, and his farming had to be done by proxy. His beautiful young wife was his only attendant and nurse, as well as a farm housekeeper; how well she performed hard and unaccustomed duties, the objects of her care shewed; everything that belonged to the house was rude but neatly arranged; the invalid, confined to an uneasy wooden chair, (they had not been able to induce any one to bring them an easy chair from the town,) looked as neat and elegant as if he had been dressed by the valet of a duke. He was of northern blood, with clear full blue eyes, calm features, a tempering of the soldier, scholar, and man of the world, in his aspect; whether that various intercourses had given himself that thorough-bred look never seen in Americans, or that it was inherited from a race who had known all these disciplines. He formed a great but pleasing contrast to his wife, whose glowing complexion and dark mellow eye bespoke an origin in some climate more familiar with the sun. He looked as if he could sit there a great while patiently, and live on his own mind, biding his time; she, as if she could bear anything for affection's sake, but would feel the weight of each moment as it passed.

Seeing the album full of drawings and verses which bespoke the circle of elegant and affectionate intercourse they had left behind, we could not but see that the young wife sometimes must need a sister, the husband a companion, and both must often miss that electricity which sparkles from the chain of congenial minds.

For man, a position is desirable in some degree proportioned to his education. Mr. Birkbeck was bred a farmer, but these were nurslings of the court and city; they may persevere, for an affectionate courage shone in their eyes, and, if so, become true lords of the soil, and informing geniuses to those around; then, perhaps, they will feel that they have not paid too dear for the tormented independence of the new settler's life. But, generally, damask roses will not thrive in the wood, and a ruder growth, if healthy and pure, we wish rather to see there.

I feel very differently about these foreigners from Americans; American men and women are inexcusable if they do not bring up children so as to be fit for vicissitudes; that is the meaning of our star, that here all men being free and equal, all should be fitted for freedom and an independence by his own resources wherever the changeful wave of our mighty stream may take him. But the star of Europe brought a different horoscope, and to mix destinies breaks the thread of both. The Arabian horse will not plough well, nor can the plough-horse be rode to play the jereed. But a man is a man wherever he goes, and something precious cannot fail to be gained by one who knows how to abide by a resolution of any kind, and pay the cost without a murmur.

Returning, the fine carriage at last fulfilled its threat of breaking down. We took refuge in a farm house. Here was a pleasant scene. A rich and beautiful estate, several happy families, who had removed together, and formed a natural community, ready to help and enliven one another. They were farmers at home, in western New York, and both men and women knew how to work. Yet even here the women did not like the change, but they were willing, "as it might be best for the young folks." Their hospitality was great, the housefull of women and pretty children seemed all of one mind.

Returning to Milwaukie much fatigued, I entertained myself for a day or two with reading. The book I had brought with me was in strong contrast with the life around me. Very strange was this vision of an exalted and sensitive existence, which seemed to invade the next sphere, in contrast with the spontaneous, instinctive life, so healthy and so near the ground I had been surveying. This was the German book entitled:

Die Seherin von Prevorst.—Eröffnungen über das innere Leben des Menschen und über das hereinragen einer Geisterwelt in die unsere. Mitgetheilt von Justinus Kerner.

The Seeress of Prevorst.—Revelations concerning the inward life of man, and the projection of a world of spirits into ours, communicated by Justinus Kerner.

This book, published in Germany some twelve years since, and which called forth there plenteous dews of admiration, as plenteous hail-storms of jeers and scorns, I never saw mentioned till some year or two since, in any English publication. Then a playful, but not sarcastic account of it, in the Dublin Magazine, so far excited my curiosity that I procured the book intending to read it so soon as I should have some leisure days, such as this journey has afforded.

Dr. Kerner, its author, is a man of distinction in his native land, both as a physician and a thinker, though always on the side of reverence, marvel, and mysticism. He was known to me only through two or three little poems of his in Catholic legends, which I much admired for the fine sense they showed of the beauty of symbols.

He here gives a biography, mental and physical, of one of the most remarkable cases of high nervous excitement that the age, so interested in such, yet affords, with all its phenomena of clairvoyance and susceptibility of magnetic influences. I insert some account of this biography at the request of many who have been interested by slight references to it. The book, a thick and heavy volume, written with true German patience, some would say clumsiness, has not, probably, and may not be translated into other languages. As to my own mental position on these subjects it may be briefly expressed by a dialogue between several persons who honor me with a portion of friendly confidence and of criticism, and myself expressed as *Free Hope*. The others may be styled *Old Church, Good Sense,* and *Self-Poise.*

Good Sense. I wonder you can take any interest in such observations or experiments. Don't you see how almost impossible it is to make them with any exactness, how entirely impossible to know anything about them unless made by yourself, when the least leaven of credulity, excited fancy, to say nothing of willing or careless imposture, spoils the whole loaf. Beside, allowing the possibility of some clear glimpses into a higher state of being, what do we want of it now? All around us lies what we neither understand nor use. Our capacities, our instincts for this our present sphere are but half developed. Let us confine ourselves to that till the lesson be learned; let us be completely natural, before we trouble ourselves with the supernatural. I never see any of these things but I long to get away and lie under a green tree and let the wind blow on me. There is marvel and charm enough in that for me.

Free Hope. And for me also. Nothing is truer than the Wordsworthian creed, on which Carlyle lays such stress, that we need only look on the miracle of every day, to sate ourselves with thought and admiration every day. But how are our faculties sharpened to do it? Precisely by apprehending the infinite results of every day.

Who sees the meaning of the flower uprooted in the ploughed field? The ploughman who does not look beyond its boundaries and does not raise his eyes from the ground? No—but the poet who sees that field in its relations with the universe, and looks oftener to the sky than on the ground. Only the dreamer shall understand realities, though, in truth, his dreaming must not be out of proportion to his waking!

The mind, roused powerfully by this existence, stretches of itself into what the French sage calls the "aromal state." From the hope thus gleaned it forms the hypothesis, under whose banner it collects its facts.

Long before these slight attempts were made to establish as a science what is at present called animal magnetism, always, in fact men were occupied more or less with this vital principle, principle of flux and influx, dynamic of our mental mechanics, human phase of electricity. Poetic observation was pure, there was no quackery in its free course, as there is so often in this wilful tampering with the hidden springs of life, for it is tampering unless done in a patient spirit and with severe truth; yet it may be, by the rude or greedy miners, some good ore is unearthed. And some there are who work in the true temper, patient and accurate in trial, not rushing to conclusions, feeling there is a mystery, not eager to call it by name, till they can know it as a reality: such may learn, such may teach.

Subject to the sudden revelations, the breaks in habitual existence caused by the aspect of death, the touch of love, the flood of music, I never lived, that I remember, what you call a common natural day. All my days are touched by the supernatural, for I feel the pressure of hidden causes, and the presence, sometimes the communion, of unseen powers. It needs not that I should ask the clairvoyant whether "a spirit-world projects into ours." As to the specific evidence, I would not tarnish my mind by hasty reception. The mind is not, I know, a highway, but a temple, and its doors should not be carelessly left open. Yet it were sin, if indolence or coldness excluded what had a claim to enter; and I doubt whether, in the eyes of pure intelligence, an ill-grounded hasty rejection be not a greater sign of weakness than an ill-grounded and hasty faith.

I will quote, as my best plea, the saying of a man old in years, but not in heart, and whose long life has been distinguished by that clear adaptation of means to ends which gives the credit of practical wisdom. He wrote to his child, "I have lived too long, and seen too much to be incredulous." Noble the thought, no less so its frank expression, instead of saws of caution, mean advices, and other modern instances. Such was the romance of Socrates when he bade his disciples "sacrifice a cock to Æsculapius."

Old Church. You are always so quick-witted and voluble, Free Hope, you don't get time to see how often you err, and even, perhaps, sin and blaspheme. The Author of all has intended to confine our knowledge within certain boundaries, has given us a short span of time for a certain probation, for which our faculties are adapted. By wild speculation and intemperate curiosity we violate his will and incur dangerous, perhaps fatal, consequences. We waste our powers, and, becoming morbid and visionary, are unfitted to obey positive precepts, and perform positive duties.

Free Hope. I do not see how it is possible to go further beyond the results of a limited human experience than those do who pretend to settle the origin and nature of sin, the final destiny of souls, and the whole plan of the causal spirit with regard to them. I think those who take your view, have not examined themselves, and do not know the ground on which they stand.

I acknowledge no limit, set up by man's opinion, as to the capacities of man. "Care is taken," I see it, "that the trees grow not up into heaven," but, to me it seems, the more vigorously they aspire the better. Only let it be a vigorous, not a partial or sickly aspiration. Let not the tree forget its root.

So long as the child insists on knowing where its dead parent is, so long as bright eyes weep at mysterious pressures, too heavy for the life, so long as that impulse is constantly arising which made the Roman emperor address his soul in a strain of such touching softness, vanishing from the thought, as the column of smoke from the eye, I know of no inquiry which the impulse of man suggests that is forbidden to the resolution of man to pursue. In every inquiry, unless sustained by a pure and reverent spirit, he gropes in the dark, or falls headlong.

Self-Poise. All this may be very true, but what is the use of all this straining? Far-sought is dear-bought. When we know that all is in each, and that the ordinary contains the extraordinary, why should we play the baby, and insist upon having the moon for a toy when a tin dish will do as well. Our deep ignorance is a chasm that we can only fill up by degrees, but the commonest rubbish will help us as well as shred silk. The God Brahma, while on earth, was set to fill up a valley, but he had only a basket given him in which to fetch earth for this purpose; so is it with us all. No leaps, no starts will avail us, by patient crystallization alone the equal temper of wisdom is attainable. Sit at home and the spirit-world will look in at your window with moonlit eyes; run out to find it, and rainbow and golden cup will have vanished and left you the beggarly child you were. The better part of wisdom is a sublime prudence, a pure and patient truth that will receive nothing it is not sure it can permanently lay to heart. Of our study there should be in proportion two-thirds of rejection to one of acceptance. And, amid the manifold infatuations and illusions of this world of emotion, a being capable of clear intelligence can do no better service than to hold himself upright, avoid nonsense, and do what chores lie in his way, acknowledging every moment that primal truth, which no fact exhibits, nor, if pressed by too warm a hope, will even indicate. I think, indeed, it is part of our lesson to give a formal consent to what is farcical, and to pick up our living and our virtue amid what is so ridiculous, hardly deigning a smile, and certainly not vexed. The work is done through all, if not by every one.

Free Hope. Thou art greatly wise, my friend, and ever respected by me, yet I find not in your theory or your scope, room enough for the lyric inspirations, or the mysterious whispers of life. To me it seems that it is madder never to abandon oneself, than often to be infatuated; better to be wounded, a captive, and a slave, than always to walk in armor. As to magnetism, that is only a matter of fancy. You sometimes need just such a field in which to wander vagrant, and if it bear a higher name, yet it may be that, in last result, the trance of Pythagoras might be classed with the more infantine transports of the Seeress of Prevorst.

What is done interests me more than what is thought and supposed. Every fact is impure, but every fact contains in it the juices of life. Every fact is a clod, from which may grow an amaranth or a palm.

Do you climb the snowy peaks from whence come the streams, where the atmosphere is rare, where you can see the sky nearer, from which you can get a commanding view of the landscape. I see great disadvantages as well as advantages in this dignified position. I had rather walk myself through all kinds of places, even at the risk of being robbed in the forest, half drowned at the ford, and covered with dust in the street.

I would beat with the living heart of the world, and understand all the moods, even the fancies or fantasies, of nature. I dare to trust to the interpreting spirit to bring me out all right at last—to establish truth through error.

Whether this be the best way is of no consequence, if it be the one individual character points out.

> For one, like me, it would be vain
> From glittering heights the eyes to strain;
> I the truth can only know,
> Tested by life's most fiery glow.
> Seeds of thought will never thrive
> Till dews of love shall bid them live.

Let me stand in my age with all its waters flowing round me. If they sometimes subdue, they must finally upbear me, for I seek the universal—and that must be the best.

The Spirit, no doubt, leads in every movement of my time: if I seek the How, I shall find it, as well as if I busied myself more with the Why.

Whatever is, is right, if only men are steadily bent to make it so, by comprehending and fulfilling its design.

May not I have an office, too, in my hospitality and ready sympathy? If I sometimes entertain guests who cannot pay with gold coin, with "fair rose nobles," that is better than to lose the chance of entertaining angels unawares.

You, my three friends, are held in heart-honor, by me. You, especially, Good-Sense, because where you do not go yourself, you do not object to another's going, if he will. You are really liberal. You, Old Church, are of use, by keeping unforgot the effigies of old religion, and reviving the tone of pure Spenserian sentiment, which this time is apt to stifle in its childish haste. But you are very faulty in censuring and wishing to limit others by your own standard. You, Self-Poise, fill a priestly office. Could but a larger intelligence of the vocations of others, and a tender sympathy with their individual natures be added, had you more of love, or more of apprehensive genius, (for either would give you the needed expansion and delicacy) you would command my entire reverence. As it is, I must at times deny and oppose you, and so must others, for you tend, by your influence, to exclude us from our full, free life. We must be content when you censure, and rejoiced when you approve; always admonished to good by your whole being, and sometimes by your judgment. And so I pass on to interest myself and others in the memoir of the Seherin von Prevorst.

Aside from Löwenstein, a town of Wirtemberg, on mountains whose highest summit is more than eighteen hundred feet above the level of the sea, lies in romantic seclusion, surrounded on all sides by woods and hills, the hamlet of Prevorst.

Its inhabitants number about four hundred and fifty, most of whom support themselves by wood-cutting, and making charcoal, and collecting wood seed.

As is usual with those who live upon the mountains, these are a vigorous race, and generally live to old age without sickness. Diseases that infest the valley, such as ague, never touch them; but they are subject in youth to attacks upon the nerves, which one would not expect in so healthy a class. In a town situated near to, and like Prevorst, the children were often attacked with a kind of St.Vitus's dance.They would foresee when it would seize upon them, and, if in the field, would hasten home to undergo the paroxysms there. From these they rose, as from magnetic sleep, without memory of what had happened.

Other symptoms show the inhabitants of this region very susceptible to magnetic and sidereal influences.

On the mountain, and indeed in the hamlet of Prevorst, was, in 1801, a woman born, in whom a peculiar inner life discovered itself from early childhood. Frederica Hauffé, whose father was gamekeeper of this district of forest, was, as the position and solitude of her birthplace made natural, brought up in the most simple manner. In the keen mountain air and long winter cold, she was not softened by tenderness either as to dress or bedding, but grew up lively and blooming; and while her brothers and sisters, under the same circumstances, were subject to rheumatic attacks, she remained free from them. On the other hand, her peculiar tendency displayed itself in her dreams. If anything affected her painfully, if her mind was excited by reproof, she had instructive warning or prophetic dreams.

While yet quite young, her parents let her go, for the advantages of instruction, to her grand-father, Johann Schmidgall, in Löwenstein.

Here were discovered in her the sensibility to magnetic and ghostly influences, which, the good Kerner assures us, her grand-parents deeply lamented, and did all in their power to repress. But, as it appears that her grandfather, also, had seen a ghost, and there were evidently legends in existence about the rooms in which the little Frederika saw ghosts, and spots where the presence of human bones caused her sudden shivering, we may be allowed to doubt whether indirect influence was not more powerful than direct repression upon these subjects.

There is the true German impartiality with regard to the scene of appearance for these imposing visitors; sometimes it is "a room in the Castle of Löwenstein, long disused," à la Radcliffe, sometimes "a deserted kitchen."

This "solemn, unhappy gift," brought no disturbance to the childish life of the maiden, she enjoyed life with more vivacity than most of her companions. The only trouble she had was the extreme irritability of the optic nerve, which, though without inflammation of the eyes, sometimes confined her to a solitary chamber. "This," says Dr. K. "was probably a sign of the development of the spiritual in the fleshly eye."

Sickness of her parents at last called her back to the lonely Prevorst, where, by trouble and watching beside sick beds, her feelings were too much excited, so that the faculty for prophetic dreams and the vision of spirits increased upon her.

From her seventeenth to her nineteenth year, when every outward relation was pleasant for her, this inward life was not so active, and she was distinguished from other girls of her circle only by the more intellectual nature, which displayed itself chiefly in the eyes, and by a greater liveliness which, however, never passed the bounds of grace and propriety.

She had none of the sentimentality so common at that age, and it can be proved that she had never an attachment, nor was disappointed in love, as has been groundlessly asserted.

In her nineteenth year, she was by her family betrothed to Herr H. The match was desirable on account of the excellence of the man, and the sure provision it afforded for her comfort through life.

But, whether from presentiment of the years of suffering that were before her, or from other hidden feelings, of which we only know with certainty that, if such there were, they were not occasioned by another attachment, she sank into a dejection, inexplicable to her family; passed whole days in weeping; scarcely slept for some weeks, and thus the life of feeling which had been too powerful in her childhood was called up anew in full force.

On the day of her solemn betrothal, took place, also, the funeral of T., the preacher of Oberstenfeld, a man of sixty and more years, whose preaching, instruction, and character, (he was goodness itself,) had had great influence upon her life. She followed the dear remains, with others, to the church-yard. Her heart till then so heavy, was suddenly relieved and calmed, as she stood beside the grave. She remained there long, enjoying her new peace, and when she went away found herself tranquil, but indifferent to all the concerns of this world. Here began the period, not indeed as yet of sickness, but of her peculiar inward life, which knew afterward no pause.

Later, in somnambulic state, she spoke of this day in the following verses. The deceased had often appeared to her as a shape of light, protecting her from evil spirits.

(These are little simple rhymes; they are not worth translating into verse, though, in the original, they have a childish grace.)

What was once so dark to me,
I see now clearly.
    In that day
When I had given in marriage myself away,

I stood quite immersed in thee,
Thou angel figure above thy grave mound.
Willingly would I have exchanged with thee,
Willingly given up to thee my earthly luck,
Which those around praised as the blessing of heaven.

I prayed upon thy grave
For one blessing only,
That the wings of this angel
Might henceforward
On the hot path of life,
Waft around me the peace of heaven.
There standest thou, angel, now; my prayer was heard.

She was, in consequence of her marriage, removed to Kürnbach, a place on the borders of Würtemberg and Baden. Its position is low, gloomy, shut in by hills; opposite in all the influences of earth and atmosphere to those of Prevorst and its vicinity.

Those of electrical susceptibility are often made sick or well by change of place. Papponi, (of whom Amoretti writes,) a man of such susceptibility, was cured of convulsive attacks by change of place. Pennet could find repose while in one part of Calabria, only by wrapping himself in an oil-cloth mantle, thus, as it were, isolating himself. That great sense of sidereal and imponderable influences, which afterward manifested itself so clearly in the Seherin, probably made this change of place very unfavorable to her. Later, it appeared, that the lower she came down from the hills, the more she suffered from spasms, but on the heights her tendency to the magnetic state was the greatest.

But also mental influences were hostile to her. Already withdrawn from the outward life, she was placed, where, as consort and house-keeper to a laboring man, the calls on her care and attention were incessant. She was obliged hourly to forsake her inner home, to pro-vide for an outer, which did not correspond with it.

She bore this seven months, though flying to solitude, whenever outward relations permitted. But longer it was not possible to conceal the inward verity by an outward action, "the body sank beneath the attempt, and the spirit took refuge in the inner circle."

One night she dreamed that she awoke and found the dead body of the preacher T. by her side; that at the same time her father, and two physicians were considering what should be done for her in a severe sickness. She called out that "the dead friend would help her; she needed no physician." Her husband, hearing her cry out in sleep, woke her.

This dream was presage of a fever, which seized her next morning. It lasted fourteen days with great violence, and was succeeded by attacks of convulsion and spasm. This was the beginning of that state of bodily suffering and mental exaltation in which she passed the remaining seven years of her life.

She seems to have been very injudiciously treated in the first stages of her illness. Bleeding was resorted to, as usual in cases of extreme suffering where the nurses know not what else to do, and, as usual, the momentary relief was paid for by an increased nervousness, and capacity for suffering.

Magnetic influences from other persons were of frequent use to her, but they were applied without care as to what characters and constitu-tions were brought into connexion with hers, and were probably in the end just as injurious to her as the loss of blood. At last she became so weak, so devoid of all power in herself, that her life seemed entirely dependent on artificial means and the influence of other men.

There is a singular story of a woman in the neighborhood, who visited her once or twice, apparently from an instinct that she should injure her, and afterwards, interfered in the same way, and with the same results, in the treatment of her child.

This demoniacal impulse and power, which were ascribed to the Canidias of ancient superstition, may be seen subtly influencing the members of every-day society. We see persons led, by an uneasy impulse, towards the persons and the topics where they are sure they can irritate and annoy. This is constantly observable among children, also in the closest relations between grown up people who have not yet the government of themselves, neither are governed by the better power.

There is also an interesting story of a quack who treated her with amulets, whose parallel may be found in the action of such persons in common society. It is an expression of the power that a vulgar and self-willed nature will attain over one delicate, poetical, but not yet clear within itself; outwardly it yields to a power which it inwardly disclaims.

A touching little passage is related of a time in the first years, when she seemed to be better, so much so as to receive an evening visit from some female friends. They grew merry and began to dance; she remained sad and thoughtful. When they stopped, she was in the attitude of prayer. One of her intimates, observing this, began to laugh. This affected her so much, that she became cold and rigid like a corpse. For some time they did not hear her breathe, and, when she did, it was with a rattling noise. They applied mustard poultices, and used foot and hand baths; she was brought back to life, but to a state of great suffering.

She recognized as her guardian spirit, who sometimes magnetized her or removed from her neighborhood substances that were hurtful to her, her grand-mother; thus coinciding with the popular opinion that traits reappear in the third generation.

Now began still greater wonders; the second sight, numerous and various visits from spirits and so forth.

The following may be mentioned in connection with theories and experiments current among ourselves.

"A friend, who was often with her at this time, wrote to me (Kerner): When I, with my finger, touch her *on the forehead between the eyebrows,* she says each time something that bears upon the state of my soul. Some of these sentences I record.

"Keep thy soul so that thou mayst bear it in thy hands."

"When thou comest into a world of bustle and folly, hold the Lord fast in thy heart."

"If any seek to veil from thee thy true feeling, pray to God for grace."

"Permit not thyself to stifle the light that springs up within thyself."

"Think often of the cross of Jesus; go forth and embrace it."

"As the dove found a resting-place in Noah's ark, so wilt thou, also, find a resting-place which God has appointed for thee."

When she was put under the care of Kerner, she had been five years in this state, and was reduced to such weakness, that she was, with difficulty, sustained from hour to hour.

He thought at first it would be best to take no notice of her magnetic states and directions, and told her he should not, but should treat her, with regard to her bodily symptoms, as he would any other invalid.

"At this time she fell every evening into magnetic sleep, and gave orders about herself; to which, however, those round her no longer paid attention.

I was now called in. I had never seen this woman, but had heard many false or perverted accounts of her condition. I must confess that I shared the evil opinion of the world as to her illness; that I advised to pay no attention to her magnetic situation, and the orders she gave in it; in her spasms, to forbear the laying of hands upon her; to deny her the support of persons of stronger nerves; in short, to do all possible to draw her out of the magnetic state, and to treat her with attention, but with absolutely none but the common medical means.

These views were shared by my friend, Dr. Off, of Löwenstein, who continued to treat her accordingly. But without good results. Hemorrhage, spasms, night-sweats continued. Her gums were scorbutically affected, and bled constantly; she lost all her teeth. Strengthening remedies affected her like being drawn up from her bed by force; she sank into a fear of all men, and a deadly weakness. Her death was to be wished, but it came not. Her relations, in despair, not knowing themselves what they could do with her, brought her, almost against my will, to me at Weinsberg.

She was brought hither an image of death, perfectly emaciated, unable to raise herself. Every three or four minutes, a teaspoonful of nourishment must be given her, else she fell into faintness or convulsion. Her somnambulic situation alternated with fever, hemorrhage, and night-sweats. Every evening, about seven o'clock, she fell into magnetic sleep. She then spread out her arms, and found herself, from that moment, in a clairvoyant state; but only when she brought them back upon her breast, did she begin to speak. (Kerner mentions that her child, too, slept with its hands and feet crossed.) In this state her eyes were shut, her face calm and bright. As she fell asleep, the first night after her arrival, she asked for me, but I bade them tell her that I now, and in future, should speak to her only when awake.

After she awoke, I went to her and declared, in brief and earnest terms, that I should pay no attention to what she said in sleep, and that her somnambulic state, which had lasted so long to the grief and

trouble of her family, must now come to an end. This declaration I accompanied by an earnest appeal, designed to awaken a firm will in her
to put down the excessive activity of brain that disordered her whole
system. Afterwards, no address was made to her on any subject when
in her sleep-waking state. She was left to lie unheeded. I pursued a
homoeopathic treatment of her case. But the medicines constantly
produced effects opposite to what I expected. She now suffered less
from spasm and somnambulism, but with increasing marks of weakness and decay. All seemed as if the end of her sufferings drew near. It
was too late for the means I wished to use. Affected so variously and
powerfully by magnetic means in the first years of her illness, she had
now no life more, so thoroughly was the force of her own organization exhausted, but what she borrowed from others. In her now more
infrequent magnetic trance, she was always seeking the true means of
her cure. It was touching to see how, retiring within herself, she sought
for help. The physician who had aided her so little with his drugs, must
often stand abashed before this inner physician, perceiving it to be far
better skilled than himself."

After some weeks forbearance, Kerner did ask her in her sleep what
he should do for her. She prescribed a magnetic treatment, which was
found of use. Afterwards, she described a machine, of which there is
a drawing in this book, which she wished to have made for her use;
it was so, and she derived benefit from it. She had indicated such a
machine in the early stages of her disease, but at that time no one attended to her. By degrees she grew better under this treatment, and
lived at Weinsberg, nearly two years, though in a state of great weakness, and more in the magnetic and clairvoyant than in the natural
human state.

How his acquaintance with her affected the physician, he thus
expresses:

"During those last months of her abode on the earth, there remained to her only the life of a sylph. I have been interested to record,
not a journal of her sickness, but the mental phenomena of such an
almost disembodied life. Such may cast light on the period when also
our Psyche may unfold her wings, free from bodily bonds, and the
hindrances of space and time. I give facts; each reader may interpret
them in his own way.

The manuals of animal magnetism and other writings have proposed many theories by which to explain such. All these are known to
me. I shall make no reference to them, but only, by use of parallel facts
here and there, show that the phenomena of this case recall many in

which there is nothing marvellous, but which are manifestly grounded in our common existence. Such apparitions cannot too frequently, if only for moments, flash across that common existence, as electric lights from the higher world.

Frau H. was, previous to my magnetic treatment, in so deep a somnambulic life, that she was, in fact, never rightly awake, even when she seemed to be; or rather, let us say, she was at all times more awake than others are; for it is strange to term sleep this state which is just that of the clearest wakefulness. Better to say she was immersed in the inward state.

In this state and the consequent excitement of the nerves, she had almost wholly lost organic force, and received it only by transmission from those of stronger condition, principally from their eyes and the ends of the fingers. The atmosphere and nerve communications of others, said she, bring me the life which I need; they do not feel it; these effusions on which I live, would flow from them and be lost, if my nerves did not attract them; only in this way can I live.

She often assured us that others did not suffer by loss of what they imparted to her; but it cannot be denied that persons were weakened by constant intercourse with her, suffered from contraction in the limbs, trembling, &c. They were weakened also in the eyes and pit of the stomach. From those related to her by blood, she could draw more benefit than from others, and, when very weak, from them only; probably on account of a natural affinity of temperament. She could not bear to have around her nervous and sick persons; those from whom she could gain nothing made her weaker.

Even so it is remarked that flowers soon lose their beauty near the sick, and suffer peculiarly under the contact or care of some persons.

Other physicians, beside myself, can vouch that the presence of some persons affected her as pabulum vitæ, while, if left with certain others or alone, she was sure to grow weaker.

From the air, too, she seemed to draw a peculiar ethereal nourishment of the same sort; she could not remain without an open window in the severest cold of winter.[*]

The spirit of things, about which we have no perception, was sensible to her, and had influence on her; she showed this sense of the spirit of metals, plants, animals, and men. Imponderable existences, such as

---

[*] Near us, this last winter, a person who suffered, and finally died, from spasms like those of the Seherin, also found relief from having the windows open, while the cold occasioned great suffering to his attendants.

the various colors of the ray, showed distinct influences upon her. The electric fluid was visible and sensible to her when it was not to us. Yea! what is incredible! even the written words of men she could discriminate by touch.*

These experiments are detailed under their several heads in the book.

From her eyes flowed a peculiar spiritual light which impressed even those who saw her for a very short time. She was in each relation more spirit than human.

Should we compare her with anything human, we would say she was as one detained at the moment of dissolution, betwixt life and death; and who is better able to discern the affairs of the world that lies before, than that behind him.

She was often in situations when one who had, like her, the power of discerning spirits, would have seen her own free from the body, which at all times enveloped it only as a light veil. She saw herself often out of the body; saw herself double. She would say, "I seem out of myself, hover above my body, and think of it as something apart from myself. But it is not a pleasant feeling, because I still sympathize with my body. If only my soul were bound more firmly to the nerve-spirit, it might be bound more closely with the nerves themselves; but the bond of my nerve-spirit is always becoming looser."

She makes a distinction between spirit as the pure intelligence; soul, the ideal of this individual man; and nerve-spirit, the dynamic of his temporal existence. Of this feeling of double identity, an invalid, now wasting under nervous disease, often speaks to me. He has it when he first awakes from sleep. Blake, the painter, whose life was almost as much a series of trances as that of our Seherin, in his designs of the Resurrection, represents spirits as rising from, or hovering over, their bodies in the same way.

Often she seemed quite freed from her body, and to have no more sense of its weight.

As to artificial culture, or dressing, (dressur,) Frau H. had nothing of it. She had learned no foreign tongue, neither history, nor geography, nor natural philosophy, nor any other of those branches now imparted to those of her sex in their schools. The Bible and hymn-book were, especially in the long years of her sickness, her only reading: her moral character was throughout blameless; she was pious without fanaticism.

---

* Facts of the same kind are asserted of late among ourselves, and believed, though "incredible."

Even her long suffering, and the peculiar manner of it, she recognized
as the grace of God; as she expresses in the following verses:

> Great God! how great is thy goodness,
>   To me thou hast given faith and love,
> Holding me firm in the distress of my sufferings.
>
> In the darkness of my sorrow,
>   I was so far led away,
> As to beg for peace in speedy death.
>
> But then came to me the mighty strong faith;
>   Hope came; and came eternal love;
> They shut my earthly eyelids.
>   When, O bliss!
>
> Dead lies my bodily frame,
>   But in the inmost mind a light burns up,
> Such as none knows in the waking life.
>   Is it a light? no! but a sun of grace!

Often in the sense of her sufferings, while in the magnetic trance,
she made prayers in verse, of which this is one:

> Father, hear me!
> Hear my prayer and supplication.
>   Father, I implore thee,
> Let not thy child perish!
>   Look on my anguish, my tears.
>
> Shed hope into my heart, and still its longing,
>   Father, on thee I call; have pity!
> Take something from me, the sick one, the poor one.
>
> Father, I leave thee not,
> Though sickness and pain consume me
>   If I the spring's light,
> See only through the mist of tears,
>   Father, I leave thee not.

These verses lose their merit of touching simplicity in an unrhymed
translation; but they will serve to show the habitual temper of her
mind.

"As I was a maker of verses," continues Dr. Kerner, "it was easy to say, Frau H. derived this talent from my magnetic influence; but she made these little verses before she came under my care." Not without deep significance was Apollo distinguished as being at once the God of poesy, of prophecy, and the medical art. Sleep-waking develops the powers of seeing, healing, and poesy. How nobly the ancients understood the inner life; how fully is it indicated in their mysteries?

I know a peasant maiden, who cannot write, but who, in the magnetic state, speaks in measured verse.

Galen was indebted to his nightly dreams for a part of his medical knowledge.

The calumnies spread about Frau H. were many and gross; this she well knew. As one day she heard so many of these as to be much affected by them, we thought she would express her feelings that night in the magnetic sleep, but she only said "they can affect my body, but not my spirit." Her mind, raised above such assaults by the consciousness of innocence, maintained its tranquillity and dwelt solely on spiritual matters.

Once in her sleep-waking she wrote thus:

> When the world declares of me
> Such cruel ill in calumny,
> And to your ears it finds a way,
> Do you believe it, yea or nay?

I answered:

> To us thou seemest true and pure,
> Let others view it as they will;
> We have our assurance still
> If our own sight can make us sure.

People of all kinds, to my great trouble, were always pressing to see her. If we refused them access to the sick room, they avenged themselves by the invention of all kinds of falsehoods.

She met all with an equal friendliness, even when it cost her bodily pain, and those who defamed her, she often defended. There came to her both good and bad men. She felt the evil in men clearly, but would not censure; lifted up a stone to cast at no sinner, but was rather likely to awake, in the faulty beings she suffered near her, faith in a spiritual life which might make them better.

Years before she was brought to me, the earth, with its atmosphere, and all that is about and upon it, human beings not excepted, was no more for her. She needed, not only a magnetizer, not only a love, an earnestness, an insight, such as scarce lies within the capacity of any man, but also what no mortal could bestow upon her, another heaven, other means of nourishment, other air than that of this earth. She belonged to the world of spirits, living here herself, as more half spirit. She belonged to the state after death, into which she had advanced more than halfway.

It is possible she might have been brought back to an adaptation for this world in the second or third year of her malady; but, in the fifth, no mode of treatment could have effected this. But by care she was aided to a greater harmony and clearness of the inward life; she enjoyed at Weinsberg, as she after said, the richest and happiest days of this life, and to us her abode here remains a point of light.

As to her outward form, we have already said it seemed but a thin veil about her spirit. She was little, her features of an oriental cast, her eye had the penetrating look of a seer's eye, which was set off by the shade of long dark eyelashes. She was a light flower that only lived on rays.

Eschenmayer writes thus of her in his "Mysteries."

"Her natural state was a mild, friendly earnestness, always disposed to prayer and devotion; her eye had a highly spiritual expression, and remained, notwithstanding her great sufferings, always bright and clear. Her look was penetrating, would quickly change in the conversation, seem to give forth sparks, and remain fixed on some one place,—this was a token that some strange apparition fettered it,—then would she resume the conversation. When I first saw her, she was in a situation which showed that her bodily life could not long endure, and that recovery to the common natural state was quite impossible. Without visible derangement of the functions, her life seemed only a wick glimmering in the socket. She was, as Kerner truly describes her, like one arrested in the act of dying and detained in the body by magnetic influences. Spirit and soul seemed often divided, and the spirit to have taken up its abode in other regions, while the soul was yet bound to the body."

I have given these extracts as being happily expressive of the relation between the physician and the clairvoyant, also of her character.

It seems to have been one of singular gentleness, and grateful piety, simple and pure, but not at all one from which we should expect extraordinary development of brain in any way; yet the excitement of her temperament from climate, scenery, the influence of traditions which evidently flowed round her, and a great constitutional impressibility did develop in her brain the germs both of poetic creation and science.

I say poetic creation, for, to my mind, the ghosts she saw were projections of herself into objective reality. The Hades she imagines is based in fact, for it is one of souls, who, having neglected their opportunities for better life, find themselves left forlorn, helpless, seeking aid from beings still ignorant and prejudiced, perhaps much below themselves in natural powers. Having forfeited their chance of direct access to God, they seek mediation from the prayers of men. But in the coloring and dress* of these ghosts, as also in their manner and mode of speech, there is a great deal which seems merely fanciful—local and peculiar.

To me, these interviews represent only prophecies of her mind; yet, considered in this way, they are, if not ghostly, spiritual facts of high beauty, and which cast light on the state of the soul after its separation from the body. Her gentle patience with them, her steady reference to a higher cause, her pure joy, when they became white in the light of happiness obtained through aspiration, are worthy of a more than half enfranchised angel.

As to the stories of mental correspondence and visits to those still engaged in this world, such as are told of her presentiment of her father's death, and connexion with him in the last moments, these are probably pure facts. Those who have sufficient strength of affection to be easily disengaged from external impressions and habits, and who dare trust their mental impulses are familiar with such.

Her invention of a language seems a simply natural motion of the mind when left to itself. The language we habitually use is so broken, and so hackneyed by ages of conventional use, that, in all deep states of being, we crave one simple and primitive in its stead. Most persons make one more or less clear from looks, tones, and symbols:—this woman, in the long leisure of her loneliness, and a mind bent upon itself, attempted to compose one of letters and words. I look upon it as no gift from without, but a growth from her own mind.

Her invention of a machine, of which she made a drawing, her power of drawing correctly her life-circle, and sun-circle, and the mathematical feeling she had of her existence, in correspondent sections of the two, are also valuable as mental facts. These figures describe

---

* The women ghosts all wear veils, put on the way admired by the Italian poets, of whom, however, she could know nothing.

her history and exemplify the position of mathematics toward the world of creative thought.

Every fact of mental existence ought to be capable of similar demonstration. I attach no especial importance to her circles:—we all live in such; all who observe themselves have the same sense of exactness and harmony in the revolutions of their destiny. But few attend to what is simple and invariable in the motions of their minds, and still fewer seek out means clearly to express them to others.

Goethe has taken up these facts in his Wanderjahre, where he speaks of his Macaria; also, one of these persons who are compensated for bodily infirmity by a more concentrated and acute state of mind, and consequent accesses of wisdom, as being bound to a star. When she was engaged by a sense of these larger revolutions, she seemed to those near her on the earth, to be sick; when she was, in fact, lower, but better adapted to the details and variations of an earthly life, these said she was well. Macaria knew the sun and life circles, also, the lives of spirit and soul, as did the forester's daughter of Prevorst.

Her power of making little verses was one of her least gifts. Many excitable persons possess this talent at versification, as all may possess it. It is merely that a certain exaltation of feeling raises the mode of expression with it, in the same way as song differs from speech. Verses of this sort do not necessarily demand the high faculties that constitute the poet,—the creative powers. Many verses, good ones, are personal or national merely. Ballads, hymns, love-lyrics, have often no claim differing from those of common prose speech, to the title of poems, except a greater keenness and terseness of expression.

The verses of this Seherin are of the simplest character, the natural garb for the sighs or aspirations of a lonely heart. She uses the shortest words, the commonest rhymes, and the verses move us by their nature and truth alone.

The most interesting of these facts to me, are her impressions from minerals and plants. Her impressions coincide with many ancient superstitions.

The hazel woke her immediately and gave her more power, therefore the witch with her hazel wand, probably found herself superior to those around her. We may also mention, in reference to witchcraft, that Dr. K asserts that, in certain moods of mind, she had no weight, but was upborne upon water, like cork, thus confirming the propriety, and justice of our forefathers' ordeal for witchcraft!

The laurel produced on her the highest magnetic effect, therefore the Sibyls had good reasons for wearing it on their brows.

"The laurel had on her, as on most sleep-wakers, a distinguished magnetic effect. We thus see why the priestess at Delphi, previous to uttering her oracles, shook a laurel tree, and then seated herself on a tripod covered with laurel boughs. In the temple of Æsculapius, and others, the laurel was used to excite sleep and dream."

From grapes she declared impressions, which corresponded with those caused by the wines made from them. Many kinds were given her, one after the other, by the person who raised them, and who gives a certificate as to the accuracy of her impressions, and his belief that she could not have derived them from any cause, but that of the touch.

She prescribed vegetable substances to be used in her machine, (as a kind of vapor bath,) and with good results to herself.

She enjoyed contact with minerals, deriving from those she liked a sense of concentrated life. Her impressions of the precious stones, corresponded with many superstitions of the ancients, which led to the preference of certain gems for amulets, on which they had engraved talismanic figures.

The ancients, in addition to their sense of the qualities that distinguish the diamond above all gems, venerated it as a talisman against wild beasts, poison, and evil spirits, thus expressing the natural influence of what is so enduring, bright, and pure. Townshend, speaking of the effect of gems on one of his sleep-wakers, said, she loved the diamond so much that she would lean her forehead towards it, whenever it was brought near her.

It is observable that these sleep-wakers, in their prescriptions, resemble the ancient sages, who culled only simples for the sick. But if they have this fine sense, also, for the qualities of animal and mineral substances, there is no reason why they should not turn bane to antidote, and prescribe at least homeopathic doses of poison, to restore the diseased to health.

The Seherin ascribed different states to the right and left sides of every body, even of the lady moon. The left is most impressible. Query: Is this the reason why the left hand has been, by the custom of nations, so almost disused, because the heart is on the left side?

She also saw different sights in the left from the right eye. In the left, the bodily state of the person; in the right, his real or destined self, how often unknown to himself, almost always obscured or perverted by his present ignorance or mistake. She had also the gift of second sight. She saw the coffins of those about to die. She saw in mirrors, cups of water; in soap-bubbles, the coming future.

We are here reminded of many beautiful superstitions and legends; of the secret pool in which the daring may, at mid-moon of night, read the future; of the magic globe, on whose pure surface Britomart sees her future love, whom she must seek, arrayed in knightly armor, through a difficult and hostile world.

> A looking-glass, right wondrously aguized,
> Whose virtues through the wyde world soon were solemnized.
> It vertue had to show in perfect sight,
> Whatever thing was in the world contayned,
> Betwixt the lowest earth and hevens hight;
> So that it to the looker appertayned,
> Whatever foe had wrought, or friend had fayned,
> Herein discovered was, ne ought mote pas,
> Ne ought in secret from the same remayned;
> Forthy it round and hollow shaped was,
> Like to the world itselfe, and seemed a World of Glas.

Faerie Queene, Book III

Such mirrors had Cornelius Aggrippa and other wizards. The soap-bubble is such a globe; only one had need of second sight or double sight to see the pictures on so transitory a mirror. Perhaps it is some vague expectation of such wonders, that makes us so fond of blowing them in childish years. But, perhaps, it is rather as a prelude to the occupation of our lives, blowing bubbles where all things may be seen, that, "to the looker appertain," if we can keep them long enough or look quick enough.

In short, were this biography of no other value, it would be most interesting as showing how the floating belief of nations, always no doubt shadowing forth in its imperfect fashion the poetic facts with their specific exposition, is found to grow up anew in a simple, but high-wrought nature.

The fashioning spirit, working upwards from the clod to man, proffers as its last, highest essay, the brain of man. In the lowest zoöphyte it aimed at this; some faint rudiments may there be discerned: but only in man has it perfected that immense galvanic battery that can be loaded from above, below, and around;—that engine, not only of perception, but of conception and consecutive thought,—whose right hand is memory, whose life is idea, the crown of nature, the platform from which spirit takes wing.

Yet, as gradation is the beautiful secret of nature, and the fashioning spirit, which loves to develop and transcend, loves no less to moderate, to modulate, and harmonize, it did not mean by thus drawing man onward to the next state of existence, to destroy his fitness for this. It did not mean to destroy his sympathies with the mineral, vegetable, and animal realms, of whose components he is in great part composed; which were the preface to his being, of whom he is to take count, whom he should govern as a reasoning head of a perfectly arranged body. He was meant to be the historian, the philosopher, the poet, the king of this world, no less than the prophet of the next.

These functions should be in equipoise, and when they are not, when we see excess either on the natural (so called as distinguished from the spiritual,) or the spiritual side, we feel that the law is transgressed. And, if it be the greatest sorrow to see brain merged in body, to see a man more hands or feet than head, so that we feel he might, with propriety, be on all fours again, or even crawl like the serpent; it is also sad to see the brain, too much excited on some one side, which we call madness, or even unduly and prematurely, so as to destroy in its bloom, the common human existence of the person, as in the case before us, and others of the poetical and prophetical existence.

We would rather minds should foresee less and see more surely, that death should ensue by gentler gradation, and the brain be the governor and interpreter, rather than the destroyer, of the animal life. But, in cases like this, where the animal life is prematurely broken up, and the brain prematurely exercised, we may as well learn what we can from it, and believe that the glimpses thus caught, if not as precious as the full view, are bright with the same light, and open to the same scene.

There is a family character about all the German ghosts. We find the same features in these stories as in those related by Jung Stilling and others. They bear the same character as the pictures by the old masters, of a deep and simple piety. She stands before as, this piety, in a full, high-necked robe, a simple, hausfrauish cap, a clear, straightforward blue eye. These are no terrible, gloomy ghosts with Spanish mantle or Italian dagger. We feel quite at home with them, and sure of their good faith.

To the Seherin, they were a real society, constantly inspiring good thoughts. The reference to them in these verses, written in her journal shortly before her death, is affecting, and shows her deep sense of their reality. She must have felt that she had been a true friend to them, by refusing always, as she did, requests she thought wrong, and referring them to a Saviour.

Farewell, my friends,
All farewell,
God bless you for your love—
Bless you for your goodness.
    All farewell!

And you, how shall I name you?
    Who have so saddened me,
I will name you also—Friends;
You have been discipline to me.
    Farewell! farewell!

Farewell! you my dear ones,
Soon will you know[*]
How hard have been my sufferings
    In the Pilgrim land.
        Farewell!

Let it not grieve you,
That my woes find an end,
    Farewell, dear ones,
Till the second meeting;
    Farewell! Farewell!

In this journal her thoughts dwell much upon those natural ties which she was not permitted to enjoy. She thought much of her children, and often fancied she had saw the one who had died, growing in the spirit land. Any allusion to them called a sweet smile on her face when in her trance.

Other interesting poems are records of these often beautiful visions, especially of that preceding her own death; the address to her life-circle, the thought of which is truly great, (this was translated in the Dublin Magazine,) and descriptions of her earthly state as an imprisonment. The story of her life, though stained like others, by partialities, and prejudices, which were not justly distinguished from what was altogether true and fair, is a poem of so pure a music, presents such gentle and holy images, that we sympathize fully in the love and gratitude Kerner and his friends felt towards her, as the friend of their best life. She was a St. Theresa in her way.

---

[*] The physician thought she here referred to the examination of her body that
    would take place after her death. The brain was found to be sound, though there
    were marks of great disease elsewhere.

His address to her, with which his volume closes, may thus be translated in homely guise. In the original it has no merit, except as uttering his affectionate and reverent feeling towards his patient, the peasant girl,—"the sick one, the poor one." But we like to see how, from the mouths of babes and sucklings, praise may be so perfected as to command this reverence from the learned and worldly-wise.

> Farewell; the debt I owe thee
>   Ever in heart I bear;
> My soul sees, since I know thee,
>   The spirit depths so clear.
>
> Whether in light or shade,
>   Thy soul now dwelling hath;
> Be, if my faith should fade,
>   The guide upon my path.
>
> Livest thou in mutual power,
>   With spirits blest and bright,
> O be, in death's dark hour,
>   My help to heaven's light.
>
> Upon thy grave is growing,
>   The plant by thee beloved,[*]
> St. Johns-wort golden glowing,
>   Like St. John's thoughts of love.
>
> Witness of sacred sorrow,
>   Whene'er thou meet'st my eye,
> O flower, from thee I borrow,
>   Thoughts for eternity.
>
> Farewell! the woes of earth
>   No more my soul affright;
> Who knows their temporal birth
>   Can easy bear their weight.

I do confess this is a paraphrase, not a translation, also, that in the other extracts, I have taken liberties with the original for the sake of condensation, and clearness. What I have written must be received as a slight and conversational account of the work.

---

[*] She received great benefit from decoctions of this herb, and often prescribed it to others.

Two or three other remarks, I had forgotten, may come in here.

The glances at the spirit-world have none of that large or universal significance, none of that value from philosophical analogy, that is felt in any picture by Swedenborg, or Dante, of permanent relations. The mind of the forester's daughter was exalted and rapidly developed; still the wild cherry tree bore no orange; she was not transformed into a philosophic or poetic organization.

Yet many of her untaught notions remind of other seers of a larger scope. She, too, receives this life as one link in a long chain; and thinks that immediately after death, the meaning of the past life will appear to us as one word.

She tends to a belief in the aromal state, and in successive existences on this earth; for behind persons she often saw another being, whether their form in the state before or after this, I know not; behind a woman a man, equipped for fight, and so forth. Her perception of character, even in cases of those whom she saw only as they passed her window, was correct.

Kerner aims many a leaden sarcasm at those who despise his credulity. He speaks of those sages as men whose brain is a glass table, incapable of receiving the electric spark, and who will not believe, because, in their mental isolation, they are incapable of feeling these facts.

Certainly, I think he would be dull, who could see no meaning or beauty in the history of the forester's daughter of Prevorst. She lived but nine-and-twenty years, yet, in that time, had traversed a larger portion of the field of thought than all her race before, in their many and long lives.

Of the abuses to which all these magical implements are prone, I have an instance, since leaving Milwaukie, in the journal of a man equally sincere, but not equally inspired, led from Germany hither by signs and wonders, as a commissioned agent of Providence, who, indeed, has arranged every detail of his life with a minuteness far beyond the promised care of the sparrow. He props himself by spiritual aid from a maiden now in this country, who was once an attendant on the Seeress, and who seems to have caught from her the contagion of trance, but not its revelations.

Do not blame me that I have written so much about Germany and Hades, while you were looking for news of the West. Here, on the pier, I see disembarking the Germans, the Norwegians, the Swedes, the Swiss. Who knows how much of old legendary lore, of modern wonder, they have already planted amid the Wisconsin forests? Soon,

soon their tales of the origin of things, and the Providence which rules them, will be so mingled with those of the Indian, that the very oak trees will not know them apart,—will not know whether itself be a Runic, a Druid, or a Winnebago oak.

Some seeds of all growths that have ever been known in this world might, no doubt, already be found in these Western wilds, if we had the power to call them to life.

I saw, in the newspaper, that the American Tract Society boasted of their agents' having exchanged, at a Western cabin door, tracts for the Devil on Two Sticks, and then burnt that more entertaining than edifying volume. No wonder, though, they study it there. Could one but have the gift of reading the dreams dreamed by men of such various birth, various history, various mind, it would afford much more extensive amusement than did the chambers of one Spanish city!

Could I but have flown at night through such mental experiences, instead of being shut up in my little bedroom at the Milwaukie boarding house, this chapter would have been worth reading. As it is, let us hasten to a close.

Had I been rich in money, I might have built a house, or set up in business, during my fortnight's stay at Milwaukie, matters move on there at so rapid a rate. But, being only rich in curiosity, I was obliged to walk the streets and pick up what I could in casual intercourse. When I left the street, indeed, and walked on the bluffs, or sat beside the lake in their shadow, my mind was rich in dreams congenial to the scene, some time to be realized, though not by me.

A boat was left, keel up, half on the sand, half in the water, swaying with each swell of the lake. It gave a picturesque grace to that part of the shore, as the only image of inaction—only object of a pensive character to be seen. Near this I sat, to dream my dreams and watch the colors of the lake, changing hourly, till the sun sank. These hours yielded impulses, wove webs, such as life will not again afford.

Returning to the boarding house, which was also a boarding school, we were sure to be greeted by gay laughter.

This school was conducted by two girls of nineteen and seventeen years; their pupils were nearly as old as themselves; the relation seemed very pleasant between them. The only superiority—that of superior knowledge—was sufficient to maintain authority—all the authority that was needed to keep daily life in good order.

In the West, people are not respected merely because they are old in years; people there have not time to keep up appearances in that way; when they cease to have a real advantage in wisdom, knowledge, or enterprise, they must stand back, and let those who are oldest in character "go ahead," however few years they may count. There are no banks of established respectability in which to bury the talent there; no napkin of precedent in which to wrap it. What cannot be made to pass current, is not esteemed coin of the realm.

To the windows of this house, where the daughter of a famous "Indian fighter," i.e. fighter against the Indians, was learning French and the piano, came wild, tawny figures, offering for sale their baskets of berries. The boys now, instead of brandishing the tomahawk, tame their hands to pick raspberries.

Here the evenings were much lightened by the gay chat of one of the party, who, with the excellent practical sense of mature experience, and the kindest heart, united a naiveté and innocence such as I never saw in any other who had walked so long life's tangled path. Like a child, she was everywhere at home, and like a child, received and bestowed entertainment from all places, all persons. I thanked her for making me laugh, as did the sick and poor, whom she was sure to find out in her briefest sojourn in any place, for more substantial aid. Happy are those who never grieve, and so often aid and enliven their fellow men!

This scene, however, I was not sorry to exchange for the much celebrated beauties of the Island of Mackinaw.

CHAPTER VI

Mackinaw

LATE AT NIGHT we reached this island, so famous for its beauty, and to which I proposed a visit of some length. It was the last week in August, when a large representation from the Chippewa and Ottawa tribes are here to receive their annual payments from the American government. As their habits make travelling easy and inexpensive to them, neither being obliged to wait for steamboats, or write to see whether hotels are full, they come hither by thousands, and those thousands in families, secure of accommodation on the beach, and food from the lake, to make a long holiday out of the occasion. There were near two thousand encamped on the island already, and more arriving every day.

As our boat came in, the captain had some rockets let off. This greatly excited the Indians, and their yells and wild cries resounded along the shore. Except for the momentary flash of the rockets, it was perfectly dark, and my sensations as I walked with a stranger to a strange hotel, through the midst of these shrieking savages, and heard the pants and snorts of the departing steamer, which carried away all my companions, were somewhat of the dismal sort; though it was pleasant, too, in the way that everything strange is; everything that breaks in upon the routine that so easily incrusts us.

I had reason to expect a room to myself at the hotel, but found none, and was obliged to take up my rest in the common parlor and eating-room, a circumstance which ensured my being an early riser.

With the first rosy streak, I was out among my Indian neighbors, whose lodges honey-combed the beautiful beach, that curved away in long, fair outline on either side the house. They were already on the alert, the children creeping out from beneath the blanket door of the lodge; the women pounding corn in their rude mortars, the

young men playing on their pipes. I had been much amused, when the
strain proper to the Winnebago courting flute was played to me on
another instrument, at any one fancying it a melody; but now, when I
heard the notes in their true tone and time, I thought it not unworthy comparison, in its graceful sequence, and the light flourish, at the
close, with the sweetest bird-songs; and this, like the bird-song, is only
practised to allure a mate. The Indian, become a citizen and a husband,
no more thinks of playing the flute than one of the "settled down"
members of our society would of choosing the "purple light of love"
as dye-stuff for a surtout.

Mackinaw has been fully described by able pens, and I can only add
my tribute to the exceeding beauty of the spot and its position. It is
charming to be on an island so small that you can sail round it in an
afternoon, yet large enough to admit of long secluded walks through
its gentle groves. You can go round it in your boat; or, on foot, you
can tread its narrow beach, resting, at times, beneath the lofty walls
of stone, richly wooded, which rise from it in various architectural
forms. In this stone, caves are continually forming, from the action of
the atmosphere; one of these is quite deep, and with a fragment left at
its mouth, wreathed with little creeping plants, that looks, as you sit
within, like a ruined pillar.

The arched rock surprised me, much as I had heard of it, from the
perfection of the arch. It is perfect whether you look up through it
from the lake, or down through it to the transparent waters. We both
ascended and descended, no very easy matter, the steep and crumbling path, and rested at the summit, beneath the trees, and at the foot
upon the cool mossy stones beside the lapsing wave. Nature has carefully decorated all this architecture with shrubs that take root within
the crevices, and small creeping vines. These natural ruins may vie for
beautiful effect with the remains of European grandeur, and have, beside, a charm as of a playful mood in nature.

The sugar-loaf rock is a fragment in the same kind as the pine
rock we saw in Illinois. It has the same air of a helmet, as seen from
an eminence at the side, which you descend by a long and steep path.
The rock itself may be ascended by the bold and agile. Half way up is
a niche, to which those, who are neither, can climb by a ladder. A very
handsome young officer and lady who were with us did so, and then,
facing round, stood there side by side, looking in the niche, if not like
saints or angels wrought by pious hands in stone, as romantically, if not
as holily, worthy the gazer's eye.

The woods which adorn the central ridge of the island are very full in foliage, and, in August, showed the tender green and pliant leaf of June elsewhere. They are rich in beautiful mosses and the wild raspberry.

From Fort Holmes, the old fort, we had the most commanding view of the lake and straits, opposite shores, and fair islets. Mackinaw, itself, is best seen from the water. Its peculiar shape is supposed to have been the origin of its name, Michilimackinac, which means the Great Turtle. One person whom I saw, wished to establish another etymology, which he fancied to be more refined; but, I doubt not, this is the true one, both because the shape might suggest such a name, and that the existence of an island in this commanding position, which did so, would seem a significant fact to the Indians. For Henry gives the details of peculiar worship paid to the Great Turtle, and the oracles received from this extraordinary Apollo of the Indian Delphos.

It is crowned most picturesquely, by the white fort, with its gay flag. From this, on one side, stretches the town. How pleasing a sight, after the raw, crude, staring assemblage of houses, everywhere else to be met in this country, an old French town, mellow in its coloring, and with the harmonious effect of a slow growth, which assimilates, naturally, with objects round it. The people in its streets, Indian, French, half-breeds, and others, walked with a leisure step, as of those who live a life of taste and inclination, rather than of the hard press of business, as in American towns elsewhere.

On the other side, along the fair, curving beach, below the white houses scattered on the declivity, clustered the Indian lodges, with their amber brown matting, so soft, and bright of hue, in the late afternoon sun. The first afternoon I was there, looking down from a near height, I felt that I never wished to see a more fascinating picture. It was an hour of the deepest serenity; bright blue and gold, rich shadows. Every moment the sunlight fell more mellow. The Indians were grouped and scattered among the lodges; the women preparing food, in the kettle or frying-pan, over the many small fires; the children, half-naked, wild as little goblins, were playing both in and out of the water. Here and there lounged a young girl, with a baby at her back, whose bright eyes glanced, as if born into a world of courage and of joy, instead of ignominious servitude and slow decay. Some girls were cutting wood, a little way from me, talking and laughing, in the low musical tone, so charming in the Indian women. Many bark canoes were upturned upon the beach, and, by that light, of almost the same amber as the lodges. Others, coming in, their square sails set, and with almost arrowy speed, though heavily laden with dusky forms, and all the apparatus of their household. Here and there a sail-boat glided by, with a different, but scarce less pleasing motion.

It was a scene of ideal loveliness, and these wild forms adorned it, as looking so at home in it. All seemed happy, and they were happy that day, for they had no firewater to madden them, as it was Sunday, and the shops were shut.

From my window, at the boarding house, my eye was constantly attracted by these picturesque groups. I was never tired of seeing the canoes come in, and the new arrivals set up their temporary dwellings. The women ran to set up the tent-poles, and spread the mats on the ground. The men brought the chests, kettles, &c.; the mats were then laid on the outside, the cedar boughs strewed on the ground, the blanket hung up for a door, and all was completed in less than twenty minutes. Then they began to prepare the night meal, and to learn of their neighbors the news of the day.

The habit of preparing food out of doors, gave all the gipsy charm and variety to their conduct. Continually I wanted Sir Walter Scott to have been there. If such romantic sketches were suggested to him, by the sight of a few gipsies, not a group near one of these fires but would have furnished him material for a separate canvass. I was so taken up with the spirit of the scene, that I could not follow out the stories suggested by these weather-beaten, sullen, but eloquent figures.

They talked a great deal, and with much variety of gesture, so that I often had a good guess at the meaning of their discourse. I saw that, whatever the Indian may be among the whites, he is anything but taciturn with his own people. And he often would declaim, or narrate at length, as indeed it is obvious, that these tribes possess great power that way, if only from the fables taken from their stores, by Mr. Schoolcraft.

I liked very much to walk or sit among them. With the women I held much communication by signs. They are almost invariably coarse and ugly, with the exception of their eyes, with a peculiarly awkward gait, and forms bent by burthens. This gait, so different from the steady and noble step of the men, marks the inferior position they occupy. I had heard much eloquent contradiction of this. Mrs. Schoolcraft had maintained to a friend, that they were in fact as nearly on a par with their husbands as the white woman with hers. "Although," said she, "on account of inevitable causes, the Indian woman is subjected to many hardships of a peculiar nature, yet her position, compared with that of the man, is higher and freer than that of the white woman. Why will people look only on one side? They either exalt the Red man into a Demigod or degrade him into a beast. They say that he compels his wife to do all the drudgery, while he does nothing but hunt and amuse himself; forgetting that, upon his activity and power of endurance as a hunter, depends the support of his family; that this is labor of the most fatiguing kind, and that it is absolutely necessary that he should keep his frame unbent by burdens and unworn by toil, that he may be able to obtain the means of subsistence. I have witnessed scenes of conjugal and parental love in the Indian's wigwam from which I have often, often thought the educated white man, proud of his superior civilization, might learn an useful lesson. When he returns from hunting, worn out with fatigue, having tasted nothing since dawn, his wife, if she is a good wife, will take off his moccasins and replace them with dry ones, and will prepare his game for their repast, while his children will climb upon him, and he will caress them with all the tenderness of a woman; and in the evening the Indian wigwam is the scene of the purest domestic pleasures. The father will relate for the amusement of the wife, and for the instruction of the children, all the events of the day's hunt, while they will treasure up every word that falls, and thus learn the theory of the art whose practice is to be the occupation of their lives.

Mrs. Grant speaks thus of the position of woman amid the Mohawk Indians:

"Lady Mary Montague says, that the court of Vienna was the paradise of old women, and that there is no other place in the world where a woman past fifty excites the least interest. Had her travels extended to the interior of North America, she would have seen another instance of this inversion of the common mode of thinking. Here a woman never was of consequence, till she had a son old enough to fight the battles of his country. From that date she held a superior rank in society; was allowed to live at ease, and even called to consultations on national affairs. In savage and warlike countries, the reign of beauty is very short, and its influence comparatively limited. The girls in childhood had a very pleasing appearance; but excepting their fine hair, eyes, and teeth, every external grace was soon banished by perpetual drudgery, carrying burdens too heavy to be borne, and other slavish employments considered beneath the dignity of the men. These walked before erect and graceful, decked with ornaments which set off to advantage the symmetry of their well-formed persons, while the poor women followed, meanly attired, bent under the weight of the children and utensils, which they carried everywhere with them, and disfigured and degraded by ceaseless toils. They were very early married, for a Mohawk had no other servant but his wife, and, whenever he commenced hunter, it was requisite he should have some one to carry his load, cook his kettle, make his moccasins, and, above all, produce the young warriors who were to succeed him in the honors of the chase and of the tomahawk. Wherever man is a mere hunter, woman is a mere slave. It is domestic intercourse that softens man, and elevates woman; and of that there can be but little, where the employments and amusements are not in common; the ancient Caledonians honored the fair; but then it is to be observed, they were fair huntresses, and moved in the light of their beauty to the hill of roes; and the culinary toils were entirely left to the rougher sex. When the young warrior made his appearance, it softened the cares of his mother, who well knew that, when he grew up, every deficiency in tenderness to his wife would be made up in superabundant duty and affection to her. If it were possible to carry filial veneration to excess, it was done here; for all other charities were absorbed in it. I wonder this system of depressing the sex in their early years, to exalt them when all their juvenile attractions were flown, and when mind alone can distinguish them, has not occurred to our modern reformers. The Mohawks took good care not to admit their women to share their prerogatives, till they approved themselves good wives and mothers."

The observations of women upon the position of woman are always more valuable than those of men; but, of these two, Mrs. Grant's seems much nearer the truth than Mrs. Schoolcraft's, because, though her opportunities for observation did not bring her so close, she looked more at both sides to find the truth.

Carver, in his travels among the Winnebagoes, describes two queens, one nominally so, like Queen Victoria; the other invested with a genuine royalty, springing from her own conduct.

In the great town of the Winnebagoes, he found a queen presiding over the tribe, instead of a sachem. He adds, that, in some tribes, the descent is given to the female line in preference to the male, that is, a sister's son will succeed to the authority, rather than a brother's son.

The position of this Winnebago queen, reminded me forcibly of Queen Victoria's.

"She sat in the council, but only asked a few questions, or gave some trifling directions in matters relative to the state, for women are never allowed to sit in their councils, except they happen to be invested with the supreme authority, and then it is not customary for

them to make any formal speeches, as the chiefs do. She was a very ancient woman, small in stature, and not much distinguished by her dress
from several young women that attended her. These, her attendants,
seemed greatly pleased whenever I showed any tokens of respect to
their queen, especially when I saluted her, which I frequently did
to acquire her favor."

The other was a woman, who being taken captive, found means to
kill her captor, and make her escape, and the tribe were so struck with
admiration at the courage and calmness she displayed on the occasion,
as to make her chieftainess in her own right.

Notwithstanding the homage paid to women, and the consequence
allowed her in some cases, it is impossible to look upon the Indian
women, without feeling that they *do* occupy a lower place than women
among the nations of European civilization. The habits of drudgery
expressed in their form and gesture, the soft and wild but melancholy expression of their eye, reminded me of the tribe mentioned by
Mackenzie, where the women destroy their female children, whenever
they have a good opportunity; and of the eloquent reproaches addressed by the Paraguay woman to her mother, that she had not, in the
same way, saved her from the anguish and weariness of her lot.

More weariness than anguish, no doubt, falls to the lot of most of
these women. They inherit submission, and the minds of the generality accommodate themselves more or less to any posture. Perhaps
they suffer less than their white sisters, who have more aspiration and
refinement, with little power of self-sustenance. But their place is certainly lower, and their share of the human inheritance less.

Their decorum and delicacy are striking, and show that when these
are native to the mind, no habits of life make any difference. Their
whole gesture is timid, yet self-possessed. They used to crowd round
me, to inspect little things I had to show them, but never press near;
on the contrary, would reprove and keep off the children. Anything
they took from my hand, was held with care, then shut or folded, and
returned with an air of lady-like precision. They would not stare, however curious they might be, but cast sidelong glances.

A locket that I wore, was an object of untiring interest; they seemed
to regard it as a talisman. My little sun-shade was still more fascinating to them; apparently they had never before seen one. For an umbrella
they entertain profound regard, probably looking upon it as the most
luxurious superfluity a person can possess, and therefore a badge of
great wealth. I used to see an old squaw, whose sullied skin and coarse,
tanned locks, told that she had braved sun and storm, without a doubt

or care, for sixty years at the least, sitting gravely at the door of her lodge, with an old green umbrella over her head, happy for hours together in the dignified shade. For her happiness pomp came not, as it so often does, too late; she received it with grateful enjoyment.

One day, as I was seated on one of the canoes, a woman came and sat beside me, with her baby in its cradle set up at her feet. She asked me by a gesture, to let her take my sun-shade, and then to show her how to open it. Then she put it into her baby's hand, and held it over its head, looking at me the while with a sweet, mischievous laugh, as much as to say, "you carry a thing that is only fit for a baby;" her pantomime was very pretty. She, like the other women, had a glance, and shy, sweet expression in the eye; the men have a steady gaze.

That noblest and loveliest of modern Preux, Lord Edward Fitzgerald, who came through Buffalo to Detroit and Mackinaw, with Brant, and was adopted into the Bear tribe by the name of Eghnidal, was struck, in the same way, by the delicacy of manners in the women. He says, "Notwithstanding the life they lead, which would make most women rough and masculine, they are as soft, meek and modest, as the best brought up girls in England. Somewhat coquettish too! Imagine the manners of Mimi in a poor *squaw*, that has been carrying packs in the woods all her life."

McKenney mentions that the young wife, during the short bloom of her beauty, is an object of homage and tenderness to her husband. One Indian woman, the Flying Pigeon, a beautiful, an excellent woman, of whom he gives some particulars, is an instance of the power uncommon characters will always exert of breaking down the barriers custom has erected round them. She captivated by her charms, and inspired with reverence for her character, her husband and son. The simple praise with which the husband indicates the religion, the judgment, and the generosity he saw in her, are as satisfying as Count Zinzendorf's more labored eulogium on his "noble consort." The conduct of her son, when, many years after her death, he saw her picture at Washington, is unspeakably affecting. Catlin gives anecdotes of the grief of a chief for the loss of a daughter, and the princely gifts he offers in exchange for her portrait, worthy not merely of European, but of Troubadour sentiment. It is also evident that, as Mrs. Schoolcraft says, the women have great power at home. It can never be otherwise, men being dependent upon them for the comfort of their lives. Just so among ourselves, wives who are neither esteemed nor loved by their husbands, have great power over their conduct by the friction of every

day, and over the formation of their opinions by the daily opportunities so close a relation affords, of perverting testimony and instilling
doubts. But these sentiments should not come in brief flashes, but burn
as a steady flame, then there would be more women worthy to inspire
them. This power is good for nothing, unless the woman be wise to
use it aright. Has the Indian, has the white woman, as noble a feeling of
life and its uses, as religious a self-respect, as worthy a field of thought
and action, as man? If not, the white woman, the Indian woman, oc-
cupies an inferior position to that of man. It is not so much a question
of power, as of privilege.

The men of these subjugated tribes, now accustomed to drunk-
enness and every way degraded, bear but a faint impress of the lost
grandeur of the race. They are no longer strong, tall, or finely proportioned. Yet as you see them stealing along a height, or striding boldly
forward, they remind you of what *was* majestic in the red man.

On the shores of lake Superior, it is said, if you visit them at home,
you may still see a remnant of the noble blood. The Pillagers—
(Pilleurs)—a band celebrated by the old travellers, are still existant there.

"Still some, 'the eagles of their tribe,' may rush."

I have spoken of the hatred felt by the white man for the Indian:
with white women it seems to amount to disgust, to loathing. How
I could endure the dirt, the peculiar smell of the Indians, and their
dwellings, was a great marvel in the eyes of my lady acquaintance;
indeed, I wonder why they did not quite give me up, as they certainly
looked on me with great distaste for it. "Get you gone, you Indian
dog," was the felt, if not the breathed, expression towards the hapless
owners of the soil. All their claims, all their sorrows quite forgot, in
abhorrence of their dirt, their tawny skins, and the vices the whites
have taught them.

A person who had seen them during great part of a life, expressed
his prejudices to me with such violence, that I was no longer surprised that the Indian children threw sticks at him as he passed. A
lady said, "do what you will for them, they will be ungrateful. The
savage cannot be washed out of them. Bring up an Indian child and
see if you can attach it to you." The next moment, she expressed, in
the presence of one of those children whom she was bringing up,
loathing at the odor left by one of her people, and one of the most
respected, as he passed through the room. When the child is grown
she will consider it basely ungrateful not to love her, as it certainly

will not; and this will be cited as an instance of the impossibility of attaching the Indian.

Whether the Indian could, by any efforts of love and intelligence from the white man, have been civilized and made a valuable ingredient in the new state, I will not say; but this we are sure of; the French Catholics, at least, did not harm them, nor disturb their minds merely to corrupt them. The French they loved. But the stern Presbyterian, with his dogmas and his task-work, the city circle and the college, with their niggard concessions and unfeeling stare, have never tried the experiment. It has not been tried. Our people and our government have sinned alike against the first-born of the soil, and if they are the fated agents of a new era, they have done nothing—have invoked no god to keep them sinless while they do the hest of fate.

Worst of all, when they invoke the holy power only to mask their iniquity; when the felon trader, who, all the week, has been besotting and degrading the Indian with rum mixed with red pepper, and damaged tobacco, kneels with him on Sunday before a common altar, to tell the rosary which recalls the thought of him crucified for love of suffering men, and to listen to sermons in praise of "purity"!!

My savage friends, cries the old fat priest, you must, above all things, aim at *purity*.

Oh, my heart swelled when I saw them in a Christian church. Better their own dog-feasts and bloody rites than such mockery of that other faith.

"The dog," said an Indian, "was once a spirit; he has fallen for his sin, and was given by the Great Spirit, in this shape, to man, as his most intelligent companion. Therefore we sacrifice it in highest honor to our friends in this world,—to our protecting geniuses in another."

There was religion in that thought. The white man sacrifices his own brother, and to Mammon, yet he turns in loathing from the dog-feast.

"You say," said the Indian of the South to the missionary, "that Christianity is pleasing to God. How can that be?—Those men at Savannah are Christians."

Yes! slave-drivers and Indian traders are called Christians, and the Indian is to be deemed less like the Son of Mary than they! Wonderful is the deceit of man's heart!

I have not, on seeing something of them in their own haunts, found reason to change the sentiments expressed in the following lines, when a deputation of the Sacs and Foxes visited Boston in 1837, and were, by one person at least, received in a dignified and courteous manner.

GOVERNOR EVERETT RECEIVING THE INDIAN CHIEFS

November, 1837

Who says that Poesy is on the wane,
And that the Muses tune their lyres in vain?
'Mid all the treasures of romantic story,
When thought was fresh and fancy in her glory,
Has ever Art found out a richer theme,
More dark a shadow, or more soft a gleam,
Than fall upon the scene, sketched carelessly,
In the newspaper column of to-day?

American romance is somewhat stale.
Talk of the hatchet, and the faces pale,
Wampum and calumets and forests dreary,
Once so attractive, now begins to weary.
Uncas and Magawisca please us still,
Unreal, yet idealized with skill;
But every poetaster scribbling witling,
From the majestic oak his stylus whittling,
Has helped to tire us, and to make us fear
The monotone in which so much we hear
Of "stoics of the wood," and "men without a tear"

Yet Nature, ever buoyant, ever young,
If let alone, will sing as erst she sung;
The course of circumstance gives back again
The Picturesque, erewhile pursued in vain;
Shows us the fount of Romance is not wasted—
The lights and shades of contrast not exhausted.

Shorn of his strength, the Samson now must sue
    For fragments from the feast his fathers gave,
The Indian dare not claim what is his due,
    But as a boon his heritage must crave;
His stately form shall soon be seen no more
Through all his father's land, th' Atlantic shore,
Beneath the sun, to *us* so kind, *they* melt,
More heavily each day our rule is felt;
The tale is old,—we do as mortals must:
Might makes right here, but God and Time are just.

So near the drama hastens to its close,
On this last scene awhile your eyes repose;
The polished Greek and Scythian meet again,
The ancient life is lived by modern man—
The savage through our busy cities walks,—
He in his untouched grandeur silent stalks.
Unmoved by all our gaieties and shows,
Wonder nor shame can touch him as he goes;
He gazes on the marvels we have wrought,
But knows the models from whence all was brought;
In God's first temples he has stood so oft,
And listened to the natural organ loft—
Has watched the eagle's flight, the muttering thunder heard,
Art cannot move him to a wondering word;
Perhaps he sees that all this luxury
Brings less food to the mind than to the eye;
Perhaps a simple sentiment has brought
More to him than your arts had ever taught.
What are the petty triumphs *Art* has given,
To eyes familiar with the naked heaven?

All has been seen—dock, railroad, and canal,
Fort, market, bridge, college, and arsenal,
Asylum, hospital, and cotton mill,
The theatre, the lighthouse, and the jail.
The Braves each novelty, reflecting, saw,
And now and then growled out the earnest *yaw*
And now the time is come, 't is understood,
When, having seen and thought so much, a *talk* may do some
    good.

A well-dressed mob have thronged the sight to greet,
And motley figures throng the spacious street;
Majestical and calm through all they stride,
Wearing the blanket with a monarch's pride;
The gazers stare and shrug, but can't deny
Their noble forms and blameless symmetry.

If the Great Spirit their morale has slighted,
And wigwam smoke their mental culture blighted,
Yet the physique, at least, perfection reaches,
In wilds where neither Combe nor Spurzheim teaches;

Where whispering trees invite man to the chase,
And bounding deer allure him to the race.

Would thou hadst seen it! That dark, stately band,
Whose ancestors enjoyed all this fair land,
Whence they, by force or fraud, were made to flee,
Are brought, the white man's victory to see.
Can kind emotions in their proud hearts glow,
As through these realms, now decked by Art, they go?
The church, the school, the railroad and the mart—
Can these a pleasure to their minds impart?
All once was theirs—Earth, ocean, forest, sky—
How can they joy in what now meets the eye?
Not yet Religion has unlocked the soul,
Nor Each has learned to glory in the Whole!

Must they not think, so strange and sad their lot,
That they by the Great Spirit are forgot?
From the far border to which they are driven,
They might look up in trust to the clear heaven;
But *here*—what tales doth every object tell
Where Massasoit sleeps—where Philip fell!

We take our turn, and the Philosopher
Sees through the clouds a hand which cannot err,
An unimproving race, with all their graces
And all their vices, must resign their places;
And Human Culture rolls its onward flood
Over the broad plains steeped in Indian blood.

Such thoughts steady our faith; yet there will rise
Some natural tears into the calmest eyes—
Which gaze where forest princes haughty go,
Made for a gaping crowd a raree show.

But *this* a scene seems where, in courtesy,
The pale face with the forest prince could vie,
For One presided, who, for tact and grace,
In any age had held an honored place,—
In Beauty's own dear day, had shone a polished Phidian vase!

Oft have I listened to his accents bland,
    And owned the magic of his silvery voice,

In all the graces which life's arts demand,
    Delighted by the justness of his choice.
Not his the stream of lavish, fervid thought,—
The rhetoric by passion's magic wrought;
Not his the massive style, the lion port,
Which with the granite class of mind assort;
But, in a range of excellence his own,
With all the charms to soft persuasion known,
Amid our busy people we admire him—"elegant and lone."

He scarce needs words, so exquisite the skill
Which modulates the tones to do his will,
That the mere sound enough would charm the ear,
And lap in its Elysium all who hear.
The intellectual paleness of his cheek,
    The heavy eyelids and slow, tranquil smile,
The well cut lips from which the graces speak,
    Fit him alike to win or to beguile,
Then those words so well chosen, fit, though few,
Their linked sweetness as our thoughts pursue,
We deem them spoken pearls, or radiant diamond dew.

And never yet did I admire the power
    Which makes so lustrous every threadbare theme—
Which won for Lafayette one other hour,
    And e'en on July Fourth could cast a gleam—
As now, when I behold him play the host,
With all the dignity which red men boast—
With all the courtesy the whites have lost;—
Assume the very hue of savage mind,
Yet in rude accents show the thought refined;—
Assume the naiveté of infant age,
And in such prattle seem still more a sage;
The golden mean with tact unerring scized,
A courtly critic shone, a simple savage pleased;
The stoic of the woods his skill confessed,
As all the Father answered in his breast,
To the sure mark the silver arrow sped,
The man without a tear a tear has shed;
And thou hadst wept, hadst thou been there, to see
How true one sentiment must ever be,
In court or camp, the city or the wild,
To rouse the Father's heart, you need but name his Child.

'T was a fair scene—and acted well by all;
So here's a health to Indian braves so tall—
Our Governor and Boston people all!

I will copy the admirable speech of Governor Everett on that occasion, as I think it the happiest attempt ever made to meet the Indian in his own way, and catch the tone of his mind. It was said, in the newspapers, that Keokuck did actually shed tears when addressed as a father. If he did not with his eyes, he well might in his heart.

Everett's Speech

CHIEFS and warriors of the Sauks and Foxes, you are welcome to our hall of council.

Brothers! you have come a long way from home to visit your white brethren; we rejoice to take you by the hand.

Brothers! we have heard the names of your chiefs and warriors; our brothers, who have travelled into the West, have told us a great deal of the Sauks and Foxes; we rejoice to see you with our own eyes, and take you by the hand.

Brothers! we are called the Massachusetts. This is the name of the red men that once lived here. Their wigwams filled yonder field; their council fire was kindled on this spot. They were of the same great race as the Sauks and Misquakuiks.

Brothers! when our fathers came over the great waters, they were a small band. The red man stood upon the rock by the seaside, and saw our fathers. He might have pushed them into the water and drowned them. But he stretched out his arm to our fathers and said, "Welcome, white men!" Our fathers were hungry, and the red men gave them corn and venison. Our fathers were cold, and the red man wrapped them up in his blanket. We are now numerous and powerful, but we remember the kindness of the red man to our fathers. Brothers, you are welcome; we are glad to see you.

Brothers! our faces are pale, and your faces are dark; but our hearts are alike. The Great Spirit has made his children of different colors, but he loves them all.

Brothers! you dwell between the Mississippi and the Missouri. They are mighty rivers. They have one branch far East in the Alleghanies, and the other far West in the Rocky Mountains; but they flow together at last into one great stream, and run down together into the sea. In like manner, the red man dwells in the West, and the white man in the East, by the great waters; but they are all one branch, one family; it has many branches and one head.

Brothers! as you entered our council house, you beheld the image of our great Father Washington. It is a cold stone—it cannot speak. But he was the friend of the red man, and had his children live in peace with their red brethren. He is gone to the world of spirits. But his words have made a very deep print in our hearts, like the step of a strong buffalo on the soft clay of the prairie.

Brother! I perceive your little son between your knees. God preserve his life, my brother. He grows up before you like the tender sapling by the side of the mighty oak. May the oak and the sapling flourish a long time together. And when the mighty oak is fallen to the ground, may the young tree fill its place in the forest, and spread out its branches over the tribe like the parent trunk.

Brothers! I make you a short talk and again bid you welcome to our council hall.

NOT OFTEN have they been addressed with such intelligence and tact. The few who have not approached them with sordid rapacity, but from love to them, as men, and souls to be redeemed, have most frequently been persons intellectually too narrow, too straightly bound in sects or opinions, to throw themselves into the character or position of the Indians, or impart to them anything they can make available. The Christ shown them by these missionaries, is to them but a new and more powerful Manito; the signs of the new religion, but the fetiches that have aided the conquerors.

Here I will copy some remarks made by a discerning observer, on the methods used by the missionaries, and their natural results.

"Mr.— and myself had a very interesting conversation, upon the subject of the Indians, their character, capabilities, &c. After ten years' experience among them, he was forced to acknowledge, that the results of the missionary efforts had produced nothing calculated to encourage. He thought that there was an intrinsic disability in them, to rise above, or go beyond the sphere in which they had so long moved. He said, that even those Indians who had been converted, and who had adopted the habits of civilization, were very little improved in their real character; they were as selfish, as deceitful, and as indolent, as those who were still heathens. They had repaid the kindnesses of the missionaries with the basest ingratitude, killing their cattle and swine, and robbing them of their harvests, which they wantonly destroyed. He had abandoned the idea of effecting any general good to the Indians.

He had conscientious scruples, as to promoting an enterprise so hopeless, as that of missions among the Indians, by sending accounts to the east, that might induce philanthropic individuals to contribute to their support. In fact, the whole experience of his intercourse with them, seemed to have convinced him of the irremediable degradation of the race. Their fortitude under suffering, he considered the result of physical and mental insensibility; their courage, a mere animal excitement, which they found it necessary to inflame, before daring to meet a foe They have no constancy of purpose; and are, in fact, but little superior to the brutes, in point of moral development. It is not astonishing, that one looking upon the Indian character, from Mr.—'s point of view, should entertain such sentiments. The object of his intercourse with them was, to make them apprehend the mysteries of a theology, which, to the most enlightened, is an abstruse, metaphysical study; and it is not singular they should prefer their pagan superstitions, which address themselves more directly to the senses. Failing in the attempt to christianize, before civilizing them, he inferred, that, in the intrinsic degradation of their faculties, the obstacle was to be found."

Thus the missionary vainly attempts, by once or twice holding up the cross, to turn deer and tigers into lambs; vainly attempts to convince the red man that a heavenly mandate takes from him his broad lands. He bows his head, but does not at heart acquiesce. He cannot. It is not true; and if it were, the descent of blood through the same channels, for centuries, had formed habits of thought not so easily to be disturbed.

Amalgamation would afford the only true and profound means of civilization. But nature seems, like all else, to declare, that this race is fated to perish. Those of mixed blood fade early, and are not generally a fine race. They lose what is best in either type, rather than enhance the value of each, by mingling. There are exceptions, one or two such I know of, but this, it is said, is the general rule.

A traveller observes, that the white settlers, who live in the woods, soon become sallow, lanky, and dejected; the atmosphere of the trees does not agree with Caucasian lungs; and it is, perhaps, in part, an instinct of this, which causes the hatred of the new settlers towards trees. The Indian breathed the atmosphere of the forests freely; he loved their shade. As they are effaced from the land, he fleets too; a part of the same manifestation, which cannot linger behind its proper era.

The Chippewas have lately petitioned the state of Michigan, that they may be admitted as citizens; but this would be vain, unless they could be admitted, as brothers, to the heart of the white man. And while the latter feels that conviction of superiority, which enabled our Wisconsin friend to throw away the gun, and send the Indian to fetch it, he had need to be very good, and very wise, not to abuse his position. But the white man, as yet, is a half-tamed pirate, and avails himself, as much as ever, of the maxim, "Might makes right." All that civilization does for the generality, is to cover up this with a veil of subtle evasions and chicane, and here and there to rouse the individual mind to appeal to heaven against it.

I have no hope of liberalizing the missionary, of humanizing the sharks of trade, of infusing the conscientious drop into the flinty bosom of policy, of saving the Indian from immediate degradation, and speedy death. The whole sermon may be preached from the text, "Needs be that offences must come, yet wo them by whom they come." Yet, ere they depart, I wish there might be some masterly attempt to reproduce, in art or literature, what is proper to them, a kind of beauty and grandeur, which few of the every-day crowd have hearts to feel, yet which ought to leave in the world its monuments, to inspire the thought of genius through all ages. Nothing in this kind has been done masterly; since it was Clevenger's ambition, 'tis pity he had not opportunity to try fully his powers. We hope some other mind may be bent upon it, ere too late.

At present the only lively impress of their passage through the world is to be found in such books as Catlin's and some stories told by the old travellers, of which I purpose a brief account.

First, let me give another brief tale of the power exerted by the white man over the savage in a trying case, but, in this case, it was righteous, was moral power.

"We were looking over McKenney's trip to the Lakes, and, on observing the picture of Key-way-no-wut, or the Going Cloud, Mr. B. observed "Ah, that is the fellow I came near having a fight with," and he detailed at length the circumstances. This Indian was a very desperate character, and whom all the Leech lake band stood in fear of. He would shoot down any Indian who offended him, without the least hesitation, and had become quite the bully of that part of the tribe. The trader at Leech lake warned Mr. B. to beware of him, and said that he once, when he (the trader) refused to give up to him his stock of wild rice, went and got his gun and tomahawk, and shook the tomahawk over his head saying, "*Now,* give me your wild rice." The trader complied with his exaction, but not so did Mr. B. in the adventure which I am about to relate. Key-way-no-wut came frequently to him with furs, wishing him to give for them cotton cloth, sugar, flour, &c. Mr. B.

explained to him that he could not trade for furs, as he was sent there as a teacher, and that it would be like putting his hand into the fire to do so, as the traders would inform against him, and he would be sent out of the country. At the same time, he *gave* him the articles which he wished. Key-way-no-wut found this a very convenient way of getting what he wanted, and followed up this sort of game, until, at last, it became insupportable. One day the Indian brought a very large otter skin, and said "I want to get for this ten pounds of sugar, and some flour and cloth," adding, "I am not like other Indians, *I* want to pay for what I get." Mr. B. found that he must either be robbed of all he had by submitting to these exactions, or take a stand at once. He thought, however, he would try to avoid a scrape, and told his customer he had not so much sugar to spare. "Give me then," said he, "what you can spare," and Mr. B. thinking to make him back out, told him he would give him five pounds of sugar for his skin. "Take it," said the Indian. He left the skin, telling Mr. B. to take good care of it. Mr. B. took it at once to the trader's store, and related the circumstance, congratulating himself that he had got rid of the Indian's exactions. But, in about a month, Key-way-no-wut appeared bringing some dirty Indian sugar, and said "I have brought back the sugar that I borrowed of you, and I want my otter skin back." Mr. B. told him, "I *bought* an otter skin of you, but if you will return the other articles you have got for it, perhaps I can get it for you." "Where is the skin?" said he very quickly, "what have you done with it?" Mr. B. replied it was in the trader's store, where he (the Indian) could not get it. At this information he was furious, laid his hands on his knife and tomahawk, and commanded Mr. B. to bring it at once. Mr. B. found this was the crisis, where he must take a stand or be "rode over rough shod" by this man; his wife, who was present was much alarmed, and begged he would get the skin for the Indian, but he told her that "either he or the Indian would soon be master of his house, and if she was afraid to see it decided which was to be so, she had better retire." He turned to Key-way-no-wut, and addressed him in a stern voice as follows: "I will *not* give you the skin. How often have you come to my house, and I have shared with you what I had. I gave you tobacco when you were well, and medicine when you were sick, and you never went away from my wigwam with your hands empty. And this is the way you return my treatment to you. I had thought you were a man and a chief, but you are not, you are nothing but an old woman. Leave this house, and never enter it again." Mr. B. said he expected the Indian would attempt his life when he said this, but that he had placed himself in a position so that he could defend himself, and he looked straight into the Indian's eye, and like other wild beasts he quailed before the glance of mental and moral courage. He calmed down at once, and soon began to make apologies. Mr. B. then told him kindly, but firmly, that, if he wished to walk in the same path with him, he must walk as straight as the crack on the floor before them; adding that he would not walk with anybody who would jostle him by walking so crooked as he had done. He was perfectly tamed, and Mr. B. said he never had any more trouble with him."

The conviction here livingly enforced of the superiority on the side of the white man, was thus expressed by the Indian orator at Mackinaw while we were there. After the customary compliments about sun, dew, &c., "This," said he, "is the difference between the white and the red man; the white man looks to the future and paves the way for posterity." This is a statement uncommonly refined for an Indian; but one of the gentlemen present, who understood the Chippeway, vouched for it as a literal rendering of his phrases; and he did indeed touch the vital point of difference. But the Indian, if he understands, cannot make use of his intelligence. The fate of his people is against it, and Pontiac and Philip have no more chance, than Julian in the times of old.

Now that I am engaged on this subject, let me give some notices of writings upon it, read either at Mackinaw or since my return.

Mrs. Jameson made such good use of her brief visit to these regions, as leaves great cause to regret she did not stay longer and go farther; also, that she did not make more use of her acquaintance with, indeed, adoption by, the Johnson family. Mr. Johnson seems to have been almost the only white man who knew how to regard with due intelligence and nobleness, his connexion with the race. Neither French or English, of any powers of sympathy, or poetical apprehension, have lived among the Indians without high feelings of enjoyment. Perhaps no luxury has been greater, than that experienced by the persons, who, sent either by trade or war, during the last century, into these majestic regions, found guides and shelter amid the children of the soil, and recognized in a form so new and of such varied, yet simple, charms, the tie of brotherhood.

But these, even Sir William Johnson, whose life, surrounded by the Indians in his castle on the Mohawk, is described with such vivacity by Mrs. Grant, have been men better fitted to enjoy and adapt themselves to this life, than to observe and record it. The very faculties that made it so easy for them to live in the present moment, were likely to unfit them for keeping its chronicle. Men, whose life is full and instinctive, care little for the pen. But the father of Mrs. Schoolcraft seems to have taken pleasure in observation and comparison, and to have imparted the same tastes to his children. They have enough of European culture to have a standard, by which to judge their native habits and inherited lore.

By the premature death of Mrs. Schoolcraft was lost a mine of poesy, to which few had access, and from which Mrs. Jameson would have known how to coin a series of medals for the history of this ancient people. We might have known in clear outline, as now we shall not, the growths of religion and philosophy, under the influences of this climate and scenery, from such suggestions as nature and the teachings of the inward mind presented.

Now we can only gather that they had their own theory of the history of this globe; had perceived a gap in its genesis, and tried to fill it up by the intervention of some secondary power, with moral sympathies. They have observed the action of fire and water upon this earth; also that the dynasty of animals has yielded to that of man. With these animals they have profound sympathy, and are always trying to restore to them their lost honors. On the rattlesnake, the beaver, and the bear, they seem to look with a mixture of sympathy and veneration, as on their fellow settlers in these realms. There is something that appeals powerfully to the imagination in the ceremonies they observe, even in case of destroying one of these animals. I will say more of this by-and-by.

The dog they cherish as having been once a spirit of high intelligence; and now in its fallen and imprisoned state, given to man as his special companion. He is therefore to them a sacrifice of peculiar worth: whether to a guardian spirit or a human friend. Yet nothing would be a greater violation than giving the remains of a sacrificial feast to the dogs, or even suffering them to touch the bones.

Similar inconsistences may be observed in the treatment of the dog by the white man. He is the most cherished companion in the familiar walks of many men; his virtues form the theme of poetry and history; the nobler races present grand traits, and are treated with proportionate respect. Yet the epithets dog and hound, are there set apart to express the uttermost contempt.

Goethe, who abhorred dogs, has selected that animal for the embodiment of the modern devil, who, in earlier times, chose rather the form of the serpent.

There is, indeed, something that peculiarly breaks in on the harmony of nature, in the bark of the dog, and that does not at all correspond with the softness and sagacity observable in his eye. The baying the moon, I have been inclined to set down as an unfavorable indication; but, since Fourier has found out that the moon is dead, and "no better than carrion;" and the Greeks have designated her as Hecate, the deity of suicide and witchcraft, the dogs are perhaps in the right.

They have among them the legend of the carbuncle, so famous in oriental mythos. Adair states that they believe this fabulous gem may be found on the spot where the rattlesnake has been destroyed.

If they have not the archetypal man, they have the archetypal animal, "the grandfather of all beavers;" to them, who do not know the elephant, this is the symbol of wisdom, as the rattlesnake and bear of power.

I will insert here a little tale about the bear, which has not before appeared in print, as representing their human way of looking on these animals, even when engaged in their pursuit. To me such stories give a fine sense of the lively perceptions and exercise of fancy, enjoyed by them in their lives of woodcraft:

Muckwa, or the Bear

A YOUNG INDIAN, who lived a great while ago, when he was quite young killed a bear; and the tribe from that circumstance called him Muckwa. As he grew up he became an expert hunter, and his favorite game was the bear, many of which he killed. One day he started off to a river far remote from the lodges of his tribe, and where berries and grapes were very plenty, in pursuit of bears. He hunted all day but found nothing; and just at night he came to some lodges which he thought to be those of some of his tribe. He approached the largest of them, lifted the curtain at its entrance, and went in, when he perceived the inmates to be bears, who were seated around the fire smoking. He said nothing, but seated himself also and smoked the pipe which they offered him, in silence. An old grey bear, who was the chief, ordered supper to be brought for him, and after he had eaten it, addressed him as follows: "My son, I am glad to see you come among us in a friendly manner. You have been a great hunter, and all the she-bears of our tribe tremble when they hear your name. But cease to trouble us, and come and live with me; we have a very pleasant life, living upon the fruits of the earth; and in the winter, instead of being obliged to hunt and travel through the deep snow, we sleep soundly until the sun unchains the streams, and makes the tender buds put forth for our subsistence. I will give you my daughter for a wife, and we will live happily together." Muckwa was inclined to accept the old bear's offer; but when he saw the daughter, who came and took off his wet moccasins, and gave him dry ones, he thought that he had never seen any Indian woman so beautiful. He accepted the offer of the chief of the bears, and lived with his wife very happily for some time. He had by her two sons, one of whom was like an Indian, and the other like a bear. When the bear-child was oppressed with heat, his mother would take him into the deep cool caves, while the Indian-child would shiver with cold, and cry after her in vain. As the autumn advanced, the bears began to go out in search of acorns, and then the she-bear said to Muckwa, "Stay at home here and watch our house, while I go to gather some nuts." She departed and was gone for some days with her people. By-and-by Muckwa became tired of staying at home, and thought that he would go off to a distance and resume his favorite bear-hunting. He accordingly started off, and at last came to a grove of lofty oaks, which were full of large acorns. He found signs of bear, and soon espied a fat she-bear on the top of a tree. He shot at her with a good aim, and she fell, pierced by his unerring arrow. He went up to her, and found it was his sister-in-law, who reproached him with his cruelty, and told him to return to his own people. Muckwa returned quietly home, and pretended not to have left his lodge. However, the old chief understood, and was disposed to kill him in revenge; but his wife found means to avert her father's anger. The winter season now coming on, Muckwa prepared to accompany his wife into winter quarters; they selected a large tamarack tree, which was hollow, and lived there comfortably until a party of hunters discovered their retreat. The she-bear told Muckwa to remain quietly in the tree, and that she would decoy off the hunters. She came out of the hollow, jumped from a bough of the tree, and escaped unharmed, although the hunters shot after her. Some time after, she returned to the tree, and told Muckwa that he had better go back to his own people. "Since you have lived among us," said she, "we have nothing but ill-fortune; you have killed my sister; and now your friends have followed your footsteps to our retreats to kill us. The Indian and the bear cannot live in the same lodge, for the Master of Life has appointed for them different habitations." So Muckwa returned with his son to his own people; but he never after would shoot a she-bear, for fear that he should kill his wife.

I admire this story for the *savoir faire,* the nonchalance, the Vivian Greyism of Indian life. It is also a poetical expression of the sorrows of unequal relations; those in which the Master of Life was not consulted. Is it not pathetic; the picture of the mother carrying off the child that was like herself into the deep, cool caves, while the other, shivering with cold, cried after her in vain? The moral, too, of Muckwa's return to the bear lodges, thinking to hide his sin by silence, while it was at once discerned by those connected with him, is fine.

We have a nursery tale, of which children never weary, of a little boy visiting a bear house and holding intercourse with them on terms as free as Muckwa did. So, perhaps, the child of Norman-Saxon blood, no less than the Indian, finds some pulse of the Orson in his veins.

As they loved to draw the lower forms of nature up to them, divining their histories, and imitating their ways, in their wild dances and paintings; even so did they love to look upward and people the atmosphere that enfolds the earth, with fairies and manitoes. The sister, obliged to leave her brother on the earth, bids him look up at evening, and he will see her painting her face in the west.

All places, distinguished in any way by nature, aroused the feelings of worship, which, however ignorant, are always elevating. See as instances in this kind, the stories of Nanabojou, and the Winnebago Prince, at the falls of St. Anthony.

As with the Greeks, beautiful legends grow up which express the aspects of various localities. From the distant sand-banks in the lakes, glittering in the sun, come stories of enchantresses combing, on the shore, the long golden hair of a beautiful daughter. The Lorelei of the Rhine, with her syren song, and the sad events that follow, is found on the lonely rocks of Lake Superior.

The story to which I now refer, may be found in a book called Life on the Lakes, or, a Trip to the Pictured Rocks. There are two which purport to be Indian tales; one is simply a romantic narrative, connected with a spot at Mackinaw, called Robinson's Folly. This, no less than the other, was unknown to those persons I saw on the island; but as they seem entirely beyond the powers of the person who writes them down, and the other one has the profound and original meaning of Greek tragedy, I believe they must be genuine legends.

The one I admire is the story of a young warrior, who goes to keep, on these lonely rocks, the fast which is to secure him vision of his tutelary spirit. There the loneliness is broken by the voice of sweet music from the water. The Indian knows well that to break the fast, which is the crisis of his life, by turning his attention from seeking the Great Spirit, to any lower object, will deprive him through life of heavenly protection, probably call down the severest punishment.

But the temptation is too strong for him; like the victims of the Lorelei, he looks, like them beholds a maiden of unearthly beauty, to him the harbinger of earthly wo.

The development of his fate, that succeeds; of love, of heart-break, of terrible revenge, which back upon itself recoils, may vie with anything I have ever known of stern tragedy, is altogether unlike any other form, and with all the peculiar expression we see lurking in the Indian eye. The demon is not frightful and fantastic, like those that haunt the German forest; but terribly human, as if of full manhood, reared in the shadow of the black forests. An Indian sarcasm vibrates through it, which, with Indian fortitude, defies the inevitable torture.

The Indian is steady to that simple creed, which forms the basis of all this mythology; that there is a God, and a life beyond this; a right and wrong which each man can see, betwixt which each man should choose; that good brings with it its reward and vice its punishment. Their moral code, if not refined as that of civilized nations, is clear and noble in the stress laid upon truth and fidelity. And all unprejudiced observers bear testimony that the Indians, until broken from their old anchorage by intercourse with the whites, who offer them, instead, a religion of which they furnish neither interpretation nor example, were singularly virtuous, if virtue be allowed to consist in a man's acting up to his own ideas of right.

Old Adair, who lived forty years among the Indians; not these tribes, indeed, but the southern Indians, does great justice to their religious aspiration. He is persuaded that they are Jews, and his main object is to identify their manifold ritual, and customs connected with it, with that of the Jews. His narrative contains much that is worthless, and is written in the most tedious manner of the folios. But his devotion to the records of ancient Jewry, has really given him power to discern congenial traits elsewhere, and for the sake of what he has expressed of the noble side of Indian character, we pardon him our having to wade through so many imbecilities.

An infidel, he says, is, in their language, "one who has shaken hands with the accursed speech;" a religious man, "one who has shaken hands with the beloved speech." If this be a correct definition, we could wish Adair more religious.

He gives a fine account of their methods of purification. These show a deep reliance on the sustaining Spirit. By fasting and prayer they make ready for all important decisions and actions. Even for the war path, on which he is likely to endure such privations, the brave prepares by a solemn fast. His reliance is on the spirit in which he goes forth.

We may contrast with the opinion of the missionary, as given on a former page, the testimony of one, who knew them as Adair did, to their heroism under torture.

He gives several stories, illustrative both of their courage, fortitude, and resource in time of peril, of which I will cite only the two first.

"The Shawano Indians took a Muskohge warrior, known by the name of "Old Scrany;" they bastinadoed him in the usual manner, and condemned him to the fiery torture. He underwent a great deal, without showing any concern; his countenance and behavior were as if he suffered not the least pain, and was formed beyond the common laws of nature. He told them, with a bold voice, that he was a very noted warrior, and gained most of his martial preferments at the expense of their nation, and was desirous of showing them in the act of dying that he was still as much their superior, as when he headed his gallant countrymen against them. That, although he had fallen into their hands, in forfeiting the protection of the divine power, by some impurity or other, yet he had still so much virtue remaining, as would enable him to punish himself more exquisitely than all their despicable, ignorant crowd could possibly do, if they gave him liberty by untying him, and would hand to him one of the red hot gun-barrels out of the fire. The proposal, and his method of address, appeared so exceedingly bold and uncommon, that his request was granted. Then he suddenly seized one end of the red hot barrel, and, brandishing it from side to side, he found his way through the armed and surprised multitude, and leaped down a prodigious steep and high bank into a branch of the river, dived through it, ran over a small island, passed the other branch amidst a shower of bullets, and, though numbers of his eager enemies were in close pursuit of him, he got to a bramble swamp, and in that naked, mangled condition, reached his own country. He proved a sharp thorn in their side afterwards, to the day of his death.

The Shawano also captivated a warrior of the Anantooiah, and put him to the stake, according to their usual cruel solemnities. Having unconcernedly suffered much sharp torture, he told them with scorn, they did not know how to punish a noted enemy, therefore he was willing to teach them, and would confirm the truth of his assertion, if they allowed him the opportunity. Accordingly he requested of them a pipe and some tobacco, which was given him; as soon as he lighted it, he sat down, naked as he was, on the women's burning torches, that were within his circle, and continued smoking his pipe without the least discomposure. On this a head warrior leaped up, and said they had seen, plain enough, that he was a warrior, and not afraid of dying; nor should he have died, but that he was both spoiled by the fire, and devoted to it by their laws; however, though he was a very dangerous enemy, and his nation a treacherous people, it should appear they paid a regard to bravery, even in one, who was marked over the body with war streaks at the cost of many lives of their beloved kindred. And then, by way of favor, he, with his friendly tomahawk, put an end to all his pains: though this merciful but bloody instrument was ready some minutes before it gave the blow, yet, I was assured, the spectators could not perceive the sufferer to change, either his posture, or his steady, erect countenance in the least."

Some stories as fine, but longer, follow. In reference to which Adair says, "The intrepid behavior of these red stoics, their surprising contempt of and indifference to life or death, instead of lessening, helps to confirm our belief of that supernatural power, which supported the great number of primitive martyrs, who sealed the Christian faith with their blood. The Indians have as much belief and expectation of a future state, as the greater part of the Israelites seem to have. But the Christians of the first centuries, may justly be said to exceed even the most heroic American Indians, for they bore the bitterest persecution with steady patience, in imitation of their divine leader Messiah, in full confidence of divine support and of a glorious recompense of reward; and, instead of even wishing for revenge on their cruel enemies and malicious tormentors, (which is the chief principle that actuates the Indians,) they not only forgave them, but, in the midst of their tortures, earnestly prayed for them, with composed countenances, sincere love, and unabated fervor. And not only men of different conditions, but the delicate women and children suffered with constancy, and died praying for their tormentors: the Indian women and children, and their young men untrained to war, are incapable of displaying the like patience and magnanimity."

Thus impartially looks the old trader. I meant to have inserted other passages, that of the encampment at Yowanne, and the horse race to which he challenged them, to show how well he could convey in his garrulous fashion the whole presence of Indian life. That of Yowanne, especially, takes my fancy much, by its wild and subtle air, and the old-nurse fashion in which every look and gesture is detailed. His enjoyment, too, at outwitting the Indians in their own fashion is contagious. There is a fine history of a young man driven by a presentiment to run upon his death. But I find, to copy these stories, as they stand, would half fill this little book, and compression would spoil them, so I must wait some other occasion.

The story, later, of giving an Indian liquid fire to swallow, I give at full length, to show how a kind-hearted man and one well disposed towards them, can treat them, and view his barbarity as a joke. It is not then so much wonder, if the trader, with this same feeling that they may be treated, (as however brutes should not be,) brutally, mixes red pepper and damaged tobacco with the rum, intending in their fever to fleece them of all they possess.

Like Murray and Henry, he has his great Indian chief, who represents what the people should be, as Pericles and Phocion what the Greek people should be. If we are entitled to judge by its best fruits of the goodness of the tree, Adair's Red Shoes, and Henry's Wawatam, should make us respect the first possessors of our country, and doubt whether we are in all ways worthy to fill their place. Of the whole tone of character, judgment may be formed by what is said of the death of Red Shoes.

"This chief, by his several transcendent qualities had arrived at the highest pitch of the red glory. . . .

He was murdered, for the sake of a French reward, by one of his own countrymen. He had the misfortune to be taken very sick on the road, and to lodge apart from the camp, according to their custom. A Judas, tempted by the high reward of the French for killing him, officiously pretended to take great care of him. While Red Shoes kept his face toward him, the barbarian had such feelings of awe and pity that he had not power to perpetrate his wicked design; but when he turned his back, then gave the fatal shot. In this manner fell this valuable brave man, by hands that would have trembled to attack him on an equality."

Adair, with all his sympathy for the Indian, mixes quite unconsciously some white man's views of the most decided sort. For instance, he recommends that the tribes be stimulated as much as possible to war with each other, that they may the more easily and completely be kept under the dominion of the whites, and he gives the following record of brutality as quite a jocose and adroit procedure.

"I told him, on his importuning me further, that I had a full bottle of the water of *ane hoome,* "bitter ears," meaning long pepper, of which he was ignorant. We were of opinion that his eager thirst for liquor, as well as his ignorance of the burning quality of the pepper, would induce the bacchanal to try it. He accordingly applauded my generous disposition, and said his heart had all along told him I would not act beneath the character I bore among his country people. The bottle was brought, I laid it on the table, and then told him, as he was spitting very much, (a general custom among the Indians when they are eager for anything,) if I drank it all at one sitting it would cause me to spit in earnest, as I used it only when I ate, and then very moderately; but though I loved it, if his heart was very poor for it, I should be silent, and not the least grudge him for pleasing his mouth. He said, 'your heart is honest, indeed; I thank you, for it is good to my heart, and makes it greatly to rejoice.' Without any further ceremony he seized the bottle, uncorked it, and swallowed a large quantity of the burning liquid, till he was nearly strangled. He gasped for a considerable time, and as soon as he recovered his breath, he said *Hah,* and soon after kept stroking his throat with his right hand. When the violence of this burning draught was pretty well over, he began to flourish away in praise of the strength of the liquor and bounty of the giver. He then went to his companion and held the liquor to his mouth according to custom, till he took several hearty swallows. This Indian seemed rather more sensible of its fiery quality than the other, for it suffocated him for a considerable time; but as soon as he recovered his breath, he tumbled about the floor like a drunken person. In this manner they finished the whole bottle, into which two others had been decanted. The burning liquor so highly inflamed their bodies, that one of the Choctaws, to cool his inward parts, drank water till he almost burst; the other, rather than bear the ridicule of the people, and the inward fire that distracted him, drowned himself the second night after in a broad and shallow clay hole.

There was an incident similar, which happened among the Cherokees. When all the liquor was expended the Indians went home, leading with them, at my request, those that were drunk. One, however, soon came back, and earnestly importuned me for more Nawahti, which signifies both physic and spirituous liquor. They, as they are now become great liars, suspect all others of being infected with their own disposition and principles. The more I excused myself, the more anxious he grew, so as to become offensive. I then told him I had only one quarter of a bottle of strong physic, which sick people might drink in small quantities, for the cure of inward pains: and, laying it down before him, I declared I did not on any account choose to part with it, but as his speech had become very long and troublesome, he might do just as his heart directed him concerning it. He took it up, saying, his heart was very poor for physic, but he would cure it, and make it quite straight. The bottle contained three gills of strong spirits of turpentine, which, in a short time he drank off. Such a quantity would have demolished me or any white person. The Indians, in general, are either capable of suffering exquisite pain longer than we are, or of showing more constancy and composure in their torments. The troublesome visiter soon tumbled down and foamed prodigiously. I then sent for some of his relations to carry him home. They came; I told them he drank greedily, and too much of the physic. They said, it was his usual custom, when the red people bought the English physic. They gave him a decoction of proper herbs and roots, the next day sweated him, repeated the former draught, and he got well. As these turpentine spirits did not inebriate him, but only inflamed his intestines, he well remembered the burning quality of my favorite physic, and cautioned the rest from ever teasing me for any physic I had concealed in any sort of bottles for my own use; otherwise they might be sure it would spoil them like the eating of fire."

We are pleased to note that the same white man, who so resolutely resisted the encroachments of Key-way-no-wut, devised a more humane experiment in a similar dilemma.

"Mr. B. told me that, when he first went into the Indian country, they got the taste of his peppermint, and, after that, colics prevailed among them to an alarming extent, till Mrs. B. made a strong decoction of flagroot, and gave them in place of their favorite medicine. This effected, as might be supposed, a radical cure."

I am inclined to recommend Adair to the patient reader, if such may be found in these United States, with the assurance that, if he will have tolerance for its intolerable prolixity and dryness, he will find, on rising from the book, that he has partaken of an infusion of real Indian bitters, such as may not be drawn from any of the more attractive memoirs on the same subject.

Another book of interest, from its fidelity and candid spirit, though written without vivacity, and by a person neither of large mind nor prepared for various inquiry, is Carver's Travels, "for three years throughout the interior parts of America, for more than five thousand miles."

He set out from Boston in "June, 1786, and proceeded, by way of Albany and Niagara, to Michilimackinac, a fort situated between the Lakes Huron and Michigan, and distant from Boston 1300 miles."

It is interesting to follow his footsteps in these localities, though they be not bold footsteps.

He mentions the town of the Sacs, on the Wisconsin, as the largest and best built he saw, "composed of ninety houses, each large enough for several families. These are built of hewn plank, neatly jointed, and covered with bark so compactly as to keep out the most penetrating rains. Before the doors are placed comfortable sheds, in which the inhabitants sit, when the weather will permit, and smoke their pipes. The streets are regular and spacious. In their plantations, which lie adjacent to their houses, and which are neatly laid out, they raise great quantities of Indian corn, beans and melons."

Such settlements compare very well with those which were found on the Mohawk. It was of such that the poor Indian was thinking, whom our host saw gazing on the shore of Nomabbin lake.

He mentions the rise and fall of the lake-waters, by a tide of three feet, once in seven years,—a phenomenon not yet accounted for.

His view of the Indian character is truly impartial. He did not see it so fully drawn out by circumstances as Henry did, (of whose narrative we shall presently speak,) but we come to similar results from the two witnesses. They are in every feature Romans, as described by Carver, and patriotism their leading impulse. He deserves the more credit for the justice he is able to do them, that he had undergone the terrors of death at their hands, when present at the surrender of one of the forts, and had seen them in that mood which they express by drinking the blood and eating the hearts of their enemies, yet is able to understand the position of their minds, and allow for their notions of duty.

No selfish views, says he, influence their advice, or obstruct their consultations.

Let me mention here the use they make of their vapor baths. "When about to decide on some important measure, they go into them, thus cleansing the skin and carrying off any peccant humors, so that the body may, as little as possible, impede the mind by any ill conditions."

They prepare the bath for one another when any arrangement is to be made between families, on the opposite principle to the whites, who make them drunk before bargaining with them. The bath serves them instead of a cup of coffee, to stimulate the thinking powers.

He mentions other instances of their kind of delicacy, which, if different from ours, was, perhaps, more rigidly observed.

Lovers never spoke of love till the daylight was quite gone.

"If an Indian goes to visit any particular person in a family, he mentions for whom his visit is intended, and the rest of the family, immediately retiring to the other end of the hut or tent, are careful not to come near enough to interrupt them during the whole of the conversation."

In cases of divorce, which was easily obtained, the advantage rested with the woman. The reason given is indeed contemptuous toward her, but a chivalric direction is given to the contempt.

"The children of the Indians are always distinguished by the name of the mother, and, if a woman marries several husbands, and has issue by each of them, they are called after her. The reason they give for this is, that, 'as their offspring are indebted to the father for the soul, the invisible part of their essence, and to the mother for their corporeal and apparent part, it is most rational that they should be distinguished by the name of the latter, from whom they indubitably derive their present being.' "

This is precisely the division of functions made by Ovid, as the father sees Hercules perishing on the funeral pyre.

> "Nec nisi materna Vulcanum parte potentem
> Sentiet. Æternuum est a me quod traxit et expers
> Atque immune necis, nullaqe domabile flamma."

He is not enough acquainted with natural history to make valuable observations. He mentions, however, as did my friend, the Indian girl, that those splendid flowers, the Wickapee and the root of the Wake-Robin, afford valuable medicines. Here, as in the case of the Lobelia, nature has blazoned her drug in higher colors than did ever quack doctor.

He observes some points of resemblance between the Indians and Tartars, but they are trivial, and not well considered. He mentions that the Tartars have the same custom, with some of these tribes, of shaving all the head except a tuft on the crown. Catlin says this is intended to afford a convenient means by which to take away the scalp; for they consider it a great disgrace to have the foeman neglect this, as if he considered the conquest, of which the scalp is the certificate, no addition to his honors.

"The Tartars," he says, "had a similar custom of sacrificing the dog; and among the Kamschatkans was a dance resembling the dog-dance of our Indians."

My friend, who joined me at Mackinaw, happened, on the homeward journey, to see a little Chinese girl, who had been sent over by one of the missions, and observed that, in features, complexion, and gesture, she was a counterpart to the little Indian girls she had just seen playing about on the lake shore.

The parentage of these tribes is still an interesting subject of speculation, though, if they be not created for this region, they have become so assimilated to it as to retain little trace of any other. To me it seems most probable, that a peculiar race was bestowed on each region, as the lion on one latitude and the white bear on another. As man has two natures—one, like that of the plants and animals, adapted to the uses and enjoyments of this planet, another, which presages and demands a higher sphere—he is constantly breaking bounds, in proportion as the mental gets the better of the mere instinctive existence. As yet, he loses in harmony of being what he gains in height and extension; the civilized man is a larger mind, but a more imperfect nature than the savage.

It is pleasant to meet, on the borders of these two states, one of those persons who combines some of the good qualities of both; not, as so many of these adventurers do, the rapaciousness and cunning of the white, with the narrowness and ferocity of the savage, but the sentiment and thoughtfulness of the one, with the boldness, personal resource, and fortitude of the other.

Such a person was Alexander Henry, who left Quebec in 1760, for Mackinaw and the Sault St. Marie, and remained in those regions, of which he has given us a most lively account, sixteen years.

His visit to Mackinaw was premature; the Indians were far from satisfied; they hated their new masters. From the first, the omens were threatening, and before many months passed, the discontent ended in the seizing of the fort at Mackinaw and massacre of its garrison; on which occasion Henry's life was saved by a fine act of Indian chivalry.

Wawatam, a distinguished chief, had found himself drawn, by strong affinity, to the English stranger. He had adopted him as a brother, in the Indian mode. When he found that his tribe had determined on the slaughter of the whites, he obtained permission to take Henry away with him, if he could. But not being able to prevail on him, as he could not assign the true reasons, he went away deeply saddened, but not without obtaining a promise that his brother should not be injured. The reason he was obliged to go, was, that his tribe felt his affections were so engaged, that his self-command could not be depended on to keep their secret. Their promise was not carefully observed, and, in consequence of the baseness of a French Canadian in whose house Henry took refuge,—baseness such as has not, even by their foes, been recorded of any Indian, his life was placed in great hazard. But Wawatam returned in time to save him. The scene in which he appears, accompanied by his wife—who seems to have gone hand in hand with him in this matter—lays down all his best things in a heap, in the middle of the hall, as a ransom for the captive, and his little, quiet speech, are as good as the Iliad. They have the same simplicity, the same lively force and tenderness.

Henry goes away with his adopted brother, and lives for some time among the tribe. The details of this life are truly interesting. One time he is lost for several days while on the chase. The description of these weary, groping days, the aspect of natural objects and of the feelings thus inspired, and the mental change after a good night's sleep, form a little episode worthy the epic muse. He stripped off the entire bark of a tree for a coverlet in the snow-storm, going to sleep with "the most distracted thoughts in the world, while the wolves around seemed to know the distress to which he was reduced;" but he waked in the morning another man, clear-headed, able to think out the way to safety.

When living in the lodge, he says: "At one time much scarcity of food prevailed. We were often twenty-four hours without eating; and when in the morning we had no victuals for the day before us, the custom was to black our faces with grease and charcoal, and exhibit, through resignation, a temper as cheerful as in the midst of plenty." This wise and dignified proceeding reminds one of a charming expression of what is best in French character, as described by Rigolette, in the Mysteries of Paris, of the household of Père Cretu and Ramonette.

He bears witness to much virtue among them. Their superstitions, as described by him, seem childlike and touching. He gives with much humor, traits that show their sympathy with the lower animals, such as I have mentioned. He speaks of them as, on the whole, taciturn, because their range of topics is so limited, and seems to have seen nothing of their talent for narration. Catlin, on the contrary, describes them as lively and garrulous, and says, that their apparent taciturnity among the whites is owing to their being surprised at what they see, and unwilling, from pride, to show that they are so, as well as that they have little to communicate on their side, that they think will be valuable.

After peace was restored, and Henry lived long at Mackinaw and the Sault St. Marie, as a trader, the traits of his biography and intercourse with the Indians, are told in the same bold and lively style. I wish I had room for many extracts, as the book is rare.

He made a journey one winter on snow shoes, to Prairie du Chien, which is of romantic interest as displaying his character. His companions could not travel nearly so fast as he did, and detained him on the way. Provisions fell short; soon they were ready to perish of starvation. Apprehending this, on a long journey, in the depth of winter, broken by no hospitable station, Henry had secreted some chocolate. When he saw his companions ready to lie down and die, he would heat water, boil in it a square of this, and give them. By the heat of the water and the fancy of nourishment, they would be revived, and induced to proceed a little further. At last they saw antlers sticking up from the ice, and found the body of an elk, which had sunk in and been frozen there, and thus preserved to save their lives. On this "and excellent soup" made from bones they found they were sustained to their journey's end; thus furnishing, says Henry, one other confirmation of the truth, that "despair was not made for man;" this expression, and his calm consideration for the Canadian women that was willing to betray him to death, denote the two sides of a fine character.

He gives an interesting account of the tribe called "The Weepers," on account of the rites with which they interrupt their feasts in honor of their friends.

He gives this humorous notice of a chief, called "The Great Road."

"The chief, to whose kindly reception we were so much indebted, was of a complexion rather darker than that of the Indians in general. His appearance was greatly injured by the condition of his hair, and this was the result of an extraordinary superstition.

"The Indians universally fix upon a particular object as sacred to themselves—as the giver of prosperity and as their preserver from evil. The choice is determined either by a dream or some strong predilection of fancy, and usually falls upon an animal, part of an animal, or something else which is to be met with by land, or by water; but the Great Road had made choice of his hair, placing, like Samson, all his safety in this portion of his proper substance! His hair was the fountain of all his happiness; it was his strength and his weapon—his spear and his shield. It preserved him in battle, directed him in the chase, watched over him in the march, and gave length of days to his wives and children. Hair, of a quality like this, was not to be profaned by the touch of human hands. I was assured that it never had been cut nor combed from his childhood upward, and that when any part of it fell from his head, he treasured that part with care; meanwhile, it did not escape all care, even while growing on the head, but was in the especial charge of a spirit, who dressed it while the owner slept. The spirit's style of hair-dressing was peculiar, the hair being matted into ropes, which spread in all directions."

I insert the following account of a visit from some Indians to him at Mackinaw, with a design to frighten him, and one to Carver, for the same purpose, as very descriptive of Indian manners:

"At two o'clock in the afternoon, the Chippeways came to my house, about sixty in number, and headed by Mina-va-va-na, their chief. They walked in single file, each with his tomahawk in one hand, and scalping knife in the other. Their bodies were naked, from the waist upwards, except in a few examples, where blankets were thrown loosely over the shoulders. Their faces were painted with charcoal, worked up with grease; their bodies with white clay in patterns of various fancies. Some had feathers thrust through their noses, and their heads decorated with the same. It is unnecessary to dwell on the sensations with which I beheld the approach of this uncouth, if not frightful, assemblage."

"Looking out, I saw about twenty naked young Indians, the most perfect in their shape, and by far the handsomest I had ever seen, coming towards me, and dancing as they approached to the music of their drums. At every ten or twelve yards they halted, and set up their yells and cries.

When they reached my tent I asked them to come in, which, without deigning to make me any answer, they did. As I observed they were painted red and black, as they are when they go against an enemy, and perceived that some parts of the war-dance were intermixed with their other movements, I doubted not but they were set on by the hostile chief who refused my salutation. I therefore determined to sell my life as dearly as possible. To this purpose I received them sitting on my chest, with my gun and pistols beside me; and ordered my men to keep a watchful eye on them, and be also on their guard.

The Indians being entered, they continued their dance alternately, singing at the same time of their heroic exploits, and the superiority of their race over every other people. To enforce their language, though it was uncommonly nervous and expressive, and such as would of itself have carried terror to the firmest heart; at the end of every period they struck their war-clubs against the poles of my tent with such violence, that I expected every moment it would have tumbled upon us. As each of them in dancing round passed by me, they placed their right hands over their eyes, and coming close to me, looked me steadily in the face, which I could not construe into a token of friendship. My men gave themselves up for lost; and I acknowledge for my own part, that I never found my apprehensions more tumultuous on any occasion."

He mollified them, however, in the end by presents.

It is pity that Lord Edward Fitzgerald did not leave a detailed account of his journey through the wilderness, where he was pilot of an unknown course for twenty days, as Murray and Henry have of theirs. There is nothing more interesting than to see the civilized man thus thrown wholly on himself and his manhood, and *not* found at fault.

McKenney and Hall's book upon the Indians is a valuable work. The portraits of the chiefs alone would make a history, and they are beautifully colored.

Most of the anecdotes may be found again in Drake's Book of the Indians; which will afford a useful magazine to their future historian.

I shall, however, cite a few of them, as especially interesting to myself.

Of Guess, the inventor of the Cherokee alphabet, it was observable in the picture, and observed in the text, that his face had an oriental cast. The same, we may recall, was said of that of the Seeress of Prevorst, and the circumstance presents pleasing analogies. Intellect dawning through features still simple and national, presents very different apparitions from the "expressive" and "historical" faces of a broken and cultured race, where there is always more to divine than to see.

Of the picture of the Flying Pigeon, the beautiful and excellent woman mentioned above, a keen observer said, "If you cover the forehead, you would think the face that of a Madonna, but the forehead is still savage; the perceptive faculties look so sharp, and the forehead not moulded like a European forehead." This is very true; in her the moral nature was most developed, and the effect of a higher growth upon her face is entirely different from that upon Guess.

His eye is inturned, while the proper Indian eye gazes steadily, as if on a distant object. That is half the romance of it, that it makes you think of dark and distant places in the forest.

Guess always preferred inventing his implements to receiving them from others: and, when considered as mad by his tribe, while bent on the invention of his alphabet, contented himself with teaching it to his little daughter; an unimpeachable witness.

Red Jacket's face, too, is much more intellectual than almost any other. But, in becoming so, it loses nothing of the peculiar Indian stamp, but only carries these traits to their perfection. Irony, discernment, resolution, and a deep smouldering fire, that disdains to flicker where it cannot blaze, may there be read. Nothing can better represent the sort of unfeelingness the whites have towards the Indians, than their conduct towards his remains. He had steadily opposed the introduction of white religion, or manners, among the Indians. He believed that for them to break down the barriers was to perish. On many occasions he had expressed this with all the force of his eloquence. He told the preachers, "if the Great Spirit had meant your religion for the red man, he would have given it to them. What they (the missionaries) tell us, we do not understand; and the light they ask for us, makes the straight and plain path trod by our fathers dark and dreary."

When he died, he charged his people to inter him themselves. "Dig my grave yourselves, and let not the white man pursue me there." In defiance of this last solemn request, and the invariable tenor of his life, the missionaries seized the body and performed their service over it, amid the sullen indignation of his people, at what, under the circumstances, was sacrilege.

Of Indian religion a fine specimen is given in the conduct of one of the war chiefs, who, on an important occasion, made a vow to the sun of entire renunciation in case he should be crowned with success. When he was so, he first went through a fast, and sacrificial dance, involving great personal torment, and lasting several days; then, distributing all his property, even his lodges, and mats, among the tribe, he and his family took up their lodging upon the bare ground, beneath the bare sky.

The devotion of the Stylites and the hair-cloth saints, is in act, though not in motive, less noble, because this great chief proposed to go on in common life, where he had lived as a prince—a beggar.

The memoir by Corn Plant of his early days is beautiful.

Very fine anecdotes are told of two of the Western chiefs, father and son, who had the wisdom to see the true policy toward the whites, and steadily to adhere to it.

A murder having taken place in the jurisdiction of the father, he delivered himself up, with those suspected, to imprisonment. One of his companions chafed bitterly under confinement. He told the chief, if they ever got out, he would kill him, and did so. The son, then a boy, came in his rage and sorrow, to this Indian, and insulted him in every way. The squaw, angry at this, urged her husband "to kill the boy at once." But he only replied with "the joy of the valiant," "He will be a great Brave," and then delivered himself up to atone for his victim, and met his death with the noblest Roman composure.

This boy became rather a great chief than a great brave, and the anecdotes about him are of signal beauty and significance.

There is a fine story of an old mother, who gave herself to death instead of her son. The son, at the time, accepted the sacrifice, seeing, with Indian coolness, that it was better she should give up her few solitary and useless days, than he a young existence full of promise. But he could not abide by this view, and after suffering awhile all the anguish of remorse, he put himself solemnly to death in the presence of the tribe, as the only atonement he could make. His young wife stood by, with her child in her arms, commanding her emotions, as he desired, for, no doubt, it seemed to her also, a sacred duty.

But the finest story of all is that of Petalesharro, in whose tribe at the time, and not many years since, the custom of offering human sacrifices still subsisted. The fire was kindled, the victim, a young female captive, bound to the stake, the tribe assembled round. The young brave darted through them, snatched the girl from her peril,

placed her upon his horse, and both had vanished before the astonished spectators had thought to interpose.

He placed the girl in her distant home, and then returned. Such is
the might of right, when joined with courage, that none ventured a
word of resentment or question. His father, struck by truth, endeav-
ored, and with success, to abolish the barbarous custom in the tribe.
On a later occasion, Petalesharro again offered his life, if required, but
it was not.

This young warrior visiting Washington, a medal was presented him
in honor of these acts. His reply deserves sculpture: "When I did it,
I knew not that it was good. I did it in ignorance. This medal makes
me know that it was good."

The recorder, through his playful expressions of horror at a declaration so surprising to the civilized Good, shows himself sensible to the
grand simplicity of heroic impulse it denotes. Were we, too, so good, as
to need a medal to show us that we are!

The half-breed and half-civilized chiefs, however handsome, look
vulgar beside the pure blood. They have the dignity of neither race.

The death of Osceola, (as described by Catlin,) presents a fine picture in the stern, warlike kind, taking leave with kindness, as a private
friend, of the American officers; but, as a foe in national regards, he
raised himself in his dying bed, and painted his face with the tokens
of eternal enmity.

The historian of the Indians should be one of their own race, as able
to sympathize with them, and possessing a mind as enlarged and cultivated as John Ross, and with his eye turned to the greatness of the past,
rather than the scanty promise of the future. Hearing of the wampum
belts, supposed to have been sent to our tribes by Montezuma, on the
invasion of the Spaniard, we feel that an Indian who could glean traditions familiarly from the old men, might collect much that we could
interpret.

Still, any clear outline, even of a portion of their past, is not to be
hoped, and we shall be well contented if we can have a collection of
genuine fragments, that will indicate as clearly their life, as a horse's
head from the Parthenon the genius of Greece.

Such, to me, are the stories I have cited above. And even European
sketches of this greatness, distant and imperfect though they be, yet
convey the truth, if made in a sympathizing spirit. Adair's Red Shoes,
Murray's old man, Catlin's noble Mandan chief, Henry's Wa-wa-tam,
with what we know of Philip, Pontiac, Tecumseh and Red Jacket,

would suffice to give the ages a glimpse at what was great in Indian life and Indian character.

We hope, too, there will be a national institute, containing all the remains of the Indians,—all that has been preserved by official intercourse at Washington, Catlin's collection, and a picture gallery as complete as can be made, with a collection of skulls from all parts of the country. To this should be joined the scanty library that exists on the subject.

I have not mentioned Mackenzie's Travels. He is an accurate observer, but sparing in his records, because his attention was wholly bent on his own objects. This circumstance gives a heroic charm to his scanty and simple narrative. Let what will happen, or who will go back, he cannot; he must find the sea, along those frozen rivers, through those starving countries, among tribes of stinted men, whose habitual interjection was "edui, it is hard, uttered in a querulous tone," distrusted by his followers, deserted by his guides, on, on he goes, till he sees the sea, cold, lowering, its strand bristling with foes; but he does see it.

His few observations, especially on the tribes who lived on fish, and held them in such superstitious observance, give a lively notion of the scene.

A little pamphlet has lately been published, giving an account of the massacre at Chicago, which I wish much I had seen while there, as it would have imparted an interest to spots otherwise barren. It is written with animation, and in an excellent style, telling just what we want to hear, and no more. The traits given of Indian generosity are as characteristic as those of Indian cruelty. A lady, who was saved by a friendly chief holding her under the waters of the lake, while the balls were whizzing around, received also, in the heat of the conflict, a reviving draught from a squaw, who saw she was exhausted; and, as she lay down, a mat was hung up between her and the scene of butchery, so that she was protected from the sight, though she could not be from sounds, full of horror.

I have not wished to write sentimentally about the Indians, however moved by the thought of their wrongs and speedy extinction. I know that the Europeans who took possession of this country, felt themselves justified by their superior civilization and religious ideas. Had they been truly civilized or Christianized, the conflicts which sprang from the collision of the two races, might have been avoided; but this cannot be expected in movements made by masses of men. The mass has never yet been humanized, though the age may develop a human thought.

Since those conflicts and differences did arise, the hatred which sprang, from terror and suffering, on the European side, has naturally warped the whites still farther from justice.

The Indian, brandishing the scalps of his friends and wife, drinking their blood and eating their hearts, is by him viewed as a fiend, though, at a distant day, he will no doubt be considered as having acted the Roman or Carthaginian part of heroic and patriotic self-defence, according to the standard of right and motives prescribed by his religious faith and education. Looked at by his own standard, he is virtuous when he most injures his enemy, and the white, if he be really the superior in enlargement of thought, ought to cast aside his inherited prejudices enough to see this,—to look on him in pity and brotherly goodwill, and do all he can to mitigate the doom of those who survive his past injuries.

In McKenney's book, is proposed a project for organizing the Indians under a patriarchal government, but it does not look feasible, even on paper. Could their own intelligent men be left to act unimpeded in their behalf, they would do far better for them than the white thinker, with all his general knowledge. But we dare not hope the designs of such will not always be frustrated by the same barbarous selfishness they were in Georgia. There was a chance of seeing what might have been done, now lost forever.

Yet let every man look to himself how far this blood shall be required at his hands. Let the missionary, instead of preaching to the Indian, preach to the trader who ruins him, of the dreadful account which will be demanded of the followers of Cain, in a sphere where the accents of purity and love come on the ear more decisively than in ours. Let every legislator take the subject to heart, and if he cannot undo the effects of past sin, try for that clear view and right sense that may save us from sinning still more deeply. And let every man and every woman, in their private dealings with the subjugated race, avoid all share in embittering, by insult or unfeeling prejudice, the captivity of Israel.

CHAPTER VII

Sault St. Marie

NINE DAYS I passed alone at Mackinaw, except for occasional visits from kind and agreeable residents at the fort, and Mr. and Mrs. A. Mr. A., long engaged in the fur-trade, is gratefully remembered by many travellers. From Mrs. A., also, I received kind attentions, paid in the vivacious and graceful manner of her nation.

The society at the boarding house entertained, being of a kind entirely new to me. There were many traders from the remote stations, such as La Pointe, Arbre Croche,—men who had become half wild and wholly rude, by living in the wild; but good-humored, observing, and with a store of knowledge to impart, of the kind proper to their place.

There were two little girls here, that were pleasant companions for me. One gay, frank, impetuous, but sweet and winning. She was an American, fair, and with bright brown hair. The other, a little French Canadian, used to join me in my walks, silently take my hand, and sit at my feet when I stopped in beautiful places. She seemed to understand without a word; and I never shall forget her little figure, with its light, but pensive motion, and her delicate, grave features, with the pale, clear complexion and soft eye. She was motherless, and much left alone by her father and brothers, who were boatmen. The two little girls were as pretty representatives of Allegro and Penseroso, as one would wish to see.

I had been wishing that a boat would come in to take me to the Sault St. Marie, and several times started to the window at night in hopes that the pant and dusky-red light crossing the waters belonged to such an one; but they were always boats for Chicago or Buffalo, till, on the 28th of August, Allegro, who shared my plans and wishes, rushed in to tell me that the General Scott had come, and, in this little steamer, accordingly, I set off the next morning.

I was the only lady, and attended in the cabin by a Dutch girl and an Indian woman. They both spoke English fluently, and entertained me much by accounts of their different experiences.

The Dutch girl told me of a dance among the common people at Amsterdam, called the shepherd's dance. The two leaders are dressed as shepherd and shepherdess; they invent to the music all kinds of movements, descriptive of things that may happen in the field, and the rest were obliged to follow. I have never heard of any dance which gave such free play to the fancy as this. French dances merely describe the polite movements of society; Spanish and Neapolitan, love; the beautiful Mazurkas, &c., are warlike or expressive of wild scenery. But in this one is great room both for fun and fancy.

The Indian was married, when young, by her parents, to a man she did not love. He became dissipated, and did not maintain her. She left him, taking with her their child; for whom and herself she earns a subsistence by going as chambermaid in these boats. Now and then, she said, her husband called on her, and asked if he might live with her again; but she always answered, no. Here she was far freer than she would have been in civilized life.

I was pleased by the nonchalance of this woman, and the perfectly national manner she had preserved after so many years of contact with all kinds of people. The two women, when I left the boat, made me presents of Indian work, such as travellers value, and the manner of the two was characteristic of their different nations. The Indian brought me hers, when I was alone, looked bashfully down when she gave it, and made an almost sentimental little speech. The Dutch girl brought hers in public, and, bridling her short chin with a self-complacent air, observed she had *bought* it for me. But the feeling of affectionate regard was the same in the minds of both.

Island after island we passed, all fairly shaped and clustering friendly, but with little variety of vegetation.

In the afternoon the weather became foggy, and we could not proceed after dark. That was as dull an evening as ever fell.

The next morning the fog still lay heavy, but the captain took me out in his boat on an exploring expedition, and we found the remains of the old English fort on Point St. Joseph's. All around was so wholly unmarked by anything but stress of wind and weather, the shores of these islands and their woods so like one another, wild and lonely, but nowhere rich and majestic, that there was some charm in the remains of the garden, the remains even of chimneys and a pier. They gave feature to the scene.

Here I gathered many flowers, but they were the same as at Mackinaw.

The captain, though he had been on this trip hundreds of times, had never seen this spot, and never would, but for this fog, and his desire to entertain me. He presented a striking instance how men, for the sake of getting a living, forget to live. It is just the same in the most romantic as the most dull and vulgar places. Men get the harness on so fast, that they can never shake it off, unless they guard against this danger from the very first. In Chicago, how many men, who never found time to see the prairies or learn anything unconnected with the business of the day, or about the country they were living in!

So this captain, a man of strong sense and good eyesight, rarely found time to go off the track or look about him on it. He lamented, too, that there had been no call which induced him to develop his powers of expression, so that he might communicate what he had seen, for the enjoyment or instruction of others.

This is a common fault among the active men, the truly living, who could tell what life is. It should not be so. Literature should not be left to the mere literati—eloquence to the mere orator. Every Caesar should be able to write his own commentary. We want a more equal, more thorough, more harmonious development, and there is nothing to hinder from it the men of this country, except their own supineness, or sordid views.

When the weather did clear, our course up the river was delightful. Long stretched before us the island of St. Joseph's, with its fair woods of sugar maple. A gentleman on board, who belongs to the Fort at the Sault, said their pastime was to come in the season of making sugar, and pass some time on this island,—the days at work, and the evening in dancing and other amusements.

I wished to extract here Henry's account of this, for it was just the same sixty years ago as now, but have already occupied too much room with extracts. Work of this kind done in the open air, where everything is temporary, and every utensil prepared on the spot, gives life a truly festive air. At such times, there is labor and no care—energy with gaiety, gaiety of the heart.

I think with the same pleasure of the Italian vintage, the Scotch harvest-home, with its evening dance in the barn, the Russian cabbage feast even, and our huskings and hop-gatherings—the hop-gatherings where the groups of men and girls are pulling down and filling baskets with the gay festoons, present as graceful pictures as the Italian vintage.

I should also like to insert Henry's descriptions of the method of catching trout and white fish, the delicacies of this region, for the same reason as I want his account of the Gens de Terre, the savages among savages, and his tales, dramatic, if not true, of cannibalism.

I have no less grieved to omit Carver's account of the devotion of a Winnebago prince at the Falls of St. Anthony, which he describes with a simplicity and intelligence, that are very pleasing.

I take the more pleasure in both Carver and Henry's power of appreciating what is good in the Indian character, that both had run the greatest risk of losing their lives during their intercourse with the Indians, and had seen them in the utmost exasperation, with all its revolting circumstances.

I wish I had a thread long enough to string on it all these beads that take my fancy; but, as I have not, I can only refer the reader to the books themselves, which may be found in the library of Harvard College, if not elsewhere.

How pleasant is the course along a new river, the sight of new shores; like a life, would but life flow as fast, and upbear us with as full a stream. I hoped we should come in sight of the rapids by daylight; but the beautiful sunset was quite gone, and only a young moon trembling over the scene, when we came within hearing of them.

I sat up long to hear them merely. It was a thoughtful hour. These two days, the 29th and 30th August, are memorable in my life; the latter is the birth-day of a near friend. I pass them alone, approaching Lake Superior; but I shall not enter into that truly wild and free region; shall not have the canoe voyage, whose daily adventure, with the camping out at night beneath the stars, would have given an interlude of such value to my existence. I shall not see the Pictured Rocks, their chapels and urns. It did not depend on me; it never has, whether such things shall be done or not.

My friends! may they see, and do, and be more, especially those who have before them a greater number of birthdays, and of a more healthy and unfettered existence:

TO EDITH, ON HER BIRTHDAY

If the same star our fates together bind,
Why are we thus divided, mind from mind?
If the same law one grief to both impart,
How could'st thou grieve a trusting mother's heart?

Our aspiration seeks a common aim,
Why were we tempered of such differing frame?
—But 'tis too late to turn this wrong to right;
Too cold, too damp, too deep, has fallen the night.

And yet, the angel of my life replies,
Upon that night a Morning Star shall rise,
Fairer than that which ruled the temporal birth,
Undimmed by vapors of the dreamy earth;

It says, that, where a heart thy claim denies,
Genius shall read its secret ere it flies;
The earthly form may vanish from thy side,
Pure love will make thee still the spirit's bride.

And thou, ungentle, yet much loving child,
Whose heart still shows the "untamed haggard wild,"
A heart which justly makes the highest claim,
Too easily is checked by transient blame;

Ere such an orb can ascertain its sphere,
The ordeal must be various and severe;
My prayers attend thee, though the feet may fly,
I hear thy music in the silent sky.

I should like, however, to hear some notes of earthly music to-night.
By the faint moonshine I can hardly see the banks; how they look I
have no guess, except that there are trees, and, now and then, a light
lets me know there are homes with their various interests. I should like
to hear some strains of the flute from beneath those trees, just to break
the sound of the rapids.

When no gentle eyebeam charms;
No fond hope the bosom warms;
Of thinking the lone mind is tired—
Nought seems bright to be desired;

Music, be thy sails unfurled,
Bear me to thy better world;
O'er a cold and weltering sea,
Blow thy breezes warm and free;

By sad sighs they ne'er were chilled,
By sceptic spell were never stilled;

Take me to that far-off shore,
Where lovers meet to part no more;
There doubt, and fear and sin are o'er,
The star of love shall set no more.

With the first light of dawn I was up and out, and then was glad I had not seen all the night before; it came upon me with such power in its dewy freshness. O! they are beautiful indeed, these rapids! The grace is so much more obvious than the power. I went up through the old Chippeway burying ground to their head, and sat down on a large stone to look. A little way off was one of the home lodges, unlike in shape to the temporary ones at Mackinaw, but these have been described by Mrs. Jameson. Women, too, I saw coming home from the woods, stooping under great loads of cedar boughs, that were strapped upon their backs. But in many European countries women carry great loads, even of wood, upon their backs. I used to hear the girls singing and laughing as they were cutting down boughs at Mackinaw; this part of their employment, though laborious, gives them the pleasure of being a great deal in the free woods.

I had ordered a canoe to take me down the rapids, and presently I saw it coming, with the two Indian canoe-men in pink calico shirts, moving it about with their long poles, with a grace and dexterity worthy fairyland. Now and then they cast the scoop-net; all looked just as I had fancied, only far prettier.

When they came to me, they spread a mat in the middle of the canoe; I sat down, and in less than four minutes we had descended the rapids, a distance of more than three quarters of a mile. I was somewhat disappointed in this being no more of an exploit than I found it. Having heard such expressions used as of "darting," or, "shooting down," these rapids, I had fancied there was a wall of rock somewhere, where descent would somehow be accomplished, and that there would come some one gasp of terror and delight, some sensation entirely new to me; but I found myself in smooth water, before I had time to feel anything but the buoyant pleasure of being carried so lightly through this surf amid the breakers. Now and then the Indians spoke to one another in a vehement jabber, which, however, had no tone that expressed other than pleasant excitement. It is, no doubt, an act of wonderful dexterity to steer amid these jagged rocks, when one rude touch would tear a hole in the birch canoe; but these men are evidently so used to doing it, and so adroit, that the silliest person could not feel afraid. I should like to have come down twenty times, that I might have had leisure to realize the pleasure. But the fog which had detained us on the way, shortened the boat's stay at the Sault, and I wanted my time to walk about.

While coming down the rapids, the Indians caught a white-fish for my breakfast; and certainly it was the best of breakfasts. The white-fish I found quite another thing caught on this spot, and cooked immediately, from what I had found it at Chicago or Mackinaw. Before, I had had the bad taste to prefer the trout, despite the solemn and eloquent remonstrances of the Habitués, to whom the superiority of white fish seemed a cardinal point of faith.

I am here reminded that I have omitted that indispensable part of a travelling journal, the account of what we found to eat. I cannot hope to make up, by one bold stroke, all my omissions of daily record; but that I may show myself not destitute of the common feelings of humanity, I will observe that he whose affections turn in summer towards vegetables, should not come to this region, till the subject of diet be better understood; that of fruit, too, there is little yet, even at the best hotel tables; that the prairie chickens require no praise from me, and that the trout and white-fish are worthy the transparency of the lake waters.

In this brief mention I by no means mean to give myself an air of superiority to the subject. If a dinner in the Illinois woods, on dry bread and drier meat, with water from the stream that flowed hard by, pleased me best of all, yet at one time, when living at a house where nothing was prepared for the table fit to touch, and even the bread could not be partaken of without a headache in consequence, I learnt to understand and sympathize with the anxious tone in which fathers of families, about to take their innocent children into some scene of wild beauty, ask first of all, "Is there a good table?" I shall ask just so in future. Only those whom the Powers have furnished small travelling cases of ambrosia, can take exercise all day, and be happy without even bread morning or night.

Our voyage back was all pleasure. It was the fairest day. I saw the river, the islands, the clouds to the greatest advantage.

On board was an old man, an Illinois farmer, whom I found a most agreeable companion. He had just been with his son, and eleven other young men, on an exploring expedition to the shores of lake Superior. He was the only old man of the party, but he had enjoyed, most of any, the journey. He had been the counsellor and playmate, too, of the young ones. He was one of those parents,—why so rare?— who understand and live a new life in that of their children, instead of wasting time and young happiness in trying to make them conform to an object and standard of their own. The character and history of each child may be a new and poetic experience to the parent, if he will let it. Our farmer was domestic, judicious, solid; the son, inventive, enterprising, superficial, full of follies, full of resources, always liable to failure, sure to rise above it. The father conformed to, and learnt from, a character he could not change, and won the sweet from the bitter.

His account of his life at home, and of his late adventures among the Indians, was very amusing, but I want talent to write it down. I have not heard the slang of these people intimately enough. There is a good book about Indiana, called the New Purchase, written by a person who knows the people of the country well enough to describe them in their own way. It is not witty, but penetrating, valuable for its practical wisdom and good-humored fun.

There were many sportsman stories told, too, by those from Illinois and Wisconsin. I do not retain any of these well enough, nor any that I heard earlier, to write them down, though they always interested me from bringing wild, natural scenes before the mind. It is pleasant for the sportsman to be in countries so alive with game; yet it is so plenty that one would think shooting pigeons or grouse would seem more like slaughter, than the excitement of skill to a good sportsman. Hunting the deer is full of adventure, and needs only a Scrope to describe it to invest the western woods with *historic* associations.

How pleasant it was to sit and hear rough men tell pieces out of their own common lives, in places of the frippery talk of some fine circle with its conventional sentiment, and timid, second-hand criticism. Free blew the wind, and boldly flowed the stream, named for Mary mother mild.

A fine thunder shower came on in the afternoon. It cleared at sunset, just as we came in sight of beautiful Mackinaw, over which a rainbow bent in promise of peace.

I have always wondered, in reading travels, at the childish joy travellers felt at meeting people they knew, and their sense of loneliness when they did not, in places where there was everything new to occupy the attention. So childish, I thought, always to be longing for the new in the old, and the old in the new. Yet just such sadness I felt, when I looked on the island, glittering in the sunset, canopied by the rainbow, and thought no friend would welcome me there; just such childish joy I felt, to see unexpectedly on the landing, the face of one whom I called friend.

The remaining two or three days were delightfully spent, in walking or boating, or sitting at the window to see the Indians go. This was not quite so pleasant as their coming in, though accomplished with the same rapidity; a family not taking half an hour to prepare for departure, and the departing canoe a beautiful object. But they left behind, on all the shore, the blemishes of their stay—old rags, dried boughs, fragments of food, the marks of their fires. Nature likes to cover up and gloss over spots and scars, but it would take her some time to restore that beach to the state it was in before they came.

S. and I had a mind for a canoe excursion, and we asked one of the traders to engage us two good Indians, that would not only take us out, but be sure and bring us back, as we could not hold converse with them. Two others offered their aid, beside the chief's son, a fine looking youth of about sixteen, richly dressed in blue broadcloth, scarlet sash and leggins, with a scarf of brighter red than the rest, tied around his head, its ends falling gracefully on one shoulder. They thought it, apparently, fine amusement to be attending two white women; they carried us into the path of the steamboat, which was going out, and paddled with all their force,—rather too fast, indeed, for there was something of a swell on the lake, and they sometimes threw water into the canoe. However, it flew over the waves, light as a sea-gull. They would say, "Pull away," and "Ver' warm," and, after these words, would laugh gaily. They enjoyed the hour, I believe, as much as we.

The house where we lived belonged to the widow of a French trader, an Indian by birth, and wearing the dress of her country. She spoke French fluently, and was very ladylike in her manners. She is a great character among them. They were all the time coming to pay her homage, or to get her aid and advice; for she is, I am told, a shrewd woman of business. My companion carried about her sketch-book with her, and the Indians were interested when they saw her using her pencil, though less so than about the sun-shade. This lady of the tribe wanted to borrow the sketches of the beach, with its lodges and wild groups, "to show to the *savages,*" she said.

Of the practical ability of the Indian women, a good specimen is given by McKenney, in an amusing story of one who went to Washington, and acted her part there in the "first circles," with a tact and sustained dissimulation worthy of Cagliostro. She seemed to have a thorough love of intrigue for its own sake, and much dramatic talent. Like the chiefs of her nation, when on an expedition among the foe, whether for revenge or profit, no impulses of vanity or wayside seductions had power to turn her aside from carrying out her plan as she had originally projected it.

Although I have little to tell, I feel that I have learnt a great deal of the Indians, from observing them even in this broken and degraded condition. There is a language of eye and motion which cannot be put into words, and which teaches what words never can. I feel acquainted with the soul of this race; I read its nobler thought in their defaced figures. There *was* a greatness, unique and precious, which he who does not feel will never duly appreciate the majesty of nature in this American continent.

I have mentioned that the Indian orator, who addressed the agents on this occasion, said, the difference between the white man and the red man is this: "the white man no sooner came here, than he thought of preparing the way for his posterity; the red man never thought of this." I was assured this was exactly his phrase; and it defines the true difference. We get the better because we do

> "Look before and after."

But, from the same cause, we

> "Pine for what is not."

The red man, when happy, was thoroughly happy; when good, was simply good. He needed the medal, to let him know that he *was* good.

These evenings we were happy, looking over the old-fashioned garden, over the beach, over the waters and pretty island opposite, beneath the growing moon; we did not stay to see it full at Mackinaw. At two o'clock, one night, or rather morning, the Great Western came snorting in, and we must go; and Mackinaw, and all the north-west summer, is now to me no more than picture and dream;—

> "A dream within a dream."

These last days at Mackinaw have been pleasanter than the "lonesome" nine, for I have recovered the companion with whom I set out from the East, one who sees all, prizes all, enjoys much, interrupts never.

At Detroit we stopped for half a day. This place is famous in our history, and the unjust anger at its surrender is still expressed by almost every one who passes there. I had always shared the common feeling on this subject; for the indignation at a disgrace to our arms that seemed so unnecessary, has been handed down from father to child, and few of us have taken the pains to ascertain where the blame lay. But now, upon the spot, having read all the testimony, I felt convinced

that it should rest solely with the government, which, by neglect-
ing to sustain General Hull, as he had a right to expect they would,
compelled him to take this step, or sacrifice many lives, and of the de-
fenceless inhabitants, not of soldiers, to the cruelty of a savage foe, for
the sake of his reputation.

I am a woman, and unlearned in such affairs; but, to a person with
common sense and good eyesight, it is clear, when viewing the location, that, under the circumstances, he had no prospect of successful
defence, and that to attempt it would have been an act of vanity, not
valor.

I feel that I am not biased in this judgment by my personal relations, for I have always heard both sides, and, though my feelings had
been moved by the picture of the old man sitting down, in the midst
of his children, to a retired and despoiled old age, after a life of honor
and happy intercourse with the public, yet tranquil, always secure that
justice must be done at last, I supposed, like others, that he deceived
himself, and deserved to pay the penalty for failure to the responsibility he had undertaken. Now on the spot, I change, and believe the
country at large must, ere long, change from this opinion. And I wish
to add my testimony, however trifling its weight, before it be drowned
in the voice of general assent, that I may do some justice to the feelings
which possessed me here and now.

A noble boat, the Wisconsin, was to be launched this afternoon, the
whole town was out in many-colored array, the band playing. Our boat
swept round to a good position, and all was ready but—the Wisconsin,
which could not be made to stir. This was quite a disappointment. It
would have been an imposing sight.

In the boat many signs admonished that we were floating eastward.
A shabbily dressed phrenologist laid his hand on every head which
would bend, with half-conceited, half-sheepish expression, to the
trial of his skill. Knots of people gathered here and there to discuss
points of theology. A bereaved lover was seeking religious consolation
in—Butler's Analogy, which he had purchased for that purpose. However, he did not turn over many pages before his attention was drawn
aside by the gay glances of certain damsels that came on board at
Detroit, and, though Butler might afterwards be seen sticking from his
pocket, it had not weight to impede him from many a feat of lightness
and liveliness. I doubt if it went with him from the boat. Some there
were, even, discussing the doctrines of Fourier. It seemed pity they
were not going to, rather than from, the rich and free country where
it would be so much easier, than with us, to try the great experiment

of voluntary association, and show, beyond a doubt, that "an ounce of prevention is worth a pound of cure," a maxim of the "wisdom of nations," which has proved of little practical efficacy as yet.

Better to stop before landing at Buffalo, while I have yet the advantage over some of my readers.

THE BOOK TO THE READER

Who open, as American readers often do, at the end,
with doggerel submission

To see your cousin in her country home,
If at the time of blackberries you come,
"Welcome, my friends," she cries with ready glee,
"The fruit is ripened, and the paths are free.
But, madam, you will tear that handsome gown;
The little boy be sure to tumble down;
And, in the thickets where they ripen best,
The matted ivy, too, its bower has drest.
And then, the thorns your hands are sure to rend,
Unless with heavy gloves you will defend;
Amid most thorns the sweetest roses blow,
Amid most thorns the sweetest berries grow."

If, undeterred, you to the fields must go,
   You tear your dresses and you scratch your hands;
But, in the places where the berries grow,
   A sweeter fruit the ready sense commands,
Of wild, gay feelings, fancies springing sweet—
Of bird-like pleasures, fluttering and fleet.

Another year, you cannot go yourself,
   To win the berries from the thickets wild,
And housewife skill, instead, has filled the shelf
   With blackberry jam, "by best receipts compiled.—
Not made with country sugar, for too strong
The flavors that to maple juice belong;
But foreign sugar, nicely mixed 'to suit
The taste,' spoils not the fragrance of the fruit."

" 'T is pretty good," half-tasting, you reply,
"I scarce should know it from fresh blackberry,

But the best pleasure such a fruit can yield,
Is to be gathered in the open field;
If only as an article of food,
Cherry or crab-apple are quite as good;

And, for occasions of festivity,
West India sweetmeats you had better buy."

Thus, such a dish of homely sweets as these
In neither way may chance the taste to please.

Yet try a little with the evening-bread;
Bring a good needle for the spool of thread;
Take fact with fiction, silver with the lead,
And, at the mint, you can get gold instead;
In fine, read me, even as you would be read.

Reviews and Essays

Emerson's Essays

Essays: Second Series. By R. W. Emerson. *Boston James Munroe and Company, 1844*

At the distance of three years this volume follows the first series of Essays, which have already made to themselves a circle of readers, attentive, thoughtful, more and more intelligent, and this circle is a large one if we consider the circumstances of this country, and of England, also, at this time.

In England it would seem there are a larger number of persons waiting for an invitation to calm thought and sincere intercourse than among ourselves. Copies of Mr. Emerson's first published little volume called "Nature," have there been sold by thousands in a short time, while one edition has needed seven years to get circulated here. Several of his Orations and Essays from "The Dial" have also been republished there, and met with a reverent and earnest response.

We suppose that while in England the want of such a voice is as great as here, a larger number are at leisure to recognize that want; a far larger number have set foot in the speculative region and have ears refined to appreciate these melodious accents.

Our people, heated by a partisan spirit, necessarily occupied in these first stages by bringing out the material resources of the land, not generally prepared by early training for the enjoyment of books that require attention and reflection, are still more injured by a large majority of writers and speakers, who lend all their efforts to flatter corrupt tastes and mental indolence, instead of feeling it their prerogative and their duty to admonish the community of the danger and arouse it to nobler energy. The aim of the writer or lecturer is not to say the best he knows in as few and well-chosen words as he can, making it his first aim to do justice to the subject. Rather he seeks to beat out a thought as thin as possible, and to consider what the audience will be most willing to receive.

The result of such a course is inevitable. Literature and Art must become daily more degraded; Philosophy cannot exist. A man who feels within his mind some spark of genius, or a capacity for the exercises of talent, should consider himself as endowed with a sacred commission. He is the natural priest, the shepherd of the people. He must raise his mind as high as he can toward the heaven of truth, and try to draw up with him those less gifted by nature with ethereal lightness. If he does not so, but rather employs his powers to flatter them in their poverty, and to hinder aspiration by useless words, and a mere seeming of activity, his sin is great, he is false to God, and false to man.

Much of this sin indeed is done ignorantly. The idea that literature calls men to the genuine hierarchy is almost forgotten. One, who finds himself able, uses his pen, as he might a trowel, solely to procure himself bread, without having reflected on the position in which he thereby places himself.

Apart from the troop of mercenaries, there is one, still larger, of those who use their powers merely for local and temporary ends, aiming at no excellence other than may conduce to these. Among these, rank persons of honor and the best intentions, but they neglect the lasting for the transient, as a man neglects to furnish his mind that he may provide the better for the house in which his body is to dwell for a few years.

When these sins and errors are prevalent, and threaten to become more so, how can we sufficiently prize and honor a mind which is quite pure from such? When, as in the present case, we find a man whose only aim is the discernment and interpretation of the spiritual laws by which we live and move and have our being, all whose objects are permanent, and whose every word stands for a fact.

If only as a representative of the claims of individual culture in a nation which tends to lay such stress on artificial organization and external results, Mr. Emerson would be invaluable here. History will inscribe his name as a father of the country, for he is one who pleads her cause against herself.

If New-England may be regarded as a chief mental focus to the New World, and many symptoms seem to give her this place, as to other centres the characteristics of heart and lungs to the body politic; if we may believe, as the writer does believe, that what is to be acted out in the country at large is, most frequently, first indicated there, as all the phenomena of the nervous system in the fantasies of the brain, we may hail as an auspicious omen the influence Mr. Emerson has there obtained, which is deep-rooted, increasing, and, over the younger portion of the community, far greater than that of any other person.

His books are received there with a more ready intelligence than elsewhere, partly because his range of personal experience and illustration applies to that region, partly because he has prepared the way for his books to be read by his great powers as a speaker.

The audience that waited for years upon the lectures, a part of which is incorporated into these volumes of Essays, was never large, but it was select, and it was constant. Among the hearers were some, who though, attracted by the beauty of character and manner, they were willing to hear the speaker through, always went away discontented. They were accustomed to an artificial method, whose scaffolding could easily be retraced, and desired an obvious sequence of logical inferences. They insisted there was nothing in what they had heard, because they could not give a clear account of its course and purport. They did not see that Pindar's odes might be very well arranged for their own purpose, and yet not bear translating into the methods of Mr. Locke.

Others were content to be benefitted by a good influence without a strict analysis of its means. "My wife says it is about the elevation of human nature, and so it seems to me;" was a fit reply to some of the critics. Many were satisfied to find themselves excited to congenial thought and nobler life, without an exact catalogue of the thoughts of the speaker.

Those who believed no truth could exist, unless encased by the burrs of opinion, went away utterly baffled. Sometimes they thought he was on their side, then presently would come something on the other. He really seemed to believe there were two sides to every subject, and even to intimate higher ground from which each might be seen to have an infinite number of sides or bearings, an impertinence not to be endured! The partisan heard but once and returned no more.

But some there were, simple souls, whose life had been, perhaps, without clear light, yet still a search after truth for its own sake, who were able to receive what followed on the suggestion of a subject in a natural manner, as a stream of thought. These recognized, beneath the veil of words, the still small voice of conscience, the vestal fires of lone religious hours, and the mild teachings of the summer woods.

The charm of the elocution, too, was great. His general manner was that of the reader, occasionally rising into direct address or invocation in passages where tenderness or majesty demanded more energy. At such times both eye and voice called on a remote future to give a worthy reply. A future which shall manifest more largely the universal soul as it was then manifest to this soul. The tone of the voice was a grave body tone, full and sweet rather than sonorous, yet flexible and haunted by many modulations, as even instruments of wood and brass seem to become after they have been long played on with skill and taste; how much more so the human voice! In the more expressive passages it uttered notes of silvery clearness, winning, yet still more commanding. The words uttered in those tones, floated awhile above us, then took root in the memory like winged seed.

In the union of an even rustic plainness with lyric inspirations, religious dignity with philosophic calmness, keen sagacity in details with boldness of view, we saw what brought to mind the early poets and legislators of Greece—men who taught their fellows to plow and avoid moral evil, sing hymns to the gods and watch the metamorphoses of nature. Here in civic Boston was such a man—one who could see man in his original grandeur and his original childishness, rooted in a simple nature, raising to the heavens the brow and eyes of a poet.

And these lectures seemed not so much lectures as grave didactic poems, theogonies, perhaps, adorned by odes when some Power was in question whom the poet had best learned to serve, and with eclogues wisely portraying in familiar tongue the duties of man to man and "harmless animals."

Such was the attitude in which the speaker appeared to that portion of the audience who have remained permanently attached to him.— They value his words as the signets of reality; receive his influence as a help and incentive to a nobler discipline than the age, in its general aspect, appears to require; and do not fear to anticipate the verdict of posterity in claiming for him the honors of greatness, and, in some respects, of a Master.

In New-England he thus formed for himself a class of readers, who rejoice to study in his books what they already know by heart. For, though the thought has become familiar, its beautiful garb is always fresh and bright in hue.

A similar circle of like-minded the books must and do form for themselves, though with a movement less directly powerful, as more distant from its source.

The Essays have also been obnoxious to many charges. To that of obscurity, or want of perfect articulation. Of 'Euphuism,' as an excess of fancy in proportion to imagination, and an inclination, at times, to subtlety at the expense of strength, has been styled. The human heart complains of inadequacy, either in the nature or experience of the writer, to represent its full vocation and its deeper needs. Sometimes it speaks of this want as "under-development" or a want of expansion which may yet be remedied; sometimes doubts whether "in this mansion there be either hall or portal to receive the loftier of the Passions." Sometimes the soul is deified at the expense of nature, then again nature at that of man, and we are not quite sure that we can make a true harmony by balance of the statements.—This writer has never written one good work, if such a work be one where the whole commands more attention than the parts. If such an one be produced only where, after an accumulation of materials, fire enough be applied to fuse the whole into one new substance. This second series is superior in this respect to the former, yet in no one essay is the main stress so obvious as to produce on the mind the harmonious effect of a noble river or a tree in full leaf. Single passages and sentences engage our attention too much in proportion. These essays, it has been justly said, tire like a string of mosaics or a house built of medals. We miss what we expect in the work of the great poet, or the great philosopher, the liberal air of all the zones: the glow, uniform yet various in tint, which is given to a body by free circulation of the heart's blood from the hour of birth. Here is, undoubtedly, the man of ideas, but we want the ideal man also; want the heart and genius of human life to interpret it, and here our satisfaction is not so perfect. We doubt this friend raised himself too early to the perpendicular and did not lie along the ground long enough to hear the secret whispers of our parent life. We could wish he might be thrown by conflicts on the lap of mother earth, to see if he would not rise again with added powers.

All this we may say, but it cannot excuse us from benefitting by the great gifts that have been given, and assigning them their due place.

Some painters paint on a red ground. And this color may be supposed to represent the ground work most immediately congenial to most men, as it is the color of blood and represents human vitality. The figures traced upon it are instinct with life in its fulness and depth.

But other painters paint on a gold ground. And a very different, but no less natural, because also a celestial beauty, is given to their works who choose for their foundation the color of the sunbeam, which nature has preferred for her most precious product, and that which will best bear the test of purification, gold.

If another simile may be allowed, another no less apt is at hand. Wine is the most brilliant and intense expression of the powers of earth.—It is her potable fire, her answer to the sun. It exhilarates, it inspires, but then it is liable to fever and intoxicate too the careless partaker.

Mead was the chosen drink of the Northern gods. And this essence of the honey of the mountain bee was not thought unworthy to revive the souls of the valiant who had left their bodies on the fields of strife below.

Nectar should combine the virtues of the ruby wine, the golden mead, without their defects or dangers.

Two high claims our writer can vindicate on the attention of his contemporaries. One from his sincerity. You have his thought just as it found place in the life of his own soul. Thus, however near or relatively distant its approximation to absolute truth, its action on you cannot fail to be healthful. It is a part of the free air.

He belongs to that band of whom there may be found a few in every age, and who now in human history may be counted by hundreds, who worship the one God only, the God of Truth. They worship, not saints, not creeds, nor churches, nor reliques, nor idols in any form. The mind is kept open to truth, and life only valued as a tendency toward it. This must be illustrated by acts and words of love, purity and intelligence. Such are the salt of the earth; let the minutest crystal of that salt be willingly by us held in solution.

The other is through that part of his life, which, if sometimes obstructed or chilled by the critical intellect, is yet the prevalent and the main source of his power. It is that by which he imprisons his hearer only to free him again as a "liberating God" (to use his own words). But indeed let us use them altogether, for none other, ancient or modern, can more worthily express how, making present to use the courses and destinies of nature, he invests himself with her serenity and animates us with her joy.

"Poetry was all written before time was, and whenever we are so finely organized that we can penetrate into that region where the air is music, we hear those primal warblings, and attempt to write them down, but we lose ever and anon a word, or a verse, and substitute something of our own, and thus miswrite the poem. The men of more delicate ear write down these cadences more faithfully, and these transcripts, though imperfect, become the songs of the nations.

"As the eyes of the Lyncæus were said to see through the earth, so the poet turns the world to glass, and shows us all things in their right series and procession. For, through that better perception, he stands one step nearer to things, and sees the flowing or metamorphosis; perceives that thought is multiform; that within the form of every creature is a force impelling it to ascend into a higher form; and following with his eyes the life, uses the forms which express that life, and so the speech flows with the flowing of nature."

Thus have we in a brief and unworthy manner indicated some views of these books. The only true criticism of these, or any good books, may be gained by making them the companions of our lives. Does every accession of knowledge or a juster sense of beauty make us prize them more? Then they are good, indeed, and more immortal than mortal. Let that test be applied to these; essays which will lead to great and complete poems—somewhere.

New-York Daily Tribune
7 Dec. 1844

Our City Charities

VISIT TO BELLEVUE ALMS HOUSE, TO THE FARM SCHOOL, THE ASYLUM FOR THE INSANE, AND PENITENTIARY ON BLACKWELL'S ISLAND.

The aspect of Nature was sad; what is worse, it was dull and dubious, when we set forth on these visits. The sky was leaden and lowering, the air unkind and piercing, the little birds sat mute and astonished at the departure of the beautiful days which had lured them to premature song. It was a suitable day for such visits. The pauper establishments that belong to a great city take the place of the skeleton at the banquets of old. They admonish us of stern realities, which must bear the same explanation as the frequent blight of Nature's bloom. They should be looked at by all, if only for their own sakes, that they may not sink listlessly into selfish ease, in a world so full of disease. They should be looked at by all who wish to enlighten themselves as to the means of aiding their fellow-creatures in any way, public or private. For nothing can really be done till the right principles are discovered, and it would seem they still need to be discovered or elucidated, so little is done, with a great deal of desire in the heart of the community to do what is right. Such visits are not yet calculated to encourage and exhilarate, as does the story of the Prodigal Son; they wear a grave aspect and suit the grave mood of a *cold* Spring day.

At the Alms House there is every appearance of kindness in the guardians of the poor, and there was a greater degree of cleanliness and comfort than we had expected. But the want of suitable and sufficient employment is a great evil. The persons who find here either a permanent or temporary refuge have scarcely any occupation provided except to raise vegetables for the establishment, and prepare clothing for themselves. The men especially have the most vagrant, degraded air, and so much indolence must tend to confirm them in every bad habit. We were told that, as they are under no strict discipline, their labor at the various trades could not be made profitable; yet surely the means of such should be provided, even at some expense. Employments of various kinds must be absolutely needed, if only to counteract the bad effects of such a position. Every establishment in aid of the poor should be planned with a view to their education. There should be instruction, both practical and in the use of books, openings to a better intercourse than they can obtain from their miserable homes, correct notions, as to cleanliness, diet, and fresh air. A great deal of pains would be lost in their case, as with all other arrangements for the good of the many, but here and there the seed would fall into the right places, and some members of the downtrodden million, rising a little from the mud, would raise the whole body with them.

As we saw old women enjoying their dish of gossip and their dish of tea, and mothers able for a while to take care in peace of their poor little children, we longed and hoped for that genius, who shall teach how to make, of these establishments, places of rest and instruction, not of degradation.

The causes which make the acceptance of public charity so much more injurious to the receiver than that of private are obvious, but surely not such that the human mind which has just invented the magnetic telegraph and Anastatic printing, may not obviate them. A deeper religion at the heart of Society would devise such means. Why should it be that the poor may still feel themselves men; paupers not? The poor man does not feel himself injured but benefitted by the charity of the doctor who gives him back the bill he is unable to pay, because the doctor is acting from intelligent sympathy—from love. Let Society do the same. She might raise the man, who is accepting her bounty, instead of degrading him.

Indeed, it requires great nobleness and faith in human nature, and God's will concerning it, for the officials not to take the tone toward these under their care, which their vices and bad habits prompt, but which must confirm them in the same. Men treated with respect are reminded of self-respect, and if there is a sound spot left in the character, the healthy influence spreads.

We were sorry to see mothers with their new born infants exposed to the careless scrutiny of male visitors. In the hospital, those who had children scarce a day old were not secure from the gaze of the stranger. This cannot be pleasant to them, and, if they have not refinement to dislike it, those who have should teach it to them. But we suppose there is no woman who has so entirely lost sight of the feelings of girlhood as not to dislike the scrutiny of strangers at a time which is sacred, if any in life is. Women they may like to see, even strangers, if they can approach them with delicacy.

In the yard of the hospital, we saw a little Dutch girl, a dwarf, who would have suggested a thousand poetical images and fictions to the mind of Victor Hugo or Sir Walter Scott. She had been brought here to New-York, as we understood, by some showman and then deserted, so that this place was her only refuge. No one could communicate with her or know her feelings, but she showed what they were, by running to the gate whenever it was opened, though treated with familiar kindness and seeming pleased by it. She had a large head, ragged dark hair, a glowering wizard eye, an uncouth yet pleasant smile, like an old child;—she wore a gold ring, and her complexion was as yellow as gold, if not as bright; altogether she looked like a gnome, more than any attempt we have ever known to embody in Art that fabled inhabitant of the mines and secret caves of earth.

From the Alms House we passed in an open boat to the Farm School. We were unprepared to find this, as we did, only a school upon a small farm, instead of one in which study is associated with labor. The children are simply taken care of and taught the common English branches till they are twelve years old, when they are bound out to various kinds of work. We think this plan very injudicious. It is bad enough for the children of rich parents, not likely in after life to bear a hard burden, and who are, at any rate, supplied with those various excitements required to develope the character in the earliest years; it is bad enough, we say, for these to have no kind of useful labor mingled with their plays and studies. Even these children would expand more, and be more variously called forth, and better prepared for common life, if another course were pursued. But, in schools like this at the farm, where the children, on leaving it, will be at once called on for adroitness and readiness of mind and body, and where the absence of natural ties and the various excitements that rise from them inevitably give to life a mechanical routine calculated to cramp and chill the character, it would be peculiarly desirable to provide various occupations, and such as are calculated to prepare for common life. As to economy of time, there is never time lost, by mingling other pursuits with the studies of children; they have vital energy enough for many things at once, and learn more from books when their attention is quickened by other kinds of culture.

Some of these children were pretty, and they were healthy and well-grown, considering the general poverty or vice of the class from which they were taken. That terrible scourge, ophthalmia, disfigured many among them. This disease, from some cause not yet detected, has been prevalent here for many years. We trust it may yield to the change of location next summer. There is not water enough here to give the children decent advantages as to bathing. This, too, will be remedied by the change. The Principal, who has been almost all his life connected with this establishment and that at Bellevue, seemed to feel a lively interest in his charge. He has arranged the dormitories with excellent judgment, both as to ventilation and neatness. This, alone, is a great advantage these children have over those of poor families living at home. They may pass the night in healthy sleep, and have thereby a chance for innocent and active days.

We saw with pleasure the little children engaged in the kind of drill they so much enjoy, of gesticulation regulated by singing. It was also pretty to see the babies sitting in a circle and the nurses in the midst feeding them, alternately, with a spoon. It seemed like a nest full of little birds, each opening its bill as the parent returns from her flight.

Hence we passed to the Asylum for the Insane. Only a part of this building is completed, and it is well known that the space is insufficient. Twice as many are inmates here as can be properly accommodated. A tolerable degree, however, of order and cleanliness is preserved. We could not but observe the vast difference between the appearance of the insane here and at Bloomingdale, or other Institutions where the number of attendants and nature of the arrangements permit them to be the objects of individual treatment; that is, where the wants and difficulties of each patient can be distinctly and carefully attended to. At Bloomingdale, the shades of character and feeling were nicely kept up, decorum of manners preserved, and the insane showed in every way that they felt no violent separation betwixt them and the rest of the world, and might easily return to it. The eye, though bewildered, seemed lively, and the tongue prompt. But *here,* insanity appeared in its more stupid, wild, or despairing forms. They crouched in corners; they had no eye for the stranger, no heart for hope, no habitual expectation of light. Just as at the Farm School, where the children show by their unformed features and mechanical movements that they are treated by wholesale, so do these poor sufferers. It is an evil incident to public establishments, and which only a more intelligent public attention can obviate.

One figure we saw, here also, of high poetical interest. It was a woman seated on the floor, in the corner of her cell, with a shawl wrapped gracefully around her head and chest, like a Nun's veil. Her hair was grey, her face attenuated and very pallid, her eyes large, open, fixed and bright with a still fire. She never moved them nor ceased chanting the service of the Church. She was a Catholic, who became insane while preparing to be a Nun. She is surely a Nun now in her heart; and a figure from which a painter might study for some of the most consecrated subjects.

Passing to the Penitentiary, we entered on one of the gloomiest scenes that deforms this great metropolis. Here are the twelve hundred, who receive the punishment due to the vices of so large a portion of the rest. And under what circumstances! Never was punishment treated more simply as a social convenience, without regard to pure right, or a hope of reformation.

Public attention is now so far awake to the state of the Penitentiary that it cannot be long, we trust, before proper means of classification are devised, a temporary asylum provided for those who leave this purgatory, even now, unwilling to return to the inferno from which it has for a time kept them, and means presented likely to lead some, at least, among the many, who seem hardened, to better views and hopes. It must be that the more righteous feeling which has shown itself in regard to the prisons at Sing Sing and elsewhere, must take some effect as to the Penitentiary also. The present Superintendent enters into the necessity of such improvements, and, should he remain there, will do what he can to carry them into effect.

The want of proper matrons, or any matrons, to take the care so necessary for the bodily or mental improvement or even decent condition of the seven hundred women assembled here, is an offence that cries aloud. It is impossible to take the most cursory survey of this assembly of women, especially it is impossible to see them in the Hospital, where the circumstances are a little more favorable, without seeing how many there are in whom the feelings of innocent childhood are not dead, who need only good influences and steady aid to raise them from the pit of infamy and woe into which they have fallen. And, if there was not one that could be helped, at least Society owes them the insurance of a decent condition while here. We trust that interest on this subject will not slumber.

The recognized principles of all such institutions which have any higher object than the punishment of fault, (and we believe few among us are so ignorant as to avow that as the only object, though they may, from want of thought, act as if it were,) are—Classification as the first step, that the bad may not impede those who wish to do well; 2d. Instruction, practical, oral, and by furnishing books which may open entirely new hopes and thoughts to minds oftener darkened than corrupted; 3d. A good Sanitary system, which promotes self-respect, and, through health and purity of body, the same in mind.

In visiting the Tombs the other day, we found the air in the upper galleries unendurable, and felt great regret that those confined there should be constantly subjected to it. Give the free breath of Heaven to all who are still permitted to breathe.—We cannot, however, wonder at finding this barbarity in a prison, having been subjected to it at the most fashionable places of public resort. Dr. Griscom has sent us his excellent lecture on the health of New-York, which we recommend to all who take a vital interest in the city where they live, and have intellect to discern that a cancer on the body must in time affect the head and heart also. We thought, while reading, that it was not surprising typhus fever and opthalmia should be bred in the cellars, while the families of those who live in palaces breathe such infected air at public places, and receive their visitors on New Year's day by candlelight. (That was a sad omen for the New Year—did they mean to class themselves among those who love darkness rather than light?)

We hope to see the two thousand poor people, and the poor children, better situated in their new abode, when we visit them again. The Insane Asylum will gain at once by enlargement of accommodations; but more attendance is also necessary, and, for that purpose, the best persons should be selected. We saw, with pleasure, tame pigeons walking about among the most violent of the insane, but we also saw two attendants with faces brutal and stolid. Such a charge is too delicate to be intrusted to any but excellent persons. Of the Penitentiary we shall write again. All criticism, however imperfect, should be welcome. There is no reason why New-York should not become a model for other States in these things. There is wealth enough, intelligence, and good desire enough, and *surely, need enough*. If she be not the best cared for city in the world, she threatens to surpass in corruption London and Paris. Such bane as is constantly poured into her veins demands powerful antidotes.

But nothing effectual can be achieved while both measures and men are made the sport of political changes. It is a most crying and shameful evil, which does not belong to our institutions, but is a careless distortion of them, that the men and measures are changed in these institutions with changes from Whig to Democrat, from Democrat to Whig. Churches, Schools, Colleges, the care of the Insane, and suffering Poor, should be preserved from the uneasy tossings of this delirium. The Country, the State, should look to it that only those fit for such officers should be chosen for such, apart from all considerations of political party. Let this be thought of; for without an absolute change in this respect no permanent good whatever can be effected; and farther, let not economy but utility be the rule of expenditure, for, here, parsimony is the worst prodigality.

New-York Daily Tribune
19 Mar. 1845

Prevalent Idea that Politeness is too great a Luxury to be given to the Poor

A FEW DAYS AGO, a lady, crossing in one of the ferry boats that ply from this city, saw a young boy, poorly dressed, sitting with an infant in his arms on one of the benches. She observed that the child looked sickly and coughed. This, as the day was raw, made her anxious in its behalf, and she went to the boy and asked whether he was alone there with the baby, and if he did not think the cold breeze dangerous for it. He replied that he was sent out with the child to take care of it, and that his father said the fresh air from the water would do it good.

While he made this simple answer, a number of persons had collected around to listen, and one of them, a well-dressed woman. addressed the boy in a string of such questions and remarks as these:

"What is your name? Where do you live? Are you telling us the truth? It's a shame to have that baby out in such weather; you'll be the death of it. (To the bystanders:) I would go and see his mother and tell her about it, if I was sure he had told us the truth about where he lived. How do you expect to get back? Here, (in the rudest voice,) somebody says you have not told the truth as to where you live."

The child, whose only offence consisted in taking care of the little one in public, and answering when he was spoken to, began to shed tears at the accusations thus grossly preferred against him. The bystanders stared at both; but among them all there was not one with sufficiently clear notions of propriety and moral energy to say to this impudent questioner, "Woman! do you suppose, because you wear a handsome shawl, and that boy a patched jacket, that you have any right to speak to him at all, unless he wishes it, far less to prefer against him those rude accusations. Your vulgarity is unendurable; leave the place or alter your manner."

Many such instances have we seen of insolent rudeness or more insolent affability founded on no apparent grounds, except an apparent difference in pecuniary position, for no one can suppose in such cases the offending party has really enjoyed the benefit of refined education and society, but all present let them pass as matters of course. It was sad to see how the poor would endure—mortifying to see how the purse-proud dared offend. An excellent man who was, in his early years, a missionary to the poor, used to speak afterwards with great shame of the manner in which he had conducted himself towards them.— "When I recollect," said he, "the freedom with which I entered their houses, inquired into all their affairs, commented on their conduct and disputed their statements I wonder I was never horsewhipped and feel that I ought to have been; it would have done me good, for I needed as severe a lesson on the universal obligations of politeness in its only genuine form of respect for man as man, and delicate sympathy with each in his peculiar position."

Charles Lamb, who was indeed worthy to be called a human being from those refined sympathies, said, "You call him a gentleman: does his washerwoman find him so?" We may say, if she did so, she found him a *man,* neither treating her with vulgar abruptness, nor giving himself airs of condescending liveliness, but treating her with that genuine respect which a feeling of equality inspires.

To doubt the veracity of another is an insult which in most *civilized* communities must in the so-called higher classes be atoned for by blood, but, in those same communities, the same men will, with the utmost lightness, doubt the truth of one who wears a ragged coat, and thus do all they can to injure and degrade him by assailing his self-respect, and breaking the feeling of personal honor—a wound to which hurts a man as a wound to its bark does a tree.

Then how rudely are favors conferred, just as a bone is thrown to a dog. A gentleman indeed will not do *that* without accompanying signs of sympathy and regard. Just as this woman said, "If you have told the truth I will go and see your mother," are many acts performed on which the actors pride themselves as kind and charitable.

All men might learn from the French in these matters. That people, whatever be their faults, are really well-bred, and many acts might be quoted from their romantic annals, where gifts were given from rich to poor with a graceful courtesy, equally honorable and delightful to the giver and the receiver.

In Catholic countries there is more courtesy, for charity is there a duty, and must be done for God's sake; there is less room for a man to give himself the Pharisaical tone about it. A rich man is not so surprised to find himself in contact with a poor one; nor is the custom of kneeling on the open pavement, the silk robe close to the beggar's rags, without profit. The separation by pews, even on the day when all meet nearest, is as bad for the manners as the soul.

Blessed be he or she who has passed through this world, not only with an open purse and willingness to render the aid of mere outward benefits, but with an open eye and open heart, ready to cheer the downcast, and enlighten the dull by words of comfort and looks of love. The wayside charities are the most valuable both as to sustaining hope and diffusing knowledge, and none can render them who has not an expansive nature, a heart alive to affection, and some true notion, however imperfectly developed, of the nature of human brotherhood.

Such an one can never sauce the given meat with taunts, freeze the bread by a cold glance of doubt, or plunge the man who asked for his hand deeper back into the mud by any kind of rudeness.

In the little instance with which we begun, no help *was* asked, unless by the sight of the timid little boy's old jacket. But the license which this seemed to the well-clothed woman to give to rudeness was so characteristic of a deep fault now existing, that a volume of comments might follow and a host of anecdotes be drawn from almost any one's experience in exposition of it. These few words, perhaps, may awaken thought in those who have drawn tears from other's eyes through an ignorance brutal, but not hopelessly so, if they are willing to rise above it.

New-York Daily Tribune
31 May 1845

The Wrongs of American Women
The Duty of American Women

THE SAME DAY brought us a copy of Mr. Burdett's little book, in which
the sufferings and difficulties that beset the large class of women who
must earn their subsistence in a city like New-York are delineated
with so much simplicity, feeling and exact adherence to the facts—
and a printed circular containing proposals for immediate practical
adoption of the plan more fully described in a book published
some weeks since under the title. "The Duty of American Women
to their Country," which was ascribed alternately to Mrs. Stone and
Miss Catharine Beecher, but of which we understand both those ladies
decline the responsibility. The two matters seemed linked with one
another by natural piety. Full acquaintance with the wrong must call
forth all manner of inventions for its redress.

The Circular, in showing the vast want that already exists of good
means for instructing the children of this nation, especially in the West,
states also the belief that among women, as being less immersed in
other cares and toils, from the preparation it gives for their task as
mothers, and from the necessity in which a great proportion stand of
earning a subsistence somehow, at least during the years which pre-
cede marriage, if they *do* marry, must the number of teachers wanted
be found, which is estimated already at *sixty thousand*.

We cordially sympathize with these views.

Much has been written about Woman's keeping within her sphere,
which is defined as the domestic sphere. As a little girl she is to learn
the lighter family duties, while she acquires that limited acquaintance
with the realm of literature and science that will enable her to superin-
tend the instruction of children in their earliest years. It is not generally
proposed that she should be sufficiently instructed and developed to
understand the pursuits or aims of her future husband; she is not to be

a helpmeet to him, in the way of companionship or counsel, except in the care of his house and children. Her youth is to be passed partly in learning to keep house and the use of the needle, partly in the social circle where her manners may be formed, ornamental accomplishments perfected and displayed, and the husband found who shall give her the domestic sphere for which exclusively she is to be prepared.

Were the destiny of Woman thus exactly marked out, did she invariably retain the shelter of a parent's or a guardian's roof till she married, did marriage give her a sure home and protector, were she never liable to be made a widow, or, if so, sure of finding immediate protection from a brother or new husband, so that she might never be forced to stand alone one moment, and were her mind given for this world only, with no faculties capable of eternal growth and infinite improvement, we would still demand for her a far wider and more generous culture than is proposed by those who so anxiously define her sphere. We would demand it that she might not ignorantly or frivolously thwart the designs of her husband, that she might be the respected friend of her sons no less than her daughters, that she might give more refinement, elevation and attraction to the society which is needed to give the characters of *men* polish and plasticity—no less so than to save them from vicious and sensual habits. But the most fastidious critic on the departure of Woman from her sphere, can scarcely fail to see at present that a vast proportion of the sex, if not the better half, do not, CANNOT, have this domestic sphere. Thousands and scores of thousands in this country no less than in Europe are obliged to maintain themselves alone. Far greater numbers divide with their husbands the care of earning a support for the family. In England, now, the progress of society has reached so admirable a pitch that the position of the sexes is frequently reversed, and the husband is obliged to stay at home and "mind the house and bairns" while the wife goes forth to the employment she alone can secure.

We readily admit that the picture of this is most painful—that Nature made entirely an opposite distribution of functions between the sexes. We believe the natural order to be the best, and that, if it could be followed in an enlightened spirit, it would bring to Woman all she wants, no less for her immortal than her mortal destiny. We are not surprised that men, who do not look deeply or carefully at causes or tendencies, should be led by disgust at the hardened, hackneyed characters which the present state of things too often produces in women to such conclusions as they are. We, no more than they, delight in the picture of the poor woman digging in the mines in her husband's clothes. We, no more than they, delight to hear their voices shrilly raised in the market-place, whether of apples or celebrity. But we see that at present they must do as they do for bread. Hundreds and thousands must step out of that hallowed domestic sphere, with no choice but to work or steal, or belong to men, not as wives, but as the wretched slaves of sensuality.

And this transition state, with all its revolting features, indicates, we do believe, the approach of a nobler era than the world has yet known. We trust that by the stress and emergencies of the present and coming time, the minds of women will be formed to more reflection and higher purposes than heretofore—their latent powers developed, their characters strengthened and eventually beautified and harmonized. Should the state of society then be such that each may remain, as Nature seems to have intended, the tutelary genius of a home, while men manage the out-door business of life, both may be done with a wisdom, a mutual understanding and respect unknown at present. Men will be no less the gainers by this than women, finding in pure and more religious marriages the joys of friendship and love combined—in their mothers and daughters better instruction, sweeter and nobler companionship, and in society at large an excitement to their finer powers and feelings unknown at present except in the region of the fine arts.

Blest be the generous, the wise among them who seek to forward hopes like these, instead of struggling against the fiat of Providence and the march of Fate to bind down rushing Life to the standard of the Past. Such efforts are vain, but those who make them are unhappy and unwise.

It is not, however, to such that we address ourselves, but to those who seek to make the best of things as they are, while they also strive to make them better. Such persons will have seen enough of the state of things in London, Paris, New-York, and manufacturing regions every where, to feel that there is an imperative necessity for opening more avenues of employment to women, and fitting them better to enter them, rather than keeping them back. Women have invaded many of the trades and some of the professions. Sewing, to the present killing extent, they cannot long bear. Factories seem likely to afford them permanent employment. In the culture of fruit, flowers and vegetables, even in the sale of them, we rejoice to see them engaged. In domestic service they will be aided, but can never be supplanted, by machinery. As much room as there is here for woman's mind and woman's labor will always be filled. A few have usurped the martial province, but these must always be few; the nature of woman is opposed to war. It is natural enough to see "Female Physicians," and we believe that the lace cap and workbag are as much at home here as the wig and gold-headed cane. In the priesthood they have from all time shared more or less—in many eras more than at the present. We believe there has been no female lawyer, and probably will be none. The pen, many of the fine arts they have made their own, and, in the more refined countries of the world, as writers, as musicians, as painters, as actors, women occupy as advantageous ground as men. Writing and music may be esteemed professions for them more than any other.

But there are two others where the demand must invariably be immense, and for which they are naturally better fitted than men, for which we should like to see them better prepared and better rewarded than they are. These are the profession of nurse to the sick and of teacher. The first of these professions we have warmly desired to see dignified. It is a noble one, now most unjustly regarded in the light of menial service. It is one which no menial, no servile nature can fitly occupy. We were rejoiced when an intelligent lady of Massachusetts made the refined heroine of a little romance select that calling. This lady (Mrs. George Lee) has looked on society with unusual largeness of spirit and healthiness of temper. She is well acquainted with the world of conventions, but sees beneath it the world of nature. She is a generous writer and unpretending, as the generous are wont to be. We do not recall the name of the tale, but the circumstance above mentioned marks its temper. We hope to see the time when the refined and cultivated will choose this profession and learn it, not only through experience under the direction of the doctor, but by acquainting themselves with the laws of matter and of mind, so that all they do shall be intelligently done, and afford them the means of developing intelligence as well as the nobler, tenderer feelings of humanity; for even the last part of the benefit they cannot receive if their work be done in a selfish or mercenary spirit.

The other profession is that of teacher, for which women are particularly adapted by their nature, superiority in tact, quickness of sympathy, gentleness, patience, and a clear and animated manner in narration or description. To form a good teacher should be added to this sincere modesty combined with firmness, liberal views with a power and will to liberalize them still further, a good method and habits of exact and thorough investigation. In the two last requisites women are generally deficient, but there are now many shining examples to prove that if they are immethodical and superficial as teachers it is because it is the custom so to teach them, and that when aware of these faults they can and will correct them.

The profession is of itself an excellent one for the improvement of the teacher during that interim between youth and maturity when the mind needs testing, tempering, and to review and rearrange the knowledge it has acquired. The natural method of doing this for one's self is to attempt teaching others; those years also are the best of the practical teacher. The teacher should be near the pupil both in years and feelings—no oracle, but the elder brother or sister of the pupil. More experience and years form the lecturer and the director of studies, but injure the powers as to familiar teaching.

These are just the years of leisure in the lives even of those women who are to enter the domestic sphere, and this calling most of all compatible with a constant progress as to qualifications for that.

Viewing the matter thus it may well be seen that we should hail with joy the assurance that sixty thousand *female* teachers are wanted, and more likely to be, and that a plan is projected which looks wise, liberal and generous, to afford the means of those whose hearts answer to this high calling obeying their dictates.

The plan is to have Cincinnati for a central point, where teachers shall be for a short time received, examined and prepared for their duties. By mutual agreement and cooperation of the various sects funds are to be raised and teachers provided according to the wants and tendencies of the various locations now destitute. What is to be done for them centrally, is for suitable persons to examine into their various kinds of fitness, communicate some general views whose value has been tested, and counsel adapted to the difficulties and advantages of their new positions. The Central Committee are to have the charge of raising funds and finding teachers and places where teachers are wanted.

The passage of thoughts, teachers and funds will be from East to West, the course of sunlight upon this earth.

The plan is offered as the most extensive and pliant means of doing a good and preventing ill to this nation, by means of a national education, whose normal school shall have an invariable object in the search after truth and the diffusion of the means of knowledge, while its form shall be plastic according to the wants of the time. This normal school promises to have good effects, for it proposes worthy aims through simple means, and the motive for its formation and support seems to be disinterested philanthropy.

It promises to eschew the bitter spirit of sectarianism and proselytism, else we, for one party, could have nothing to do with it. Men, no doubt, have been oftentimes kept from absolute famine by the wheat with which such tares are mingled; but we believe the time is come when a purer and more generous food is to be offered to the people at large. We believe the aim of all education to be to rouse the mind to action, show it the means of discipline and of information; then leave it free, with God, Conscience, and the love of Truth for its guardians and teachers. Woe be to those who sacrifice these aims of universal and eternal value to the propagation of a set of opinions. But on this subject we can accept such doctrine as is offered by Rev. Calvin Stowe, one of the committee, in the following passage:

"In judicious practice, I am persuaded there will seldom be any very great difficulty, especially if there be excited in the community anything like a whole-hearted honesty and enlightened sincerity in the cause of public instruction.

"It is all right for people to suit their own taste and convictions in respect to sect; and by fair means and at proper times to teach their children and those under their influence to prefer the denominations which they prefer; but farther than this no one has any right to go. It is all wrong to hazard the well being of the soul, to jeopardize great public interests for the sake of advancing the interests of a sect. People must learn to practice some self-denial, on Christian principles, in respect to their denominational preferences, as well as in respect to other things, before pure Religion can ever gain a complete victory over every form of human selfishness."

The persons who propose themselves to the examination and instruction of the teachers at Cincinnati, till the plan shall be sufficiently under way to provide regularly for the office, are Mrs. Stowe and Miss Catherine Beecher, ladies well known to fame, as possessing unusual qualifications for the task.

As to finding abundance of teachers, who that reads this little book of Mr. Burdett's, or the account of the compensation of female labor in New-York, and the hopeless, comfortless, useless, pernicious lives those who have even the advantage of getting work must live with the sufferings and almost inevitable degradation to which those who cannot are exposed, but must long to snatch such as are capable of this better profession, and among the multitude there must be many who are or could be made so, from their present toils and make them free and the means of freedom and growth to others.

To many books on such subjects, among others to "Woman in the Nineteenth Century," the objection has been made that they exhibit ills without specifying any practical means for their remedy. The writer of the last named essay does indeed think that it contains one great rule which, if laid to heart, would prove a practical remedy for many ills, and of such daily and hourly efficacy in the conduct of life that any extensive observance of it for a single year would perceptibly raise the tone of thought, feeling and conduct throughout the civilized world. But to those who ask not only such a principle, but an external method for immediate use, we say, here is one proposed that looks noble and promising, the proposers offer themselves to the work with heart and hand, with time and purse: Go ye and do likewise.

Those who wish details as to this plan, will find them in the "Duty of American Women to their Country," published by Harper & Brothers, Cliff-st. The publishers may, probably, be able to furnish also the Circular to which we have referred. At a leisure day we shall offer some suggestions and remarks as to the methods and objects there proposed.

New-York Daily Tribune
30 Sept. 1845

What fits a Man to be a Voter? Is it to be White Within,
or White Without?

THE COUNTRY had been denuded of its forests, and men cried—
"Come! we must plant anew, or there will be no shade for the homes
of our children, or fuel for their hearths. Let us find the best kernels
for a new growth."

And a basket of butternuts was offered.

But the planters rejected it with disgust. "What a black, rough coat it
has," said they; "it is entirely unfit for the dishes on a nobleman's table,
nor have we ever seen it in such places. It must have a greasy, offensive
kernel; nor can fine trees grow up from such a nut."

"Friends," said one of the planters, "this decision may be rash. The
chestnut has not a handsome outside; it is long encased in troublesome burrs, and, when disengaged, is almost as black as these nuts you
despise. Yet from it grow trees of lofty stature, graceful form and long
life. Its kernel is white and has furnished food to the most poetic and
splendid nations of the older world."

"Don't tell me," says another, "brown is entirely different from black.
I like brown very well; there is Oriental precedent for its respectability.
Perhaps we will use some of your chestnuts, if we can get fine samples.
But for the present I think we should use only English walnuts, such as
our fore-fathers delighted to honor. Here are many basketsfull of them,
quite enough for the present. We will plant them with a sprinkling
between of the chestnut and acorn." "But," rejoined the other, "many
butternuts are beneath the sod, and you cannot help a mixture of them
being in your wood at any rate."

"Well! we will grub them up and cut them down wherever we find
them. We can use the young shrubs for kindlings."

At that moment entered the council two persons of a darker complexion than most of those present, as if born beneath the glow of a

more scorching sun. First came a Woman, beautiful in the mild, pure grandeur of her look; in whose large dark eye a prophetic intelligence was mingled with infinite sweetness. She looked at the assembly with an air of surprise, as if its aspect was strange to her. She threw quite back her veil, and stepping aside made room for her companion. His form was youthful, about the age of one we have seen in many a picture, produced by the thought of eighteen centuries, as of one "instructing the Doctors." I need not describe the features; all minds have their own impressions of such an image,

> "Severe in youthful beauty."

In his hand, he bore a little white banner on which was embroidered PEACE AND GOOD WILL TO MEN. And the words seemed to glitter and give out sparks, as he paused in the assembly.

"I came hither," said he, "an uninvited guest, because I read sculptured above the door—'All men born Free and Equal,' and in this dwelling hoped to find myself at home. What is the matter in dispute?"

Then they whispered one to another, and murmurs were heard— "He is a mere boy; young people are always foolish and extravagant;" or "He looks like a fanatic." But others said, "He looks like one whom we have been taught to honor. It will be best to tell the matter in dispute."

When he heard it, he smiled and said, "It will be needful first to ascertain which of the nuts is soundest *within.*" And with a hammer he broke one, two, and more of the English walnuts, and they were mouldy.

Then he tried the other nuts, but found most of them fresh and *white,* for they were fresh from the bosom of the earth, while the others had been kept in a damp cellar.

And he said, "You had better plant them together, lest none or few of the walnuts be sound. And why are you so reluctant? Has not Heaven permitted them both to grow on the same soil? and does not that show what is intended about it?"

And they said, "But they are black and ugly to look upon." He replied, "They do not seem so to me. What my Father has fashioned in such guise offends not mine eye."

And they said, "But from one of these trees flew a bird of prey who has done great wrong. We meant, therefore, to suffer no such tree among us."

And he replied, "Amid the band of my countrymen and friends there was one guilty of the blackest crime, that of selling for a price the life of his dearest friend, yet all the others of his blood were not put under ban because of his guilt."

Then they said, "But in the Holy Book our teachers tell us, we are bid to keep in exile or distress whatsoever is black and unseemly in our eyes."

Then he put his hand to his brow and cried in a voice of the most penetrating pathos, "Have I been so long among ye and ye have not known me?"—And the Woman turned from them, the majestic hope of her glance, and both forms suddenly vanished, but the banner was left trailing in the dust.

The men stood gazing at one another. After which one mounted on high and said:

"Perhaps, my friends, we carry too far this aversion to objects merely because they are black. I heard, the other day, a wise man say that black was the color of evil—marked as such by God, and that whenever a white man struck a black man he did an act of worship to God. I could not quite believe him. I hope, in what I am about to add, I shall not be misunderstood. I am no Abolitionist. I respect above all things, divine or human, the Constitution framed by our forefathers, and the peculiar institutions hallowed by the usage of their sons. I have no sympathy with the black race in this country. I wish it to be understood that I feel toward negroes the purest personal antipathy. It is a family trait with us. My little son, scarce able to speak, will cry out "Nigger! Nigger!" whenever he sees one, and try to throw things at them. He made a whole omnibus load laugh the other day by his cunning way of doing this. The child of my political antagonist, on the other hand, says "he likes *tullared* children the best." You see he is tainted in his cradle by the loose principles of his parents, even before he can say nigger or pronounce the more refined appellation. But that is no matter. I merely mention this by the way: not to prejudice you against Mr. ————, but that you may appreciate the very different state of things in my family, and not misinterpret what I have to say. I was lately in one of our prisons where a somewhat injudicious indulgence had extended to one of the condemned felons, a lost and wretched outcast from society, the use of materials for painting, that having been his profession. He had completed at his leisure, a picture of the Lord's Supper. Most of the figures were well enough, but Judas he has represented as a black.—Now, gentlemen, I am of opinion that this is an unwarrantable liberty taken with the Holy Scriptures and shows *too much* prejudice in the community. It is my wish to be moderate and fair, and preserve a medium, neither, on the one hand, yielding the wholesome antipathies planted in our breasts as a safeguard against degradation, and our constitutional obligations, which, as I have before observed, are, with me, more binding than any other; nor on the other hand forgetting that liberality and wisdom which are the prerogative of every citizen of this free Commonwealth. I agree then with our young visitor. I hardly know, indeed, why a stranger and one so young was permitted to mingle in this council, but it was certainly thoughtful in him to crack and examine the nuts. I agree that it may be well to plant some of the black nuts among the others, so that, if many of the walnuts fail, we may make use of this inferior tree."

At this moment arose a hubbub, and such a clamor of "dangerous innovation," "political capital," "low-minded demagogue," "infidel who denies the Bible," "lower link in the chain of creation," &c. that it is impossible to say what was the decision.

New-York Daily Tribune
31 Mar. 1846

∽

Farewell

FAREWELL to New-York City, where twenty months have presented me with a richer and more varied exercise for thought and life than twenty years could in any other part of these United States.

It is the common remark about New-York that it has, at least, nothing petty or provincial in its methods and habits. The place is large enough; there is room enough and occupation enough for men to have no need or excuse for small cavils or scrutinies. A person who is independent and knows what he wants, may lead his proper life here unimpeded by others.

Vice and Crime, if flagrant and frequent, are less thickly coated by Hypocrisy than elsewhere. The air comes sometimes to the most infected subjects.

New-York is the focus, the point where American and European interests converge. There is no topic of general interest to men that will not betimes be brought before the thinker by the quick turning of the wheel.

Too quick that revolution, some object. Life rushes wide and free, but *too fast;* yet it is in the power of every one to avert from himself the evil that accompanies the good. He must build for his study, as did the German poet, a house beneath the bridge, and, then, all that passes above and by him will be heard and seen, but he will not be carried away with it.

Earlier views have been confirmed and many new ones opened. On two great leadings,—the superlative importance of promoting National Education by heightening and deepening the cultivation of individual minds, and the part which is assigned to Woman in the next stage of human progress in this country, where most important achievements are to be effected, I have received much encouragement, much instruction, and the fairest hopes of more.

On various subjects of minor importance, no less than these, I hope for good results from observation with my own eyes of Life in the Old World, and to bring home some packages of seed for Life in the New.

These words I address to my friends, for I feel that I have some. The degree of sympathetic response to the thoughts and suggestions I have offered through the columns of this paper has indeed surprised me, conscious as I am of a natural and acquired aloofness from many, if not most, popular tendencies of my time and place. It has greatly encouraged me, for none can sympathize with thoughts like mine who are permanently ensnared in the meshes of sect or party; none who prefer the formation and advancement of mere opinions to the free pursuit of Truth. I see, surely, that the topmost bubble or sparkle of the cup is no voucher for the nature of its contents throughout, and shall, in future, feel that in our age, nobler in that respect than most of the preceding, each sincere and fervent act or word is secure, not only of a final, but a speedy, response.

I go to behold the wonders of art, and the temples of old religion. But I shall see no forms of beauty and majesty beyond what my Country is capable of producing in myriad variety, if she has but the soul to will it; no temple to compare with what she might erect in the Ages, if the catchword of the time, a sense of DIVINE ORDER, should become, no more a mere word or effigy, but a deeply rooted and pregnant Idea in her life. Beneath the light of a hope that this may be, I ask of my friends once more a kind Farewell.

New-York Daily Tribune
1 Aug. 1846